3.7
6e Davis, David Howard.
        Energy politics / David Howard Davis. New York :
    St. Martin's Press, [1974]
        211 p. : diagrs. ; 22 cm.
        Includes bibliographical references and index.

            1. Power resources - United States. 2. Energy
        policy - United States.   I. Title.
    HD9502.U52D3   333.7   74-81261
    Information Design   487/1698   MARC

ENERGY POLITICS

ENERGY POLITICS

DAVID HOWARD DAVIS

St. Martin's Press   New York

To My Niece and Godchild
Jennifer Elaine Dillman

Acknowledgments

First thanks go to my students at Rutgers University, for whom I wrote this book. My Political Science 202 class in the spring semester of 1973 bore a particularly heavy burden of hearing and discussing partially thought-out ideas and hypotheses. Four friends at Rutgers deserve the next thanks for critiquing the first draft: Alan Stone, Thomas Kerr, Jane Kerr, and Carol Spader. Later, Joseph N. Crowley of the University of Nevada, Francis E. Rourke of the Johns Hopkins University, and Peter Woll of Brandeis University aided with their detailed comments. Others I wish to thank for useful criticisms are Truman Price of the U.S. Environmental Protection Agency, Robert D. Thomas of Florida Atlantic University, and Stephen H. Balch of the City University of New York. For their encouragement and patient listening, I am indebted to Michael R. Curtis, Stanley H. Friedelbaum, Charles E. Jacob, Richard W. Mansbach, and Carlton W. Sterling of Rutgers and Ralph A. Luken of the U.S. Environmental Protection Agency. Joseph Abatemarco cheerfully shouldered the task of typing the manuscript, for which I thrice thank him. Lisa Thorne typed the revisions. Finally, as an observer of the political process quickly learns, key actors are often institutions rather than people. Hence I wish to thank the Rutgers University Library, the NASPAA Public Administration Fellow Program, and the U.S. Environmental Protection Agency.

Contents

1

Introduction

The energy crisis burst on the political scene in the mid-1970's with stunning force. Suddenly the American people, who had exploited the continent's seemingly endless resources for more than three and a half centuries, faced shortages. Schools closed for lack of heat. Motorists waited for hours to buy a few gallons of gasoline. Natural gas suppliers reneged on their deliveries. City dwellers suffered through electrical blackouts and brownouts. America's insatiable appetite for energy finally came face to face with scarcity. Today its 6 percent of the world's population consumes 35 percent of its energy. Since 1947 demand for electricity has grown at a rate of 7 percent per year, enough to double every ten years. The demand for natural gas has grown at 6 percent; for oil, at 3 percent; and for coal, at 2 percent. In recent years demand has grown even faster: 9 percent for electricity and 4½ percent overall. When the energy producers were no longer able to satisfy the nation's demand, the day of reckoning was at hand.

If this judgment were to be assigned a literal date it would be October 17, 1973, for on that day, inscrutable kings, emirs, and sheiks met in the windswept Arab capital of Kuwait to proclaim the end of an era. The old era was one of cheap and dependable energy, epitomized by the easy exploitation of the crude oil lying just beneath the Middle Eastern sands. The new era was to be one of more costly and more uncertain energy. The Arabs, who controlled 60 percent of the world's oil exports, met on the shores of the Persian Gulf to institute their boycott in the wake of their war against Israel. Being unable to secure victory in real war, the Arabs turned to economic war. If American aid gave Israel an advantage on the Sinai and Golan battlefields, the United States would have to pay a

1

penalty for its intervention. If, in the Arabs' view, the United States denied them victory, the Arabs would deny the United States energy. In spite of glib western forecasts of its dissolution, the Arab unity held firm enough and long enough to push Great Britain toward economic stagnation and a new government, force the Japanese to declare their support for the Arab cause, and send the American Secretary of State to negotiate an Israeli withdrawal from captured territory.

Within the United States the boycott sparked violence on the turnpikes, fostered the birth of a new federal agency, and further undercut support of a President trying to stave off impeachment. In Washington, senators investigating American relations with the Arabs discovered a secret decision of Harry Truman's National Security Council that had quietly guided foreign policy for a quarter of a century. Other probers revealed the machinations of giant petroleum corporations aimed at enriching Texas producers of oil and natural gas in return for millions of dollars of campaign contributions. In the state capitals, governors proclaimed schemes to ration gasoline, and state legislators negotiated deals to buy from secret supplies.

Yet if October 17, 1973, symbolized judgment day for the energy crisis of the 1970's, it was not the only day of reckoning, nor was that crisis the only one. The United States had faced other such dramatic days and critical events before in its often tumultuous politics of energy. America had seen the violence of the 1902 coal strike, the Ludlow massacre, and the Mossadegh coup d'état. It had seen the desperation of the cold city dweller, the dispossessed mountaineer, and the cancer-ridden uranium miner. It had seen, too, the happier side of energy: farmers made prosperous by electrical power, homeowners able to buy cheap and clean natural gas, refinery workers paid high wages. In the past energy politics brought to the fore some of the titans of American history: Theodore Roosevelt, John D. Rockefeller, Woodrow Wilson, John L. Lewis, Franklin Roosevelt. But more often the names were less familiar: Mark Requa, David Lilienthal, Glenn Seaborg. Energy politics has shaped major social movements: the growth of trade unionism, the resurgence of the Democratic party, the federal government's regulation of the economy. Yet more often it has been less conspicuous. Energy politics is more typically a small world of its own, tightly closed against the intrusion of outsiders. It has been a world usually unnoticed by political scientists and average citizens, and those involved in the process have not sought attention. Indeed, the ignorance and inattention of outsiders has helped to make energy politics what it is. Its few early analysts wrote of its "private government" and "undemocratic features."

But events of the 1970's brought the private world of energy politics into public attention as a number of economic, social, partisan, and international streams flowed together in what soon became popularly known as "the energy crisis." Naming the phenomenon stirred concern. "Crisis" was originally a medical term describing a decisive, climactic stage in the course of a disease, after which the patient either recovered or died. By implication the United States faces such a critical point. It is claimed that the energy situation is at a climax. If successfully resolved it will usher in a new era of abundant and cheap power. If not resolved, it will lead to stagnation and even decay. Many voices have joined in giving the alarm about the crisis. Chief among them have been those of the energy producers. Oil companies warn that their wells will run dry. Natural gas suppliers announce that their supplies will soon be exhausted. The coal operators can no longer supply cheap coal. Electrical utilities that burn oil, gas, or coal to fire their boilers suffer from shortages and the high prices of these fuels. At the same time they have already dammed all the good sites for hydroelectrical generation. Even nuclear reactors are proving to be so costly and difficult to construct that their promise, which seemed so bright a few years ago, has now dimmed.

Yet not all agree that an energy crisis exists. Critics charge that it is a sham, and that it has been a phony crisis, manipulated by the public relations departments of big energy corporations. These business giants have created, or at least exacerbated, the situation as a means of securing economic advantage. In particular, the critics say, the energy crisis is a weapon to counter the success of the environmental movement. Public concern with pollution has imposed costs on energy production that the corporations find burdensome. Drillers must now clean up the oil they spill into the ocean. Refiners must stop polluting the air. Electrical generating plants must burn low sulfur coal or oil. Coal operators must occasionally restore the lands they ravage. Nuclear power stations can no longer discharge hot water into a nearby river or vent radioactive iodine into the atmosphere. The popular movement for a better environment, which began in the mid-1960's, reached fruition in a series of federal and state laws passed in the late 1960's and early 1970's. The legislative cornerstone was the National Environmental Policy Act of 1969. Other important federal legislation included the Clean Air Act, the Water Pollution Control Act, and the Solid Waste Disposal Act. Once implemented, these laws began to hurt the energy companies, thus creating a backlash. Since the environmentalists' weapon was political, the response had to be political as well.

The sudden emergence of energy as a political issue is the current manifestation of the policy fads characteristic of American public opinion. Since World War II national attention has focused successively on anti-Communism, civil rights, the Vietnam war, the environment, and the energy crisis. Each fad typically develops peaks of frenzied activity marked by mass demonstrations, presidential television speeches, congressional legislation, and the creation of new governmental agencies. Then after a few years of intense militancy popular attention drifts away to new topics. The issue receives less notice from the news media and Congress; the new bureau charged with solving the problem settles down to work. The fundamental national decisions made at the height of concern usually point the policy permanently toward the goals established at that time.

These policy fads resemble epidemics of infectious diseases. They strike suddenly. Their success depends on a large reservoir of people who have never been in contact with the affliction and are thus susceptible. Once started, the infection spreads quickly, rapidly infecting a large proportion of the population. Then it subsides. Though some may have succumbed to its ravages, the survivors are immune from a second infection. The same affliction cannot strike again as long as enough of those with immunity remain in the population. Another epidemic may occur, however, since immunity to one disease does not give immunity to another.

Policy epidemics are, of course, happier phenomena than disease. For one thing, infection is to some degree voluntary, though one seldom realizes the extent to which the forces of society determine his behavior. The outspoken critic of a popular movement is as much "infected" as an adherent. For another, those who succumb to disease are often dead or crippled, whereas those who succumb to a policy fad find a new life opening up. They find fulfillment through service to a cause. Many find a livelihood as permanent leaders or bureaucrats in the institutions that the movement spawns.

Yet if the energy crisis is the policy epidemic of the 1970's it represents only a coming to the surface of a set of concerns that have been endemic in American politics throughout the twentieth century. Energy politics has been important, though hidden, for many years. This book examines the subject over the longer term, putting it in perspective. Perspective is especially needed in analysis of energy politics because the peak of attention has brought about distortions. Talk of a crisis connotes that the problems are novel and transitory, when in fact they are much the same problems the United States has faced many times before. Indeed many of the so-called problems are not problems but merely business as usual (or politics as usual).

This book takes a public policy approach. While there are probably as many definitions of "policy analysis" as there are analysts, the approach does have a central focus. Its basic building block is a specific policy arena. Thus the focus here is on energy, as opposed to other arenas such as foreign policy, civil rights policy, or education policy. The policy approach contrasts with other political science approaches, which may be institutional, behavioral, or normative. Institutional analysis, long a favorite within the discipline, uses the major institutions of the government as its basic building blocks. Thus experts write books about Congress or the Presidency or the bureaucracy or the courts. In the 1950's and 1960's, as a reaction against what they considered to be the excessive emphasis on institutional structure, a new wave of analysts focused on behavior. The aim was to examine the dynamics of the political system rather than merely its static state. The behavioralists often, though not always, employed statistical techniques. Much of their work used surveys of voter opinion or roll-call analysis of legislatures. Still the behavioral revolution, as it was half-facetiously labeled, was not so different from the traditional approach since it continued to emphasize process rather than outcomes. Both studied how the political system worked rather than what its results were.

Normative approaches have been more oriented toward outcomes of the process. A first wave came during the 1930's emphasizing training for citizenship and public service. A second wave in the late 1960's, identifying itself as the New Left, attacked the basic conservativism of the American political system and the process-oriented analysis of it by conventional political scientists. Normative studies emphasized values. They began with the assumption that the political system would be judged according to how its results matched its goals. Foreign affairs presented an easy target for the New Left since there, more than elsewhere, analysis had focused on output. Furthermore, because national goals were articulated thoroughly, comparison of the results with the values was inescapable. Against the background of the Vietnamese war the New Left critics of American foreign policy railed against American blundering, chicanery, and hypocrisy.

Foreign policy analysis also has lent itself to the policy approach. The two chief features of this approach are that it confines itself to a single arena (such as foreign affairs) and that it emphasizes outcomes rather than process. Within these two constraints its methods vary. It may examine institutions like the National Security Council, the Senate Foreign Relations Committee, or the United Nations. It may examine behavior like the Marshall Plan, supporting the Saigon regime, or aid to Israel. Or it may examine this behavior in the light of oft proclaimed American ideals of economic development, promoting democracy, and the pacific settlement of disputes.

Current trends within political science indicate that foreign affairs is no longer the sole topic subject to the policy approach. Increasingly new books and journals favor this technique. Universities are establishing programs on urban affairs, black studies, and the environment. They now offer undergraduate courses and graduate degree programs specifically in policy studies. "Think tanks" such as the RAND Corporation, the Urban Institute, and the Brookings Institution make their influence felt at the highest levels.

All of this suggests a new trend in politics as well as in political science. In the past politicians have been the ones who decided national policies. These have been men and women without specialized training in a specific arena. Typically they come to their decision-making positions from backgrounds as lawyers, merchants, teachers, or farmers. Now as the issues become more developed such generalists cannot cope with the complexity within each arena. They will have to turn to specialists familiar with the details of the policy problem. Hence the decision-maker of the future may be not the politician but the political scientist who commands the expertise necessary to integrate the technical and the political aspects of the arena.

Current analysis of the energy situation errs, frequently because it is based on unexamined assumptions.[1] Its most conspicuous feature is alarmism. From President Nixon to popular magazines to scholarly tomes, the shared theme is that of alarm. In his fourth energy message in less than nine months, President Nixon sounded the alarm to Congress:

> As the 93rd Congress reconvenes this week, it returns to an agenda that is piled high with vital legislative questions.
>
> No single legislative area is more critical or more challenging to us as a people, however, than the subject of this first message to the Congress: The energy crisis.[2]

According to the U.S. Geological Survey's reports of proven reserves the United States has only enough oil to last 10 years, enough natural gas to last 11 years, and enough uranium to last 13 years. The sole bright spot is coal. There are enough coal reserves to last 500 years, but mining it would require destroying millions of acres of forests and farms. This points up the alarmism of the other side of the issue: the damage to the natural and human environment. Strip mining ravages the land. Coal dust causes black lung disease. Oil spills pollute harbors. Refineries pollute the air. Electrical generating plants are smoky and ugly. Nuclear reactors release radiation. The only solution, say some, is to stop the rampant increase in consumption—if necessary, to stop economic growth. The country will have to cut back. The U.S. Environmental Protection Agency has already announced plans for sharply curtailing automobile travel in Los Angeles and northern New Jersey, where high gasoline consumption translates immediately into smog. The Civil Aeronautics Board has implemented plans to save the nation's petroleum supplies by reducing the number of commercial airline flights since airplanes are the most extravagant fuel burners. Electrical utilities, under pressure from state regulatory commissions, have stopped advertising to promote increased use of electrical appliances.

The alarmism is not always justified. "Proven reserves" is a technical term geologists use to describe an oil, gas, or coal field that has been tested by actual drilling or mining. It is not necessary for the country to maintain a 50- or 25-year level of proven reserves any more than it is necessary for a grocery store to maintain a year's backlog of food. All that is necessary is that the reserves remain enough ahead of consumption for them to come on the market in an orderly and timely manner. What this time margin should be, however, is open to debate. In recent years the level of proven reserves dropped from about a 20-year supply to the present 10- to 12-year level, and this may not be adequate.

The alarmists may be overstating their case in other respects as well. Environmental damage does not follow automatically from extractive industries. When it does occur it can be minimized or repaired. Likewise the environmental risks of transporting, refining, and distributing fuel can be controlled, though in fact they seldom are.

Alarmism itself may be a political strategy. Public opinion is a resource. What better way is there to arouse the public than to frighten it? Fear can rally the apathetic to a cause. Presidents frequently use a crisis to stir support, though seldom on an energy issue. A grave emergency can boost a President's popularity five to ten points in the Gallup or Lou Harris public opinion polls. This happened to John F. Kennedy after the 1961 Bay of Pigs invasion, even though he himself admitted that the Cuban liberation scheme was a grievous blunder. Presenting a situation as a crisis invokes a primeval group instinct to come to the support of the embattled leader. At a time when the Watergate scandal was driving his popular support to a new low, President Nixon tried to exploit this instinct by using the rhetoric of a crisis in a series of energy messages to Congress. He filled a certain popular need for emotional and symbolic reassurances merely by addressing the issue in terms of a crisis, irrespective of what he proposed in the messages. The large energy-producing companies also profit from speaking of a crisis. It becomes justification for raising prices, reducing quality, and securing special privileges. The environmentalists, for their part, can follow the same strategy but in the opposite direction. To them the crisis is one of ecological disaster. People will be unable to breathe because of smog. Oil spills will kill birds. Thermal discharges will kill fish. Radiation will kill everything. This litany of doom echoes the rhetoric that brought the environmental movement into influence in the late 1960's, leading to a series of legislative and institutional victories—thus proving the value of a skillfully manipulated crisis.

The primacy of politics is the second great unexamined assumption of current analysis. Too few who consider the problem, whether in government or not, bother to ask if the solution should be sought in the political sector. In the past energy was an economic problem. The Hanna Coal Company supplied coal. Standard Oil supplied oil. If supplies were scarce, the price went up; if supplies were abundant, the price went down. Economic decision-making under the price system was the rule. But now political decision-making is assumed. The fact is that the trend represents a flight from the market. Energy producers turn from the price system to government to guide their industries. This trend, however, is not new but of long standing. Shifting decision-making from the economic to the political sector alters the balance of forces. Companies powerful economically may be weak politically. Citizen groups weak economically may be strong politically. If shifting a controversy from the economy to the polity will improve one's position, that is the logical strategy to follow.

The assumption in much analysis that political decision-making is the ultimate way does not rule out a third unexamined presupposition: that science is the panacea. In the past the nation has moved forward, wantonly exploiting its patrimony, confident that scientific research will find new energy sources by the time it exhausts the existing ones. The view of "science as the new frontier" allows inefficient consumption of oil and natural gas just as the western frontier allowed the nineteenth-century pioneers to chop down the virgin forests and plow the prairie sod. Today's sons of the pioneers trust science to provide them with the energy they will need in the future. Geologists will discover crude oil off the East Coast and blast natural gas out of Colorado rocks that hold it prisoner molecule by molecule. Petrochemical engineers will build mine-mouth plants to convert dirty coal into synthetic gas transported by pipelines. The most faith lies with the potential of nuclear power. The "fast breeder" reactor will create more fuel than it burns. Fusion of hydrogen atoms will bring the power of the hydrogen bomb under control using fuel easily obtained from ordinary water. Those looking farther into the future see science efficiently producing power from the wind, the sun, the tides and the heat inside the earth.

Yet science can not be assumed to be a panacea for the nation's energy problems. Many of the more experimental technologies have still to be proven possible. The potentially most mighty—nuclear fusion—has still to be invented, let alone made practical. Oil from shale, natural gas from sandstone, synthetic gas from coal are technically possible—but not feasible at present prices. For these processes to be economical the alternative costs of obtaining oil or gas will have to soar. Of course, this is exactly what soon may happen. Science as a panacea has a second form. This is to assume that decisions which are difficult to resolve in the political or economic sector are easy to solve in the technological sector. Thus a political decision-making body may abdicate its responsibility for choosing by passing the problem on to the scientists. If Congress cannot balance the risks of radiation against its benefits, let the Atomic Energy Commission decide. This may solve the problem for Congress but not for the people exposed to the radiation.

A fourth erring in much current analysis of the energy crisis is that it tends to be futuristic. It speculates about the energy situation in 1985 or 2000 without considering it in the 1970's. The predictions are technical and framed in a way that presupposes that the political context is immaterial. That assumption is unwarranted. As this book illustrates, past and present energy policy has been highly politicized. Every indication is that future energy politics will be so too. Focusing analysis on a nonpolitical future is an escape, intentional or not, from grappling with the ambiguous realities of the past and present situation.

Preoccupation with petroleum is the fifth error common to much analysis. If nuclear power is the panacea, oil is the problem. Virtually every newspaper or magazine article on the "energy crisis" starts with the oil shortage and ends with the atomic solution. Scholarly analysis is equally obsessed with oil. True, the petroleum situation is the most dramatic. It is conspicuous because it powers the automobile America loves so dearly. Its politics is byzantine. At home the politics depends on Washington lobbyists, generous donations to presidential candidates, and gaping tax loopholes. Abroad it depends on wars between Israel and the Arabs, deals with the Russians, and secret meetings in Kuwait. If there is a crisis, it is surely one of petroleum. Yet petroleum is not all there is to energy. Other fuels and other political settings ought not to be neglected.

The final assumption of most current analysis is that the politics of energy is a single phenomenon. It is not. It is multifaceted. Dividing it chronologically makes it easier to understand. The first set of problems belongs to the 1970's. These are primarily difficulties of distribution: heating oil for schools, gasoline for automobiles, electricity for air conditioners, crude oil for refineries. They involve remedying the shortcomings of the present system. The next set of problems belongs to the 1980's. How is the United States to maintain its supply of oil in the face of dwindling supplies and toughened Arab demands? What can it substitute for oil? This set involves changing the present system of both acquisition and consumption. It means coal and nuclear power instead of oil, subways instead of automobiles and trains instead of planes. The third set of problems is for the year 2000. How much energy can the United States furnish itself? If fusion power is then practical, the answer may be "plenty." If not, it may be "too little," and the consequence will be a lower standard of living or imperialistic wars to conquer the oil-producing countries in the Middle East and elsewhere.

This suggests that physical characteristics are the logical starting point for analysis. Geography is an important way in which the nation's energy problems are differentiated. In worldwide terms, whether a country has enough fuel domestically is of crucial importance. There is no energy crisis in Saudi Arabia, Iran, or Venezuela. Much of American energy politics revolves around avoiding dependence on these oil rich countries. Sometimes the call for energy autarky is legitimate, but more often it is self-serving. The rhetoric of national security has paid handsome dividends to Texas oil men. Geography is important at home as well as abroad. Energy issues pit one region against another according to what fuel lies beneath the surface. Coal-producing Pennsylvania is the natural adversary of petroleum-producing Texas. Being endowed with a fuel in itself has far-reaching political consequences. Coal is a dominant issue in West Virginia. Oil is a dominant one in Oklahoma. Lack of any local fuel is a key issue in New England. It is the nature of pollution that the costs are borne locally. A strip mine destroys the Appalachian mountains but lights New York City. A refinery pollutes its neighborhood but fuels cars on distant freeways. The long-term burden of extractive industry is borne locally as well. Mining and drilling are suicidal. Sooner or later they deplete their supply of coal, uranium, oil, or gas and move on, leaving behind ghost towns, wasted forests, polluted rivers, and crippled workers. This desolation, however, is a local problem hidden from national attention. Those who reaped the benefits escape the costs because geography protects them.

Neither time nor geography, however, differentiates energy politics as completely or as neatly as the type of fuel. Coal politics is independent of oil politics which is independent of nuclear politics. Politically each fuel is segmented from the others. This is a key feature too often ignored. Even when the technical characteristics of two fuels overlap, their politics are generally separate. While oil and natural gas flow from the same well, they part politically at once; different companies, different laws, and different government agencies control them as they reach the surface. While fossil fuels and nuclear fuel both produce electricity, they are politically separate. Even after the identical electricity leaves the generating station, government may maintain a jurisdictional separation. Since the political forces affecting the various fuels are so segmented, this book examines each fuel as a separate arena. Energy politics consists of not one but five arenas.

The five political arenas—coal, oil, natural gas, electricity, and nuclear energy—are considered in an order based on the degree to which government intervenes. Coal comes first because it is least subject to government control. It is the most private of the five fuels. Ownership is in private hands. Links to the government are minimal. No federal agency routinely regulates price or production. The oil industry is less autonomous. While ownership is private, the linkages to federal and state governments are extensive. No agency regulates price, but a coordinated set of state commissions does regulate production. Natural gas is third. Ownership is still private, but a federal agency heavily regulates price, production, sales, and construction of the industry. Ownership of electrical power facilities is mixed. Some are private; some are public, owned by either the federal, state, or local governments; still others are owned cooperatively. Governments at all levels regulate price, production, sales, and construction. Finally, the government intervenes most in nuclear energy. Ownership and regulation follow the same mixed pattern as in the electrical power arena. In addition the federal government enjoys monopoly ownership of the radioactive fuel that powers the reactors and subjects the utilities to detailed control in using it.

Separating energy politics into five arenas is, of course, to some extent arbitrary. The segmentation is far from absolute. The issues in one arena do spill over to affect neighboring arenas. Different fuels may share the same regulatory commissions or the same labor union. The same laws or court decisions may govern them. They may find their friends in the same political party or the same government agency. Much of the next five chapters will explore the linkages among the various arenas. Still, the separation of energy politics into the five arenas is the key feature in terms of public policy analysis and hence gives this book its basic format.

In examining the five arenas this book attempts to do more than merely review the history of energy politics in the United States. Fascinating as its chronicles may be, analysis of its processes will not be fully useful unless it tests some more general theoretical framework that promises to have applicability extending to other fields of policy. Hence the general theoretical context needs to be briefly outlined prior to any discussion of the five arenas. Figure 1 presents graphically the essential features of the conceptual scheme.

Energy politics depends on three sets of independent variables. The first is physical characteristics, including the specific physical properties of the fuel. A particular energy commodity will offer a greater or lesser degree of divisibility in its production, transportation, refining, distribution, and utilization, thus structuring these functions. It may be clean or dirty, with an attendant impact on the natural environment. Similarly, it may be safe or dangerous. Its geographic location is another physical characteristic with profound impact on its politics. Fuel produced within the United States fosters a political style radically different from that of fuel

Figure 1
Conceptual Scheme To Be Tested

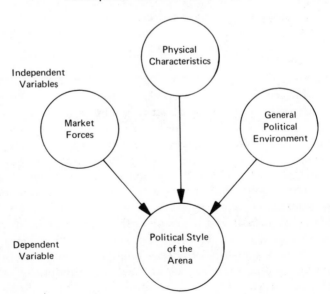

imported from abroad. Fuel produced from offshore wells on the outer continental shelf becomes involved in different political situations than fuel produced within a particular state's boundaries. Fuel found in one state presents a different set of political implications than that from another state. The absence of any natural fuel resources in New England has long arrayed this region against the fuel rich mountain and Gulf Coast states.

The second set of independent variables focuses on the market forces that structure an industry. Certain branches of energy production have experienced instability that has led to profound political impacts. The current phrase "energy crisis" implies an economic state of affairs that calls for a political solution. Its reciprocal term is "sick industry," which is likewise a description of an economic condition calling for political intervention. "Sick industry" refers to declining or unstable *demand* whereas "crisis" refers to declining or unstable *supply*. Neither of these terms technically falls within the methodology of either economics or political science, but both serve to express a call for help from the economic to the political sector. An intermediate market situation is that of a normal industry which is able to adjust without exhibiting either of the two extremes.

The third set of independent variables relates to the general political environment that has shaped the policy process. At any given time certain issues so dominate American politics that they penetrate the particular politics of each arena. These may include the trauma of wartime mobilization or the righteous spirit of reform. They may involve a crusade against a Communist specter or a battle against an economic depression. Whatever they may be, they so transcend the political issues of their specific arenas as to impose their characteristic features on other arenas. This imprinting of the general political milieu is especially critical in the era in which a particular form of energy first emerges. Those fuels that came into widespread use in the 1930's have a distinctive New Deal aura about their politics, while those already in common use were much less marked by the New Deal. Again, the politics of those fuels long in common use have been buffeted by many transcending political issues, whereas the politics of those more recently come into use show a greater impact of recent political issues. All, however, show a political style influenced by the overall political environment dominant at the time of their birth.

As the diagram illustrates, the independent variables interact to produce a particular process, here labeled the "political style." This term is a catchword to capture the essence of the political process occurring within the issue area. It is a basic thesis of this book that political style within each of the five policy arenas is distinctive. Each is characterized by its own institutions and behavior. While a policy arena may to some extent share its institutions and behavior with closely related arenas, it still has unique, individual features that distinguish it from its close relatives. To analyze these features, political science asks who the protagonists are, how decisions are made, how conflict is managed, and how resources are controlled.

Notes

1. Since the "energy crisis" is a new phenomenon most analysis has appeared in newspapers and popular magazines. In addition to these journalistic discussions this critique includes more scholarly efforts such as Lawrence Rocks and Richard Runyon, *The Energy Crisis* (New York: Crown, 1972); The National Petroleum Council, *U.S. Energy Outlook* (Washington, D.C., 1972); James E. Atkins, "The Oil Crisis: This Time the Wolf Is Here," *Foreign Affairs*, 51 (1973), 462—90; and Marc J. Roberts, "Is There an Energy Crisis?" *The Public Interest*, 31 (1973), 17—37.

2. *The New York Times*, January 24, 1974.

2

King Coal

Coal was king in nineteenth-century America. Its reign began soon after the United States won its independence from Great Britain and turned westward toward the Appalachian Mountains. The early pioneers in western Pennsylvania and Virginia soon discovered the valuable energy source lying literally underfoot. The black rock so easily dug from exposed seams yielded a fuel far superior to the wood and charcoal on which the newly freed Americans had had to rely while living along the Atlantic Coast. Throughout the nineteenth century coal fired the iron furnaces of Pittsburgh, heated the factories of New York, and drove the locomotives carrying settlers west across the continent.

Coal's physical properties led to its early development. Its high energy value per pound made it more efficient than wood. It could be burned just as it came out of the ground. Mining did not demand elaborate technology or even a large investment of capital. The Appalachian coal fields lay close to the established eastern cities and soon spawned new industrial cities such as Pittsburgh and Birmingham.

In the nineteenth century market forces made coal a vigorous, expanding industry; but before the twentieth century was two decades old it reached its peak, and thereafter its economic health declined. As a "sick industry" it spread its malaise as a pestilence. Its economic decline contaminated its politics as if the industry were called upon to act out some tragic destiny. Cruelty, corruption, and violence plagued the politics of coal to a degree unmatched in any other energy arena.

Coal's extended history carried it through a succession of general political environments longer than that of any other form of energy. Since so many transcending political issues wrought their impact upon it, coal was less influenced by any single one. The industry's development began in the laissez faire environment of the nineteenth century, when governments did not intervene in economic affairs. Because coal's political style was so firmly established in this environment, successive environments had a lesser effect. Teddy Roosevelt's progressive reforms, Woodrow Wilson's wartime mobilization, and Franklin Roosevelt's New Deal all left their marks, but not so deeply as on other forms of energy.

Old King Coal was a harsh old soul, and the story of the coal industry for the first half of the twentieth century was the story of the workers trying to bring this harsh master under control. To a greater extent than for any of the other four forms of energy to be considered in this book, the politics of coal focuses on labor.

The century opened with a long and bitter strike in the anthracite fields of northeastern Pennsylvania, which did much to redefine the government's role in labor-management relations. The first round of the conflict came during the presidential election of 1900. The United Mine Workers, a young and weak union based in the bituminous fields of western Pennsylvania and the Midwest, had launched an organizing drive in the anthracite fields. Though only about 9,000 out of the 140,000 hard-coal miners had joined, the members were eager to strike a blow against the hard conditions and the low pay that were their lot. The U.M.W. struck on September 17 and was soon joined by over 100,000 nonmembers until 125,000 miners were off the job. Yet the operators were adamant. They would not recognize the union or even meet with its saintly, thirty-year-old president, John Mitchell. The operators' obstinacy was not shared, however, by the Republican party. Party chief Mark Hanna, a coal operator himself before turning to politics, prevailed upon the coal barons to settle the strike before it endangered the party's campaign for President McKinley's reelection. They did so grudgingly. Though they refused to negotiate with Mitchell, they did raise wages 10 percent and on October 29, with the election only a few days away, the miners returned to work.[1]

This election eve settlement was fragile. For the next year and a half the operators obstructed the U.M.W. organizing drives, stockpiled big inventories, and hired more men for the Coal and Iron Police, a private force authorized by the state of Pennsylvania to enforce the coal barons' will. For their part, the miners expressed their dissatisfaction in the form of frequent wildcat strikes.

In the spring of 1902, the tenuous truce broke down. Mitchell had presented the U.M.W. demands of union recognition, a minimum wage scale, a 20 percent wage increase, and an eight-hour day. When the operators refused, 147,000 miners struck. The strike stretched through the summer, accompanied by ill will, hunger, and riots. The governor called out two regiments of the National Guard to keep order. But just when the strikers were most demoralized, their cause was unwittingly buoyed by the leader of the coal operators. In reply to a letter urging him to settle the strike in the spirit of Christian charity, George F. Baer, the president of the Reading Railroad, wrote that labor was best served "not by the labor agitators, but by the Christian men of property to whom God has given control of the property rights of the country and upon the successful management of which so much depends."[2]

The public sympathy this arrogant letter engendered was not the miners' only ally. The weather was another. As summer gave way to the chill of autumn, the strike took on a graver tone. In New York City, the price of coal went up to $20 per ton, three to four times the normal cost. The mayor feared riots. He and many other state and city officials throughout the Northeast urged the federal government to intervene.

In 1902, government intervention was not routine. Indeed it was nearly unheard of.[3] The government's policy toward the economy was still essentially the same laissez faire one that had prevailed during the nineteenth century. Mark Hanna's appeal to the operators, which had settled the strike two years before, had deviated little, if at all, from this laissez faire attitude. He made his appeal as a fellow coal operator and as the Republican party leader, not on the basis of any government office.

Theodore Roosevelt, who by 1902 was President in the wake of McKinley's assassination, had long considered intervening. He viewed the President's role as more active than had his predecessors. He considered prosecuting the operators under the

Sherman Antitrust Act, but his Attorney General believed the case to be too weak. He wrote to the coal barons, but they remained firm. At last, on October 3, with the congressional elections nearing, he convened a meeting of the U.M.W. and the operators in Washington. The conference did little except to outrage Roosevelt at the arrogance of the operators in contrast to the calm reasonableness of the miners. The President was stymied. The operators had defied his mediation. He threatened to send federal troops to Pennsylvania to mine the coal but found he could not do so legally.

Shortly after these abortive negotiations, Secretary of War Elihu Root made a new proposal to the operators specifically designed to salve their sensitive pride. This agreement, signed October 12, established an arbitration commission of six men. After much bickering all parties were satisfied with the membership: two favorable to the operators, two favorable to labor, and two neutral. These six then elected the U.S. Labor Commissioner (equivalent to the present Secretary of Labor) to join them. The strikers returned to work and the Republicans won control of Congress.

The commission began hearings in Scranton, Pennsylvania, shortly after election day. After five months of testimony and deliberation, the commission announced its award. The miners gained a 10 percent increase in pay and other improvements. But the decision did not grant formal recognition to the union. The U.M.W. was still, in the words of George F. Baer, "a set of outlaws." While the union failed to win formal recognition by the operators, it did win informal recognition by the public and the federal government. For the first time ever, the President had intervened to settle a strike. The relationship between employer and employee was being redefined in the grimy company towns of Pennsylvania and in the dignified offices of Washington. Then, as was often to be the case thereafter, the redefinition was hammered out under the threat of an energy shortage.

Although the settlement of the anthracite strikes in 1900 and 1902 pointed toward an enhanced role for the U.M.W., its defeat in the Ludlow strike of 1913-14 seemed to aim labor-management relations in another direction—that of company unions. The Colorado Fuel and Iron Company employed over 15,000 men in its mines. In the fall of 1913, 9,000 of them living in Ludlow abandoned not only the mines but their company-owned houses to set up camp in tents on the nearby hills. So began a 15-month strike aimed at union recognition and emancipation from the tyranny of the company store, the company doctor, and the company house. The encamped strikers endured a Rocky Mountain winter flecked with flurries of violence. The operators had prevailed on the governor to impose martial law. On April 22, 1914, the sporadic outbursts erupted into a full-scale battle as the National Guard fired into the tent city with rifles and machine guns. Three miners and one soldier died in the first fighting. Then the Guard moved into the camp, poured coal oil on the tents and set them afire. Women and children, hiding in foxholes under the tents, fled screaming. Not all were able to flee. When the fires died out, two women and eleven children were found suffocated or burned to death. In revenge, the striking miners launched a week of guerrilla warfare, attacking the Colorado National Guard and company guards and officials throughout southern Colorado until federal troops ordered from Forth Leavenworth, Kansas, arrived to restore order.[4]

Prior to the Ludlow massacre, President Wilson had been reluctant to send in federal troops. He did not want to seem to be favoring the Colorado Fuel and Iron Company, owned by the Rockefeller family, nor did he want to make further commitments of army units at the same time his military intervention in Mexico was going so badly politically and militarily. He had appealed to the Rockefellers to give in to the U.M.W. demands but John D. Rockefeller, Jr., had strongly rebuffed the President's request. He wanted to maintain the open shop where no worker would be compelled to join a union. After the massacre the President again put forth a truce offer, which the coal operators arrogantly rejected. The President was piqued. The U.M.W. was despondent. With its strike funds nearly depleted it called on the government to seize control of the mines. Wilson pleaded that he had no legal authority. Finally in December 1914 the union capitulated. It accepted management's terms with only a few face saving sops.

In the aftermath of the strike Rockefeller rethought his position. He hired as an advisor Mackenzie King, then the former labor minister of Canada and later to be its prime minister for 21 years.

Rockefeller and King toured the Colorado coal fields in 1915. The result was the Colorado Industrial Representative Plan, or, as it was better known, the Rockefeller Plan.

The Rockefeller Plan strove to replace labor-management hostility with cooperation. Workers and managers selected representatives to Joint Committees on Industrial Cooperation and Conciliation. The committees sought policies of industrial harmony and heard grievances of individual workers. Adopted by the other Rockefeller enterprises, this paternalism met with success in avoiding strikes and eliminating conflict. The trade union movement, however, did not share management's enthusiasm, for the plan launched the company union, which in the opinion of organized labor was a fake union, not truly dedicated to the welfare of the workers but concerned largely with the interests of the company. The unions sought legislation to outlaw such company unions and finally achieved it in 1935, when Congress passed the National Labor Relations Act.

World War I was a high point for King Coal. For the previous half-century demand had been rising rapidly. The war increased the demand to unprecedented levels, which obscured some of the underlying conflicts within the industry. One of these conflicts was a geographic one between the northern and southern mines. The mines south of the Ohio River enjoyed several advantages. Some were natural: the mines were newer and the seams better. Some were political: the Interstate Commerce Commission permitted the railroads that served the southern Appalachians to carry coal at a cheaper rate than those in the north. Since transportation often accounted for 40 percent of the cost, this conferred a major advantage. The northern operators urged the ICC to order the southern railroads to raise their rates, effectively adding a premium to the price of their competitors' coal. The southern operators enjoyed the further economy of nonunion labor. Even after World War I, when the U.M.W. was able to unionize the southern mines, the wage differential continued for many years.[5]

While the wartime prosperity smoothed over all these conflicts as the high demand brought high profits to the operators and high wages to the miners, the reconversion to a peacetime economy brought them to the fore again. The U.M.W. was determined to maintain the high wage levels. To do so, it struck on November 1, 1919. The impact was much greater than that of the 1902 strike. Then only the anthracite miners struck. This time bituminous miners struck as well. This time the union was much stronger. This time the effect was worldwide. The mines of Europe lay shattered by the war, many of their workers casualties of the fighting. Indeed, Europe had hoped to import American coal to tide it over the winter. On November 11, the first anniversary of the armistice, while steel mills were closing and cities had begun rationing fuel, the U.M.W. announced that it was ready to negotiate. The word came from John L. Lewis, just beginning his four decades as president of the United Mine Workers. The conference, convened in Washington under the auspices of the Secretary of Labor, made little progress for nearly a month. At last the President intervened personally, appointing an arbitration board chosen to give a generous settlement to labor.[6]

Once again a bitter coal strike ended with a government-appointed commission. As in the 1902 strike the commission was to save face for the operators. Again as in the 1902 strike, the U.M.W.'s bargaining stance was strengthened by a crisis situation. In both cases the public faced severe fuel shortages as the cold winter loomed. The miners were able to exploit the emergency. The Ludlow strikers had had no such advantages. The coal they mined was used for making steel, not heating homes, and even as such contributed only a small proportion to the nation's steel output.

John L. Lewis' successful settlement of the 1919 strike gave him a firm hold on the U.M.W., something he needed to carry him through the difficult decade ahead. From the early 1920's on, the coal industry began to decline in relation to other forms of energy. Demand leveled off. The high prices during the war had taught consumers how to economize on coal. The uncertain deliveries caused by strikes and transportation problems prompted them to shift to more dependable sources of energy. Technical developments made oil and natural gas more attractive. Thus, while the total American economy expanded rapidly during the roaring 20's, the consumption of coal remained the same. Despite the U.M.W.'s vigorous activities, sluggish demand actually forced it to accept reduced wages in the 1927 contract negotiations. Once the Great

Depression began with the 1929 crash, the plight of the industry became desperate. The plight of the U.M.W. was even more desperate. The union had exhausted its resources in a series of futile strikes in the late 1920's. Membership dropped to a low of 84,000 out of 522,000 bituminous miners in 1930.[7]

While the Great Depression was an era of national misery, it was also an era of profound change in the political system. American society redefined the role of its government and of its basic institutions. Among the key institutions whose places were recast was organized labor, and John L. Lewis and his United Mine Workers were in the vanguard.

Franklin D. Roosevelt won the Presidency in 1932, leading a coalition of forces in his party forged by Al Smith four years earlier. In 1928 Smith had gone down to inglorious defeat, pulling a scanty 15 million votes, primarily from the South and the northern cities. While the "solid South" had been with the party since before the Civil War, the urban North had not. Smith had cracked the Republican stranglehold there, albeit in a pitifully weak fashion. Four years later Roosevelt, opposing a Republican candidate now saddled with responsibility for the Depression, carried the same urban-southern coalition to victory. He did so in 1932, however, with little help from the groups now thought of as hard-core Democrats. Negroes, for example, deserted the party of Lincoln only in the smallest numbers. Organized labor displayed no strong shift to Roosevelt. Leaders like Lewis remained loyal to the Grand Old Party.

Although Roosevelt had been elected on a conservative platform and had pledged to cut government spending, by the time he was inaugurated on March 4, 1933, he had rethought his governing strategy. Immediately upon taking office he began a wave of action known as the Hundred Days. Among the first of these New Deal measures was the National Industrial Recovery Act. Section 7(a) of the NIRA provided that "employees shall have the right to organize and to bargain collectively through representatives of their own choosing, and shall be free from interference, restraint or coercion of employers . . . in the designation of such representatives." This was a bill of rights for the trade unions. They could now organize workers free of the heavy hand of the companies.

The U.M.W. began a massive membership drive. Its slogan was "President Roosevelt wants you to join the union."[8]

The NIRA of 1933 succumbed to a conservative, Republican-dominated Supreme Court in 1935. But before the high court declared the act unconstitutional U.M.W. membership soared to 540,000. Within a month of the NIRA decision Congress passed the National Labor Relations Act as a replacement, and, despite numerous predictions to the contrary, the Supreme Court upheld its constitutionality. Henceforth, the government was to be the friend and the protector of labor.

Though King Coal had been on a relative decline as an industry for a decade, John L. Lewis and the U.M.W. were at their acme. Lewis' control over the union was tight. During the bleak days in the early 1930's, he had taken advantage of the weakness of many of the districts and locals to install his own men in power. Earlier he had removed his troublesome vice president, William Green, by getting him elected president of the American Federation of Labor. As the 1930's moved on, Lewis felt increasingly dissatisfied with the parent group. The A.F.L. clung to a concept of organization by crafts—all carpenters, all machinists, all blasters. Lewis believed it should shift to organization by industry—all construction workers, all automobile workers, all miners. The U.M.W. had successfully followed this policy. The issue came to a head at the 1935 A.F.L. convention. When the Federation voted decisively against an industrial basis, Lewis first vented his spleen by bloodying his opponent, "Big Bill" Hutcheson, in a fist fight on the convention floor. He then led the formation of a rival organization—the Committee for Industrial Organization. The C.I.O. chose Lewis as president and at once launched a recruiting drive. In spite of A.F.L. hostility, the C.I.O. flourished. The U.M.W. furnished much of the money and leadership. The rivalry between these two powerful wings of organized labor, each led by a former coal miner, was to divide industrial labor relations for the next two decades.[9]

One of the first consequences of the split in organized labor was greater political activity. The A.F.L. had been reluctant to engage in partisanship. The new C.I.O. was eager to do so. Furthermore, labor was realigning its votes. While few union leaders had supported the Democrats in 1932, many did so in 1936. Four years of

Roosevelt's New Deal had transformed the place of the trade union. The NIRA had allowed the unions to organize, gain members, and win wage increases. The National Labor Relations Act had given them a friend in the collective bargaining process. The company union, the mainstay of the Rockefeller Plan, had been eliminated. The leaders were now ready to reward their friend the President.

To do so, Lewis in April 1936 organized the Non-Partisan League pledged to the re-election of F.D.R. The league enjoyed wide support from 59 different unions, some of them from the A.F.L. as well as the C.I.O. Most of the money and leadership, however, came from the U.M.W.[10]

Lewis' 1936 switch from the Republican to the Democratic party was indicative of the major realignment of the American electorate that occurred in the 1930's. The entire country was undergoing a shift in attitudes from one in which a majority of the voters identified with the party of Lincoln to one in which the majority identified with the party of Roosevelt. The old pattern had been based on Civil War loyalties. Southern states were Democratic; northern states were Republican. In the border states the old Copperhead counties were Democratic while the old Union counties were Republican. Outside the South the Democrats could collect enough votes from recent immigrants and others neglected by the Republicans to gain control of an occasional city. Roosevelt changed this pattern. After taking Smith's urban-southern coalition and capitalizing on Hoover's identification with the Great Depression to capture the White House in 1932, Roosevelt set about forging his coalition of two disadvantaged sectors of the nation—the South and the cities—into a permanent basis for Democratic strength; from his efforts came the New Deal programs to aid labor, Negroes, farmers, the South, and so on. The 1936 landslide victory that these groups gave him richly rewarded the President for his work. Roosevelt won 28 million votes, carrying all states except Maine and Vermont.

The short-term impact of the Non-Partisan League is hard to assess. Its leaders understandably took full credit for the massive support working men gave to Roosevelt. But the question remains whether Lewis and the other trade union officials were leading these men into the Democratic fold or following them. Many workers had voted for Roosevelt in 1932, though few labor leaders did so. Thus the many more workers and their leaders who supported F.D.R. in 1936 were flowing with the tide.

The long-term impact of this movement is easier to assess. The 1936 breaking away of Lewis and other leaders from the G.O.P. marked the beginning of the enduring allegiance to the Democratic party. Likewise the typical member's switch to Roosevelt brought the beginnings of the present pattern of political loyalty. The process was not necessarily smooth. A citizen's identification with a political party takes years to establish. Most learn it in childhood from their parents through a lengthy process of socialization. To break away from an inherited partisan loyalty not only took the shock of the Great Depression and the ensuing reforms of the New Deal but took many more years of tentative loyalty to the new party.

The U.M.W. could look back on the 1930's with pride. It had been in the forefront of the labor triumph. Starting with few members in a hostile political environment, it had grown rapidly and shared fully in the new prolabor policies of the New Deal. John L. Lewis and other leaders were now welcome visitors to the White House and the Capitol. The coal miners deserve much of the credit for this transformation. The U.M.W. furnished the top leadership for both the A.F.L. and the breakaway C.I.O. They dominated the Non-Partisan League.

Lewis used the emergency conditions of World War II and the immediate postwar period to advance aggressively the cause of his miners. In 1943, the U.M.W. struck for higher wages. President Roosevelt seized the mines to save war production from collapsing, but since Lewis had issued the call for the strike prior to the government's seizure, he was not technically in violation of the no-strike provisions of the War Labor Disputes Act and thus escaped criminal prosecution. Roosevelt could do little except quickly come to terms with the mine workers' costly demands.[11]

The U.M.W. again exploited a crisis situation in the 1946-47 strike.[12] When the government seized the mines, Lewis negotiated a contract with the Secretary of the Interior, which provided that the government would contribute a royalty of 5 cents per ton to finance an industry-wide U.M.W. welfare fund, a provision he had been unable to obtain from the operators. When the strike ended and the operators tried to undo this provision, they found that once established, it was impossible to roll back. By 1948, the royalty was 20 cents per ton.

Labor's successes during the New Deal and the war years produced a backlash. For the first time since 1930 the Republicans won control of Congress in 1946. They were pledged to a program of bringing labor under control to satisfy the voters upset by the postwar wave of strikes in coal and other industries. The Republicans' answer was the Taft-Hartley Act, passed over President Truman's veto. The law was not really antilabor. Most of its provisions represented compromises between the two points of view. It provided for an injunction giving an 80-day cooling off period during which the two sides were required to mediate their dispute. If mediation failed, the union might then walk out. Still, labor considered this a setback. The Act was invoked against the U.M.W. three times in the next three years. On one of these occasions, Lewis' disobedience of the injunction resulted in a heavy fine for contempt of court.

The passage of the Taft-Hartley Act signaled the end of an era for the coal industry.[13] The first half of the twentieth century was characterized by a growing domination of King Coal by those men who labored to dig it out of the ground. From their position of weakness and degradation, which John Mitchell sought to remedy in the 1902 strike, they had risen to a place of power epitomized by the might of John L. Lewis. In part labor could rise because it accepted the fact that the industry was in relative decline. Except for the temporary boom brought about by the World War II emergency, the tonnage of coal brought to the surface had remained stable since the end of World War I. The share it represented of the total energy supplied had dropped. Its consumers were converting to oil and gas. The U.M.W.'s response had been to accept less work as long as wages remained high. Many of the contracts negotiated had provided for three- and four-day workweeks. The effect was to stabilize production even in the face of opposition from the operators who wanted to mine more coal at a lower labor cost.

The relative decline in the demand for coal was combined with increased benefits for the miner. During the 1930's, his income rose rapidly as did that of other industrial workers. During the war and immediately thereafter, thanks to John L. Lewis's ruthless exploitation of the emergency situation, his income rose even faster than that of other industrial workers. The union built a pension fund and a series of hospitals.

This was, however, the high point for the union. The United Mine Workers' forward momentum came to a stop. The Taft-Hartley Act swung the balance slightly back to the operators' side. With this and with declining demand, relationships in the industry stabilized. Two major impacts had been made: the federal government had become the friend of labor, and the unions had found a home in the Democratic party.

Throughout the first half of the century, the politics of coal had rested on essentially social issues: What were the rights of the miners to organize? For which party should they vote? When should the government intervene? By 1950 these issues were resolved, and little was heard from the industry until the mid-1960's. This time the key political issues were based on a changing technology. While the fuel's physical properties remained the same as they had for billions of years, the producers had developed new means of digging the ore.

The extraction process was undergoing rapid change. Whereas in 1950 over two-thirds of the coal came from deep mines, by 1970 that proportion had dropped to half. The new wave was strip mining. Improved engineering technology did much to foster the growth of stripping. Giant shovels as high as a 22-story building can quickly strip off 30 to 40 feet of overburden covering a seam of coal. Then bulldozers and smaller shovels gobble up the coal to load into waiting trucks. Mammoth augers and cheap explosives can tear away fuel from inaccessible corners. This method enjoys further efficiencies over the old. Surface techniques can remove 90 percent of the coal in the seam, whereas the old tunnel and pillar mines can remove only 50 percent. Labor costs are lower with the new method. A few men can operate the giant machines, which replace dozens of the old skilled miners. The U.M.W. favors stripping because it means more pay and safer conditions even though many fewer can find employment. The union has a long history of encouraging automation, unlike many others in the less dangerous trades.

High demand for cheap coal has encouraged surface mining as well. Much of the coal goes to generate electricity, the demand for which is doubling every ten years. Much goes abroad. The Japanese buy tremendous amounts to fuel their voracious industrial machine. Likewise, Europeans find American coal cheaper than their own even after it is shipped across the Atlantic. Ironically, one reason European coal is expensive is the strictly enforced laws requiring full restoration of land after strip mining.

The concern with air pollution that emerged during the past decade has further shifted the balance toward surface mining.[14] While much of the eastern coal from deep mines is high in sulfur, the western coal is low. Since many power generating plants must decrease their sulfur emissions they now buy the coal lying 30 to 40 feet under the prairies of Montana, Wyoming, and the Dakotas. Before air pollution controls placed a premium on low sulfur fuels the western fields could not compete with the eastern. Shipping the coal to market was too costly. But now Chicago and other midwestern cities find they must buy the western coal since the locally mined product is too sulfurous. Elsewhere, concern with pollution dictates that the electric generating plant be located near the coal fields and the electricity transmitted hundreds of miles to the consuming cities. Hence the Four Corners plant in New Mexico supplies power for Los Angeles.[15]

This site is good for Los Angeles but not necessarily good for New Mexico. The plant and the mines that feed it are located on Navajo and Hopi lands. The Indians view the plant with mixed feelings. For some it means prosperity. Salaries of over $10,000 can revolutionize a reservation where the average income is less than $3,000. The two tribes will earn $100 million in royalties over the next 35 years. But it also means destruction of the land, and to the Indian, the land is sacred. As archeologists are discovering, his culture literally lies buried in it. The Indians traditionally believe that God himself lives in the nearby Black Mesa soon to fall victim to the shovel. Even the less spiritual residents regret the ravages of the earthmovers and the smoke of the generators.

The coal company mining the Black Mesa has agreed to restore the land afterwards. Those living near hundreds of other surface mines are not so lucky. Restoration is a costly and difficult task, and in the past few operators even tried. More are trying today because several of the chief mining states have passed laws requiring it. Pennsylvania, West Virginia, and Kentucky have such laws, which work when they are enforced.

Kentucky in particular owes it to its citizens to enforce its laws as a way to repay them for the past tribulations they have suffered at the hands of the state's legislature and courts.[16] The particular evil perpetuated on the people of the Bluegrass State is the "broad form deed." In the early days of the coal boom, agents of the operators systematically crisscrossed the highlands purchasing the mineral rights. For a few dollars per acre the naive mountaineers sold thousands of dollars worth of buried coal. Worse yet, they conveyed to the companies the right to excavate, to build roads and structures, to use the timber, to divert and pollute the water, and to cover the land with spoil. The farmers retained the right to plant a little corn and pay taxes. Disastrous as this conveyance was, it caused comparatively little trouble as long as the mining was subsurface. But once an operator chose to strip mine, the destruction was complete. Bulldozers and shovels would move in, chewing up timber, crops, and even the family cemetery. If after a spring rain the ravaged mountain slid down into the valley destroying all the houses, as in a 1949 case before the Kentucky Court of Appeals, that was an act of God for which the coal company could not be held responsible. A few years later when the court at first decided in favor of a farmer, the coal companies were able to bring enough pressure to bear that the court reversed itself on a rehearing. This decision guaranteed the rights of strip mining for another prosperous decade.

Kentucky politicians, like those in other states, were reluctant to bear down hard on the coal companies because they believed that what was good for the operators was good for the state, not just the politicians but the people as well. Were the laws too harsh, the coal companies would simply move to a neighboring state where economic conditions would be more favorable. Reclamation itself was a dubious concept. First, the costs were uncertain. If too much was demanded the mining would no longer be profitable. Second, the benefits were uncertain. To what standard should the land be restored? Ohio requires that the land be returned to the same contours as before. This has produced some impressive reclamation projects with the former mine site dotted with lakes, trees, and campsites. But these showcases tend to be expensive public relations gimmicks far too costly to be built routinely. Even minimal grading and planting with fast growing legumes adds an expense most operators would prefer to avoid. Only the compulsion of state enforcement makes them comply. Difficult as the problem is in Ohio, it is worse in Kentucky and West Virginia, where the rugged mountain geography leads to different mining techniques. In the rolling hills of Ohio and the plains of the Midwest and West, the operators practice area mining. This leaves the overburden covering the coal seam handy for refilling the pit. But in the mountains they must practice contour and auger mining in which the soil overburden cannot be recovered to repair the cuts. Thus rigid enforcement of laws is of little use since there is no practical technique by which to reclaim the land.

The technology of strip mining and reclamation is not entirely a dismal battle against the odds. Improvements in engineering mean land that has been mined out once may be remined using more massive equipment. Newer shovels can reach deeper seams that could not be economically exploited 10 to 20 years previously. Operators find it advantageous to dig again in abandoned strip mines. This often means that "orphan banks" of spoil that have been lying treeless and acidic for years will be reworked and then restored by the new operator. The digging will also collapse old tunnels from underground mines, which may have been polluting the water table, or slowly burning for years.

The process of periodic remining of the same land suggests a long-run solution to the question of what is to become of the property. It will simply be held by the coal company until improvements in mining equipment make it possible to dig once more to exploit some deeper bed of coal. While this is preferable to the company's merely abandoning the land, thereby depriving the state of taxes at the same time that it saddles the state with the responsibility, continued company ownership does not guarantee that the land will be returned to anything approaching a natural condition for the time in between. For this the states must vigorously enforce reclamation standards.

While the states have adequate reclamation laws on the books, they are not enforced. The state bureaus charged with the responsibility fail to obtain satisfactory results. The companies restore a few small areas for display; the bulk remains unrepaired. To overcome this common failing of state ineffectiveness, environmentalists have proposed a federal law. The fight is led by the COALition Against Strip Mining along with the Sierra Club and other ecology lobbyists. In 1972 the House of Representatives passed such a bill, but the Senate did not. The antistrippers are opposed by the National Coal Association. The N.C.A.'s lobbying strategy in Congress, as it has been against similar legislation in the states, has been to give token support to the bill while working behind the scenes to kill it. Another lobbying technique is to support a weak law in order to avoid a strong one.

As the coal industry abandoned the deep mines in favor of strip mines and abandoned the hills of Kentucky, Pennsylvania, and West Virginia in favor of the prairies of Montana and the Dakotas, it left a legacy of unemployment and despair. The misery of the West Virginians so shocked John F. Kennedy when he campaigned there in that state's 1960 presidential primary that he resolved to bring federal aid to the region. The program developed slowly, however, and was still being planned when Kennedy was assassinated. Lyndon Johnson announced that its enactment would have first priority as a memorial to the martyred President. Johnson coined the word "Appalachia" to describe the region of 360 counties in 12 states running from upstate New York to central Alabama. Nearly every part of the region could trace its poverty to the decline of deep coal mining. As the companies laid off skilled miners, the young deserted the highlands for cities like Detroit, Cleveland, and Baltimore, while the old were condemned to remain behind. The educated who could more easily find jobs left the hills to the ignorant who could not. The strong and healthy left, and the weak and ill stayed. Those remaining had few among them who possessed the education and energy for a political career. Where the people did mobilize for politics, their leaders were 80-year-old men and frail widows.

The Appalachian Regional Development Act of 1965 approached the area's problems from two directions: (1) a federal-state commission worked to develop the region's economy, and (2) Congress appropriated funds to develop the economic infrastructure and repair some of the damage from strip mining and deforestation. Thirty-seven million dollars were voted to seal mine entrances, extinguish underground fires, and restore strip mines on public (but not private) land.[17]

The impact of the act was mixed. The 1965 law failed to spark an Appalachian renaissance. Indeed one of the commission's conclusions was that the most rural and mountainous sections had no economic future. The best solution was to build highways so that those residents could drive to the nearby cities in which economic growth was occurring. Those too old, ill, ignorant, or remote would have to continue on public welfare and money from sons and daughters who could leave. On the other hand the federal funds channeled into the 12 states of Appalachia aroused the envy of other disadvantaged states. This led Congress in 1967 to establish similar programs for 5 other regions: New England, Upper Great Lakes, Ozarks, Coastal Plains, and Four Corners.

In granting aid to Appalachia, Congress dealt with the human costs of the coal industry indirectly. In 1969 it dealt with them directly by passing legislation on health and safety. The first such laws had been passed in 1941. When John L. Lewis negotiated his agreement with the Secretary of the Interior at the time of the 1946 government seizures, he included provisions for health and safety along with the pension fund royalties and hefty wage hikes he squeezed out of Uncle Sam. These standards were incorporated in the 1947 law, revised in 1952. Then for nearly two decades the matter was ignored while conditions grew worse. Improved mining techniques produced more coal dust in the mines as mechanical equipment replaced manual methods. The dust entered the miners' lungs, causing black lung disease. It was only in the 1960's that this syndrome was recognized as a specific illness. Previously physicians believed that the shortness of breath characteristic of veteran miners was silicosis, caused by inhaling silica (sand) dust. Black lung disease is a progressive affliction. After 20 years a miner's lungs will be half blackened with deposits of coal dust. After 30 to 40 years his lungs will be completely black. The disease causes coughing, wheezing, and difficulty in breathing, then an early death. This terrible price charged to support American industry was long paid by the miner alone. Later the U.M.W. ameliorated his burden with the establishment of the pension fund and regional hospitals.[18]

Black lung disease brings a slow death; mine accidents bring a quick one. Since 1907, 90,000 have died in the mines. Since 1930 1½ million have been seriously injured. Some horrifying disasters in the late 1960's directed national attention to the problem. In 1968, 78 men died when explosions and fires 600 feet below the surface trapped the night shift in Mine #9 of the Mountaineer Coal Company in West Virginia. After nine days of attempting rescue the mine was sealed off to extinguish the fire, which continued to rage underground. The miners criticized the Bureau of Mines of the Department of the Interior for failing to enforce the 1952 laws.

The twin concerns with safety and black lung disease finally merged with enough strength to stir Congress to pass a new law in December of 1969. The act directed the Secretary of the Interior to establish safety standards and the Secretary of Health, Education, and Welfare to establish health standards. The Bureau of Mines was to inspect more often. The penalties for violation were raised. Less coal dust was allowed, and free, periodic chest X-rays were provided. The federal government would pay $136 per month to a miner disabled by black lung disease or to his widow. President Nixon opposed this provision and threatened to veto the law unless it were removed. He said that this was workmen's compensation, an area traditionally and properly left to the states. The federal government could not afford to begin taking on such expensive commitments. But in the end he signed the law, since no President could afford to offend organized labor by denying $136 per month to cripples and widows.

The Coal Mine Health and Safety Act had been in effect only a few months when the miners expressed their dissatisfaction with it. In a series of wildcat strikes affecting 150 mines in western Pennsylvania, they protested against lax enforcement of its provisions. The new law was of little use unless the Bureau of Mines was vigilant in its execution. The miners' union was itself a target of the strikers' wrath for failing to take a strong, adversarial stance in defense of the workers' health and safety.

This was probably the least worry of the U.M.W. leadership

during 1970, for its sins were far greater than mere neglect of the members' health and safety. On December 9, 1969, W. A. "Tony" Boyle, the union president whom John L. Lewis handpicked in 1963, won a bitterly fought campaign for re-election as union president. His opponent was "Jock" Yablonski, U.M.W. officer and leader of a movement to clean up the union. The cleanup was to correct such wrongs as misuse of the pension fund, kickbacks from bankers, collusion with management, and illegal voting procedures. Even before the days of John L. Lewis the U.M.W. had been a rowdy organization characterized by internal violence, dictatorship, and financial sleight-of-hand. Boyle saw no reason to let Yablonski end this style of operation. Defeating the challenger at the polls was insufficient. Shortly after Christmas three U.M.W. thugs broke into the Yablonskis' Pennsylvania home where they murdered him along with his wife and daughter. The F.B.I. investigation and testimony at their assassins' trial revealed the sordid details of U.M.W. involvement. Boyle and his top lieutenants were implicated. Contemporaneously Boyle himself was convicted of conspiracy and making illegal political contributions with union funds.

In the wake of this trial the Department of Labor moved in 1972 to set aside as illegal the 1969 election of Boyle. The court that voided the election directed the Labor Department to manage the union in the meantime and supervise the new vote to assure that it would be fair. Boyle's challenger this time was Arnold Miller, a partially disabled victim of black lung disease and leader of a reform faction known as the Miners for Democracy. Miller won, but even then Boyle tried a few last tricks. He resigned and had the union vote him an annual pension of $50,000. When the courts validated Miller's election four days later, the President rescinded the pension, fired all of Boyle's appointees from the executive board and called for their replacement, this time by election rather than appointment. Tony Boyle's fall from power fit the violent destiny King Coal decrees. In 1973 both the federal and state prosecutors indicted him for instigating the Yablonski murders. The night before he was to appear in the federal court, Boyle, then age 70, attempted suicide. As he lay unconscious in a Washington hospital newscasters spoke of the symbolic end of an era for coal.

Yet Boyle even cheated death. After two months he recovered enough to enter prison for misusing union funds and to stand trial for the three murders, for which he was convicted on April 11, 1974.

Seen over the past decade, the political characteristics of the coal industry have displayed a far different orientation than they did in the first half of the century. Then coal was at the vortex of the forces that radically altered American society. The U.M.W. led the labor movement in asserting its rights. The trade unions fought to establish their place, to define their rights. In the process they were in the forefront of the great electoral realignments when labor shifted the balance of the electorate from the Republicans to the Democrats. John L. Lewis and his U.M.W. led the more militant out of the A.F.L. and out of the G.O.P.

By the late 1940's, however, most of the battles were over, frequently because they had been won. Trade unions were established. The militants had their industry-based C.I.O. The working class voters had a home in the Democratic party. The tide began to turn. Already during the 1940's the U.M.W. strikes had aimed more at wages and less at rights. The trend continued. In 1947, the Taft-Hartley Act slowed the progress of labor even though it did little to roll back gains made during the New Deal and the war. The C.I.O. ended its schism with the A.F.L., leading to their merger in 1955. Labor demanded little from the Democrats other than continued domination of the Labor Department. With the A.F.L.-C.I.O. merger, the accomplishment of many of its goals, and the decline of underground mining and hence members, the U.M.W. lost its dominance in the trade union movement.

The U.M.W. has been drawn into politics in recent years in terms of the most traditional functions of government: law and order and health and safety. The government's concern that its citizens not be murdered is one of its most ancient. The medieval British monarch was able to extend his authority over all of England because he sent out sheriffs and judges who would punish those criminals who broke the king's peace. Later governments assumed the responsibility to see that trustees guarded the funds for which they were responsible. Thus when the federal courts tried Jock Yablonski's murderers and the U.M.W. pension fund's embezzlers, the government was exercising its most basic functions in contrast to the New Deal, when it was experimenting with innovative new relationships between government and industry. Similarly the federal government's concern with the health and safety of the miners was a traditional one. The physical well-being of their citizens long ago prompted governments to enact laws regulating public health and safety. The coal industry was contributing nothing new to the American political system here either.

The new political issue that King Coal presents today is environmental protection. One aspect is strip mining. The increasing concern with ecology has inflamed the passions of nearly all who study the problem of surface mining. The massive scope of the technique is the most distressing aspect. Monster machines gouge the earth open, then dump spoil where it will lie barren and ugly for a generation. Yet there is no solution, for the economic advantages all lie with stripping. It is cheap. It is safe. It does not cause black lung disease. The demand is high. If it offends environmentalists and evicts mountaineers, those in the industry say that is the penalty to be paid for the energy.

The other aspect is air pollution. In the face of oil shortages after the Arab boycott began in October 1973 the U.S. Environmental Protection Agency suspended clean air standards so that electrical utility plants could convert to coal. Many had abandoned coal only a short time before to comply with EPA emission standards. The power companies had chosen conversion to oil because it was then cheaper than either buying low sulfur coal from the West or installing "stack gas scrubbers" to remove the pollutants before they escaped into the atmosphere. Coal seemed to offer at least some relief from the "energy crisis." But there was to be a price. In part the price was economic. The cost of coal immediately leapt 20 percent and threatened to double quickly. In part the price was political. Producers clamored for favored treatment and relief from environmental and mine safety regulations. The president of the National Coal Association, Carl E. Bagge, asked that "the levers of governmental power be pulled to give us a 'go' sign, a green light." He claimed coal could meet the crisis "if present handicaps to production are removed," "by removing impediments," and with the "full cooperation of both government and coal miners."[19] Bagge's pronouncements recalled a faint echo of George F. Baer's 1902 stand. Coal barons still survive; King Coal is still a harsh old soul.

As this chapter illustrates, the politics of coal derives first from the physical properties of the fuel. The fact that it is solid, found close to the surface, and high in energy for its volume led to its early exploitation by a simple technology. Hence small privately owned business set the pattern for later development. The fact that it is found most frequently in the Appalachian mountains led to its coming to dominate the politics of a few states such as Pennsylvania, West Virginia, and Kentucky while their coastal neighbors such as New Jersey, Delaware, and the New England states remained unscarred. The recent discovery that coal may be mined profitably in Montana has brought turmoil to the Big Sky Country, pitting the established ranchers against the interloping coal companies. Many a cattleman feels suddenly victimized by the black rock buried under his grasslands, for if he is to garner its wealth he must sacrifice his way of life.

If the physical characteristics of coal in part explain its politics, so too do its market characteristics. Coal is the quintessential "sick industry." Demand has declined relatively (and often absolutely) since the post World War I year of 1919. This decline has cast a pall over the politics of coal. Decreasing need for the fuel caused unemployment in the 1920's and John L. Lewis' backlash in the 1930's, when he found an ally in Franklin D. Roosevelt. The industry's sickness continued, however, even after the New Deal's assistance and still afflicts its politics. The corruption, violence, and criminality plaguing the United Mine Workers could not have been so widespread in a healthy, expanding industry.

The third set of independent variables explaining an arena's policy process relates to its general political environment. Since coal has such a long history, it is the product of many transcending issues. As it entered the twentieth century it was firmly rooted in laissez faire attitudes. Private ownership and the free market held sway. Government regulations had no place. These nineteenth-century attitudes continue to dominate coal to a greater extent than any other form of energy. Yet the arena has not escaped totally the impact of other trends. The New Deal profoundly affected the process, greatly enhancing the role of the union. Today the environmental movement is a predominant influence, but it clashes head-on with the sudden resurgence in demand generated by the energy crisis of the 1970's.

The interaction of these three sets of variables results in an industry in which the government plays a smaller role than in the other forms of energy considered in this book. Government intervention is not extensive and is focused in traditional areas of concern such as health and safety, law and order. In comparison to other fuels, coal is unregulated. Private ownership is the rule at all levels, and the market determines the price and quantity produced. The unique feature of coal politics has been the role of the trade union movement. Yet titanic labor conflicts no longer batter the industry and help shape the course of national politics as they did in the first half of this century. Coal is no longer king.

Notes

1. Robert L. Reynolds, "The Coal Kings Come to Judgment," *American Heritage*, 11 (1960), 54.

2. George F. Baer, "Mr. Baer on Management Responsibilities," in E. Wright Bakke, Clark Kerr, and Charles W. Anrod, *Unions, Management and the Public*, 2nd ed. (New York: Harcourt, Brace and World, 1960), pp. 186–87.

3. John L. Blackman, Jr., *Presidential Seizure in Labor Disputes* (Cambridge, Mass: Harvard, 1967), pp. 12–14.

4. George S. McGovern and Leonard F. Guttridge, *The Great Coalfield War* (Boston: Houghton Mifflin, 1972), *passim*.

5. Morton Baratz, *The Union and the Coal Industry* (New Haven, Conn: Yale, 1955), pp. 100–23.

6. C. L. Sulzberger, *Sit Down with John L. Lewis* (New York: Random House, 1938), pp. 44–46; Cecil Carnes, *John L. Lewis* (New York: Speller, 1936), pp. 28–37; Blackman, *op. cit.*, pp. 237–38.

7. Baratz, *op. cit.*, pp. 58–62.

8. *Ibid.*, pp. 49, 84; Carnes, *op. cit.*, pp. 238–53.

9. Carnes, *op. cit.*, pp. 254–65; Sulzberger, *op cit.*, pp. 58–67.

10. Carnes, *op. cit.*, pp. 282–83, 288–95; Baratz, *op. cit.*, p. 86.

11. Baratz, *op. cit.*, p. 84; Blackman, *op. cit.*, pp. 236–39.

12. Blackman, *op. cit.*, pp. 177—79, 211—13; Baratz, *op. cit.*, pp. 82—83.

13. See Herbert R. Northrup and Gordon F. Bloom, *Government and Labor* (Homewood, Ill: Irwin, 1963), pp. 69—144.

14. U.S. Senate, Committee on Interior, Subcommittee on Minerals, Materials and Fuels, *Surface Mining*, 92nd Congress, 1971—72, *passim; idem, The Issues Related to Surface Mining*, 92nd Congress, 1971—72, *passim.*

15. U.S. Senate, *The Issues Related to Surface Mining*, pp. 174—76.

16. Harry M. Caudill, *Night Comes to the Cumberlands* (Boston: Little, Brown, 1963), *passim;* Harry M. Caudill, *My Land Is Dying* (New York: Dutton, 1971), *passim.*

17. Congressional Quarterly Service, *Congress and the Nation*, Vol. II (Washington, D.C.: Congressional Quarterly, 1968), p. 286.

18. U.S. Senate, Committee on Labor and Public Welfare, Subcommittee on Labor, *Coal Mine Health and Safety*, 91st Congress, 1st Session, 1969, *passim.*

19. "Coal Forecast Hopeful, Hedged," *Washington Star News (The New York Times* News Service), December 21, 1974.

3

Oil: The New King

If coal was the old king of energy, oil is surely the new one. In 1900 coal accounted for 71 percent of the energy consumed as compared to 2 percent for petroleum. By midcentury oil had jumped to 36 percent, while coal had dropped to 37 percent. Recent figures show oil supplying 44 percent with coal even lower at 22 percent.[1]

In its rise to pre-eminence in the energy market oil has followed a political path far different from King Coal's. It has been spared much of the latter's tragic destiny. The influence of labor, which so dominated the politics of coal, has been nil. The politics of oil has been management oriented, and indeed management has often displayed a cozy familiarity with government, seeking its intervention in the industry.

Physical differences account for some of the political differences. Crude oil lies deep underground. Its exploitation requires more advanced technology and greater capital than does coal's. Though first discovered in the Appalachian mountains, its geographical locus soon shifted westward and then abroad. Easily tapped pools close to the sea in the Middle East and Venezuela today give oil an international orientation.

Market forces account for other of the political differences. The "energy crisis" is a symptom of a decline in the supply of oil. But shortages of *supply* have not been the sole market characteristic to shape the policy arena. Many of oil's unique political features were shaped by inadequate or unstable *demand*. The volatile swings from feast to famine in the 1910's and 1920's brought about many of the laws and institutions that still guide the industry. Thus oil was often a "sick industry" like coal.

While oil is a newer industry than coal, its origins stretch far enough back to be rooted firmly in the government's laissez faire policies of the nineteenth century. Its private enterprise heritage proved strong enough to survive the buffeting of reforms, wars, the New Deal, environmentalism, and consumerism. Indeed the issue has often been the reverse: Do oil interests control the government?

The government's first major attempt to intervene in the oil arena reached its climax in 1911, when the Supreme Court ruled on *Standard Oil Company* v. *the United States.* John D. Rockefeller, Sr., had begun to fashion the Standard Oil Company in 1862, only three years after Colonel Drake drilled the world's first oil well in Titusville, Pennsylvania. By the turn of the century, Rockefeller's cartel controlled 87 percent of the crude oil supplies, 82 percent of the refining capacity, and 85 percent of the kerosene, fuel oil, and gasoline sold. Standard was a vertically integrated company. The company, with the aid of its 37 subsidiaries, owned the leases to the oil fields, the drills and pumps, the pipelines and railroad tank cars, the refineries, and the service stations that distributed the finished products. From this position of economic power the company was the logical target for attacks on its monopolistic mode. Journalists struck the first blows. The states then launched a series of prosecutions of the petroleum giant. In 1906 alone state governments filed at least 13 lawsuits. The federal government joined in the crusade. The Bureau of Corporations of the Commerce Department issued its highly publicized report on the entire petroleum industry. This study concluded that the Rockefeller enterprises dominated the business. The cartel was guilty of railroad rebates, discriminatory pricing, and non-competitive distribution. Based on the evidence gathered by the Bureau of Corporations, the government sued in the federal district court in St. Louis to break up the oil empire under provisions of the Sherman Antitrust Act of 1890. The decision of the district court, eventually sustained by the Supreme Court, was that the Standard Oil Company should be broken up into its component companies. Once the 1911 decree was effected the successor companies found themselves in difficult competitive positions. Although the total cartel had been vertically integrated, the component companies tended to be horizontal. One would produce the oil, a second would refine it, a third would distribute it. The short-term result was that the now separated divisions maintained their old business patterns, thereby foiling much of the purpose of the cartel's dissolution. The long-run result was that the major successor companies began to integrate vertically. Standard of Indiana and Standard of Ohio, for example, soon acquired wells and pipelines to get the crude oil to their refineries.[2]

Some have questioned whether the government was effective in its lawsuit against the Rockefeller empire. In its own defense at the trial Standard had argued that the practices of which it was accused were legal and that stiff competition drove it to the more marginal business techniques. The competition was stiffening as the market forces shifted rapidly. A series of new oil fields opened up in which Standard was unable to obtain leases. The most famous was Spindletop in east Texas. There on January 10, 1901, oil, gas, and wreckage of the drilling rig spurted hundreds of feet into the air to proclaim the first Texas gusher. Within a year the field produced 6.1 million barrels of crude oil. The Gulf oil fields began an era of rapid exploitation and quick exhaustion. As the east Texas and Louisiana wells began to run dry, drillers began striking oil in Oklahoma and Kansas. This midcontinent field proved to be both richer and more stable than the Gulf fields. Contemporaneously California wells began flowing. The only new area discovered during this period in which Standard was able to maintain monopolistic control was the Illinois field. The other fields spawned a series of rival companies that would have been likely to break the Standard oil monopoly without the federal government's prosecution: Gulf, Texaco, Phillips, Union, and Sunoco. By 1910, these competitors had reduced Standard's share of the market to 60 percent, down from 90 percent in 1880.[3]

The wide open exploitation of these newly discovered oil fields resulted, in part, from the legal structure. Ownership of the oil was determined by the "rule of capture." This rule came into the oil industry via a nineteenth-century Pennsylvania case defining the rights to natural gas. Stated briefly, the rule is that the owner of the well is entitled to everything he can pump out of it regardless of whether this flows from under his neighbor's land. Thus the optimum strategy was to drill fast and pump hard, to place the wells close to the neighbor and even drill at an angle under his property. The cumulative effect was a disaster. Each operator was in a race to drain his neighbor's wealth. The waste was tremendous. Entire pools ran dry in a few years.[4]

The glut of production prompted state governments to establish procedures to conserve the oil by limiting the number of wells that could be drilled and regulating the amount that could be pumped. This concern with conservation meshed neatly with the producers' economic self-interest. The flood of oil from these newly developed fields quickly set the price per barrel tumbling. Pipelines could not carry it, and refineries could not process it. Oklahoma passed a law setting the minimum price at 65 cents per barrel. When this was ignored, the legislature repealed it and passed a new law prorating production. This had the desired effect of keeping the price high and was soon copied by other oil-producing states.

The oil boom in Oklahoma gave the federal government an opportunity to do one of its few good deeds for the Indians. The Department of the Interior undertook to protect the Indians' property interests by supervising the leasing of the oil rights. Operators were required to pay royalties of one-eighth or one-sixth, to avoid waste, and to post bond to guarantee their performance. Interior Department supervision made many economically naive Cherokees, Seminoles, and Osages rich men. Side benefits included conservation and prevention of monopoly control.

The federal government also participated in the oil boom through the U.S. Geological Survey. The agency's first concern was to aid the drillers in their search through the application of modern science. At first the oil men were skeptical, but with increased success in locating oil pools by their relation to geological features, the operators turned grateful. Government science had won an early victory. The Geological Survey was also instrumental in urging conservation measures to reduce the flagrant waste of the period.

The Geological Survey's scientific aid to the petroleum industry in this period began a trend of government aid, not only to that industry, but to other forms of energy that were to come to prominence as the century progressed. Washington had provided some scientific and technical advice to the coal industry. The Interior Department had established the Bureau of Mines for that purpose in 1884, but the coal operators never made much use of the Bureau of Mines' aid. Coal mining held few scientific puzzles for which research was helpful. Indeed the bureau shifted some of its own attention to the emerging oil business by establishing a Petroleum Division in 1915.

The oil industry's place in the American political system was defined largely in the crucible of World War I. Ten years before, the federal and state governments were concerned primarily with breaking up the cartel arrangements. Once war broke out the government switched to trying to restore the broad integration of the industry.

President Wilson's Administration recognized the importance of oil in modern warfare. Warships, which had formerly burned coal, now burned oil. During the prewar period, the Royal Navy had been one of the chief buyers in the newly discovered Texas and Louisiana fields. Once hostilities began, American wells supplied up to 85 percent of Britain's even greater demands. Warfare on land demanded petroleum also. The civilian popularity of the automobile had its equivalent in the military popularity of the staff car, truck, and tank. This too increased demand.[5]

The Wilson Administration's response to the enhanced demand was to create a Petroleum Advisory Committee as one in a series of committees to coordinate the nation's industrial effort. The members were chiefly the greats of the oil business—the heads of the major corporations—but there was a leavening of three members from the trade associations who were to represent the smaller producers and refiners, the so-called independents. The Advisory Committee coordinated the industry's efforts by surveying the American capabilities and allocating supplies between domestic civilian needs and Allied combat needs. Once the United States entered the war, the federal government reorganized the industrial effort. The Advisory Committee became the National Petroleum War Service Committee without a major change in personnel or function. This proved unsatisfactory to some of its critics, who charged that since it was still a committee of private businesses it could not represent the national interest. The members were simply seeking preference for their own companies. Under the mantle of patriotism the petroleum barons had forged a cartel greater than the old Standard Oil Company.

To meet these criticisms, Wilson established the U.S. Fuel Administration in 1917. Mark Requa, a California engineer and friend of Herbert Hoover, headed its Oil Division. Requa took firm control, pooling production, promoting conservation, and allocating supplies, but he did so in a manner that paralleled the interests of the private companies. The Fuel Administration worked through the businessmen on the War Service Committee, and its policies did not challenge the advantages of the industry. Requa relied largely on compromise and voluntary compliance. Since business gained, the companies were happy to cooperate. When the Federal Trade Commission accused the industry of profiteering and monopolistic practices, Requa counterattacked on behalf of oil. Finally the FTC and the Fuel Administration agreed to a deal. The FTC could prosecute some lesser charges against Standard Oil of Indiana but would not attack the overall pooling arrangement. The Fuel Administration further agreed unofficially to quash any future price rises.[6]

In their policy clash the two agencies displayed typical bureaucratic behavior. Each had sought to accomplish its goals. The FTC's mission was to prevent restraint of trade; the Fuel Administration's was to supply fuel. When these two contradictory goals conflicted, the two agencies had to resolve them in the context of the particular situation. Each brought to the bargaining table certain strengths and weaknesses. The FTC had the weight of the law on its side, but the Fuel Administration had the wartime emergency on its side. In the resulting compromise the war might have given Requa the bargaining advantage, yet the FTC won much of its objective. Since the goals of the two agencies were not completely at odds both could gain. The FTC sought freer trade, which did not directly counter the Fuel Administration's goals of maximum petroleum production. Thus the eventual interagency agreement satisfied both bureaus just as a business transaction exchanging money for goods or services satisfies both parties to it.

Wilson's policy at the end of the war was to dismantle the elaborate structure of government-business cooperation as rapidly as was practical. To many oilmen this seemed a mistake. They had grown fond of the cozy arrangement and had prospered. Many feared that when the high war demand subsided, the industry would be in trouble. They would need govenment control to "stabilize" business, by which they meant to avoid harsh competition. While the official component of the war apparatus expired, the unofficial furnished the basis of a new industry organization. The U.S. Fuel Administration discontinued operations in 1919, but the government National Petroleum War Service Committee transformed itself into the private American Petroleum Institute. Mark Requa and the War Service Committee members moved into positions of authority in the new A.P.I. If the unified cooperation of the war effort could not continue under government leadership, perhaps it could continue privately.[7]

Despite the end of demand to fuel battleships and tanks, the immediate postwar years were ones of a threatened oil shortage. Much of the blame for this 1919 energy crisis goes to the alarmists. The head of the U.S. Geological Survey predicated that on the basis of his calculations, the United States would run out of oil in ten years. The U.S. Navy went so far as to send six destroyers alongside a San Francisco refinery to seize the fuel by force. The surging popularity of automobiles pointed in the same direction. In fact the oil crisis turned out to be false. Domestic discoveries kept up with the increasing demand—albeit in a tumultuous manner, as a major discovery would drive down the price of crude or the exhaustion of an old field would boost it.

This volatile and free-wheeling era furnished the backdrop for the most serious scandal to touch the Presidency between the Grant and Nixon administrations. Teapot Dome brought together the greed of ambitious men, the poor judgment of a President, and the secrecy of the Washington bureaucracy. In 1912, President Taft, anxious that the Navy have enough oil, set aside large segments of publicly owned lands in California, Montana, and Wyoming on which oil had been discovered. Teapot Dome was one of these. The oil on these lands was to be reserved for future naval needs. In 1922 Albert Fall, the Secretary of the Interior, initiated the swindle by persuading President Harding and the Secretary of the Navy to transfer these reserves from the Navy to the Interior Department. The Navy's reward for sacrificing its patrimony was that the oil companies would build a storage facility at Pearl Harbor, Hawaii. Fall next leased the reserves—secretly and without competitive bidding—to Harry Sinclair and E. L. Doheny at piddling rates in return for several bribes. When the scandal came to light after Harding's death, Fall was tried, convicted, and sentenced to prison, the first Cabinet secretary so disgraced.[8]

Calvin Coolidge was anxious to erase the bad name that the oil scandal had given to the Presidency. His response was to create the Federal Oil Conservation Board. The underlying purpose of the board was to prevent another Teapot Dome scandal. More broadly it was to oversee the oil industry without actually controlling it, as the U.S. Fuel Administration had during the First World War. It was charged particularly with preventing waste and assuring adequate supplies for the Navy. While it lacked power to enforce its views on the companies the federal government's role as landlord for the many wells on public land gave it leverage on the industry. At first business was favorable to the board, but when it became apparent that the board was working for conservation while the companies wanted exploitation the cooperation broke down. The American Petroleum Institute switched from supporting the board to attacking it.

If the producers could get little help from the Interior Department in smoothing out the boom and bust chaos of the 1920's, they made up for it in the tax advantages the federal government gave them. The origin of the notorious depletion allowance, which Congress voted in 1926, lay in two areas. First was the fear of an oil shortage that was current in the mid-1920's. Second was the Internal Revenue Service's complex system of determining the value of a well. The IRS valuations were flexible and often appeared arbitrary. A standardized policy would be a reform. The logic behind a depletion allowance is that the value of the well drops each year as more of the oil is pumped out until, when the last drop is gone, the well is worthless. Manufacturers have a similar problem, which they handle by depreciating the cost of a machine every year until it is worn out. But a machine has an easily predictable life expectancy whereas a well does not. No one can tell when an oil pool will run dry. Hence any valuation of a well must be based on some extrinsic measure. This is what the IRS had been doing, but in an individual case by case manner, which caused the oilmen to complain to Congress. Congress first decided to base the value of the depletion on a percentage of annual gross sales. While the connection between gross sales and the decline in value may not make sense to an economist, it satisfied the congressmen. The next problem was to decide the particular percentage to use. Lobbyists for the Mid-Continent Oil Producers Association recommended a 25 percent minimum to the Senate. That chamber, being dominated by pro-business Republicans, saw no reason to quarrel with the figure. The House of Representatives, however, thought that it was not good enough for the dedicated exemplars of free enterprise. It voted for a 30 percent rate. The conference committee of the two houses resolved the difference by compromising at the predictable figure of 27½ percent. Thus that magic number entered the political process, to endure without being changed a fraction of a point for 43 years. Indeed the petroleum industry grew so fond of the figure that it would not even lobby to have it raised for fear that any tampering would call the industry's whole privileged position into question. When the North Dakota legislature was enacting its own oil laws at the time of that state's oil boom in the early 1950's, the industry lobbyists insisted that the 27½ percent figure be used.

The depletion allowance permits a petroleum company to deduct 27½ percent of its gross (not merely net) from its taxable income, providing the deduction does not exceed 50 percent of taxable income. Related tax advantages that Congress bestowed upon the oilmen included deductions for the costs of exploration, drilling, and development. Even before the onset of the Great Depression the boom and bust cycles that characterized the petroleum industry became increasingly destabilizing. The industry's very successes led to its disasters. In 1929 a major pool was found directly below Oklahoma City. The enthusiastic citizens literally drilled in their backyards and on the lawn of the state capitol. If this was not enough to drive the prices down, the following year the producers discovered the east Texas field. By the end of 1931 this pool had 3,600 wells producing. The price of oil dropped as low as 10 cents a barrel.

Despite repeated urgings by the industry, President Hoover refused to intervene. In the absence of federal intervention the state governments acted. Oklahoma had begun to regulate production in 1917 in order to conserve its natural resource. With the great discoveries of the 1920's it shifted the emphasis to include economic considerations. Less oil pumped meant a higher price per barrel. But this regulatory system was challenged in federal court and declared invalid. The fields were in confusion. Violence flared. The governor declared martial law and sent the National Guard to maintain order. Faced with this disorder the federal court eventually reversed its decision and upheld Oklahoma's right to regulate oil production.[9]

The situation in Texas was even worse. Like Oklahoma, Texas had developed a regulatory system to conserve its natural resources and eventually to maintain a high price as well. At first this proration was voluntary; later it became mandatory. The grudging acceptance the drillers first gave to these quotas collapsed with the discovery of the east Texas field. The oilmen refused to limit their production. As in Oklahoma they sued in federal court and won. The court said that the Texas Railroad Commission, the state agency responsible for enforcement, could not prorate production in the interest of maintaining a high price. With this, production soared and price plummeted. Companies threatened to vandalize their rivals' wells and blow up their pipelines. After two months of chaos the Texas governor declared martial law. The troops stayed in the fields until the U.S. Supreme Court handed down a decision on the similar Oklahoma situation. Since in the Oklahoma case state control was upheld, Texas used this to justify its own regulations. Thus the power of the Texas Railroad Commission to restrict the production of the state's wells in order to maintain a high price was firmly fixed.

The governments of Texas and Oklahoma realized that even though they could control production within their own borders, they could do little to keep the price high if the other states did not similarly restrict production. To this end they led a fight for a comprehensive nationwide system. They met with little success, however, until after the election of Franklin D. Roosevelt.

The New Deal had much less of an impact on the oil industry

than it did on coal, largely because many of the key decisions with respect to petroleum were already fully debated by the time Roosevelt became President. The New Deal merely ratified the oil decisions, whereas in the coal industry the New Deal began the debate. The chief vehicle for ratifying the government role in petroleum was the National Industrial Recovery Act. The National Recovery Administration, established under the provisions of the NIRA, chose to focus first on oil because of the industry's desperate straits.

In keeping with the NIRA provisions the NRA delegated the actual drafting of the specific rules to nongovernment boards drawn from the industry. These boards were nominated and dominated by the American Petroleum Institute. The A.P.I. members could not agree on whether the federal government should have authority to set mandatory quotas on production. Those favoring mandatory quotas allied with Secretary of the Interior Harold Ickes, while those opposed allied with NRA Administrator Hugh Johnson. Both men appealed to President Roosevelt, and Roosevelt, as he frequently did, played them off against each other without revealing his own position. Finally he told them to work out a compromise. Ickes lost in his desire to have permanent mandatory production quotas, but he more than made up for it by having administration of the code moved from Johnson's NRA to his Interior Department.

A section of the NIRA was addressed to a special problem of the petroleum industry: hot oil—that is, crude oil pumped in excess of state quotas. It was "hot" because it could not legally be sold. It could, however, be sold illegally, and a black market soon developed. Since the hot oil was undercutting the artificially high price of the quota oil, the states sought federal aid in preventing its sale. Section 9c of the NIRA provided that aid, but it was only partially effective, since producers could evade its provisions. Within two years the Supreme Court invalidated Section 9c. Congress quickly repassed the provision as a separate law, the Connally Act, named for Texas Senator Tom Connally, who along with Congressman Sam Rayburn sponsored it. It is frequently known, however, as the Hot Oil Act.

The definition of the role of government in the petroleum industry so recently sanctified with the NIRA came to an abrupt end in June 1935. The Supreme Court declared the entire National Industrial Recovery Act unconstitutional. The American Petroleum Institute led the search for a substitute. Industry had found the NRA-fostered cooperation to their liking. It offered a wide latitude for private decision-making under the protective shield of the federal government. The oil companies could form cartels, fix prices, enforce quotas, and so on, without fear of government prosecution for monopoly practices because it was the government itself that encouraged the behavior. What Standard Oil was doing wrong in 1911 the NRA was doing right in 1935. With the NIRA declared unconstitutional, the ˙industry feared its replacement might be extensive government control rather than the titular supervision it had grown to cherish. To head this off the A.P.I. backed a plan put forth by the government of Oklahoma to establish an Interstate Compact to Conserve Oil and Gas. The 6 original states have since added over 20 more to their ranks. As an interstate treaty the Compact was submitted to Congress for approval. By voting to accept it, Congress effectively chose this approach in preference to passing a law of its own to regulate the industry. Thus the A.P.I. successfully averted the possibility of more stringent federal regulations.

The New Deal was not the blessing for the oil workers that it was for the coal miners. First, the oil workers lacked many of the incentives to unionize that the miners had. There were fewer of them. Their pay was higher and their working conditions better. Many were already represented in company unions. After the Ludlow coal strike of 1913, Rockefeller had extended the Rockefeller Plan to his industry-dominating Standard Oil Company (New Jersey). From Jersey Standard the plan spread to other oil companies. Insidious as they were to the real unions, the company unions satisfied many of their workers' demands.

Like the United Mine Workers, the International Association of Oil Field, Gas Well, and Refinery Workers benefited from the pro-union provisions of the National Industrial Recovery Act. Membership rose from a pitifully shrunken 300, to which poor leadership and lost strikes had reduced it in 1933, to 40,000 dues payers in 1936. This still was a minority of the petroleum labor force. When a membership drive among refinery workers flagged in 1935, the union reorganized. It changed its name to the Oil Workers International Union and joined John L. Lewis' new C.I.O. The switch to militancy did nothing to help. Membership sagged to 20,000 by 1940. Most workers seemed to be satisfied with their high pay and representation in a company union. Petroleum workers never came close to generating the flamboyant leadership, the critical votes, the high drama, or the low violence that the coal miners contributed to the American political system.[10]

So by the end of the 1930's the place of government in the oil industry was defined. The federal government felt a need for regulation, but this need was somehow felt to be satisfied through providing an umbrella under which the privileged companies could determine their own fate. The key producing states had a much greater role. The Texas Railroad Commission and the equivalent agencies in other states still effectively control the amount of oil pumped. Their work is coordinated by the statistics gathered and published by the Interstate Oil Compact and buttressed by the Hot Oil Act, but it is essentially state action. The dominance of the A.P.I. as an authoritative industry organization, likewise, was fully established by this time. It led the campaign for stabilization during the booms and busts of the 1920's, then was able to impose its will via the NRA and later the Interstate Compact.

Economists describe the oil companies' eagerness for government regulation as a flight from the market. Businesses seek to be governed less by economic laws and more by political laws. Rather than establish price and quantity by supply and demand, they prefer to establish it by means of legislative and administrative decision-making. The effect of this shift from the economic sphere to the political sphere is conservative. It favors established firms and hurts new firms. It is also likely to hurt the consumer, since the result of government-administered prices is virtually always to distort the supply schedule. If prices are set too high the consumer must bear the burden; if they are set too low he faces a shortage. Government interference often hurts business profits too, since it distorts the market for the producers as well as for consumers. But some economists now question whether businesses truly seek to maximize profits and suggest that they seek to maximize something else—such as their own welfare. This notion would fit the stated aims of the petroleum companies during the 1920's and 1930's, when they urged government regulation of production as a means to "stabilize" the industry. Stabilizing meant protecting established forms from strong new competition. It did not necessarily mean increasing profits. The situation in Oklahoma illustrated the conservative bias of government regulation. Prior to 1929 there had been little call for state interference. Then with the discovery of the rich pool beneath Oklahoma City the drillers in the Seminole fields, up to then the richest oil pool in production, suddenly called for regulation to stabilize the market. What they were really saying was that with the appearance of serious competition, the state of Oklahoma should restrict output, particularly from the newly discovered rival source. Yet only a few years before, the discovery of the Seminole field had brought a similar outcry for curbs on production, and a year later the discovery of the east Texas fields sent the Oklahoma governor to Washington to seek federal government limitations on production. These appeals for restrictions on output were generally disguised in rhetoric alluding to conservation of a natural resource. Waste was a problem and a legitimate concern of the government. The U.S. Geological Survey was alarmed that the national wealth might be depleted rapidly. Many of the state laws were framed in terms of conservation. But this was not a particular concern of the producers. Their goal was to pump as much crude oil as quickly as possible. To this end they lobbied for state conservation laws that included economic loss due to low prices in their definitions of waste. What is more wasteful than losing money?

Although the consumer is classically the loser in a regulated industry, there is little evidence that this was the case during the 1920's. While there was much agitation for limits to production, none was effectively achieved until the Hot Oil Act and the Interstate Oil Compact made the proration scheme work. Until then the frequent discoveries of new oil pools expanded the supply too fast for effective limits on the market. Black market buyers maintained a steady stream of cheap crude to the refineries. Later, as new sources came less frequently and the laws backing up the prorationing were passed, the producers did achieve the stability they sought, and the consumers began to pay a premium for it.

The elaborate pattern of government-business boundaries worked out in the 1920's and 1930's survived the trauma of World War II remarkably unscarred. The demands of fighting a massive war temporarily transformed the industry into a highly centralized one in which the federal government made all the big decisions. Secretary of the Interior Ickes used the emergency to move to extensive government control, something he had been unable to accomplish during peacetime. President Roosevelt appointed him Petroleum Coordinator for National Defense in June 1941. Once named, Ickes got the Department of Justice to suspend prosecutions of oil companies in violation of the Sherman Antitrust Act and Federal Trade Act. He got the producers to pool their supplies and transportation. He built special refineries to produce 100 octane gasoline for aviation. When German submarines began sinking tankers sailing between the Gulf and the East Coast Ickes proposed one of his most ambitious schemes: to build a pipeline from the Texas fields to pump the crude directly to the eastern refineries. The pipeline, named the Big Inch, was completed by September 1943. Ickes then built a companion, the Little Big Inch, to pump refined products eastward from Illinois.[11]

Once the war ended, this federal supervision ended, and the industry reverted to its prewar status. This was not entirely to Secretary Ickes's liking. He soon quarreled with President Truman and resigned from the Cabinet. Truman was determined to dismantle the apparatus of federal control in an orderly way. He did not want to maintain the wartime arrangements, but neither did he want to repeat the abrupt dislocations of the reconversion after World War I. Rationing of fuel oil and gasoline ended at once. This program had been under Ickes' control but had been handled by the Office of Price Administration. Indeed Ickes had contested some of the OPA's decisions to put a ceiling on the price the producers could charge for crude. In general there had been little dissatisfaction with the gasoline program. Each automobile owner received a booklet of coupons entitling him to buy gasoline. The

OPA varied the number of gallons each coupon was worth according to the supplies available in each area.

The 3,000 miles of government-built pipeline presented a greater problem. The oil transportation companies, fearing that the Big Inch and Little Big Inch would put their ships and railroad cars out of business, proposed that the government simply abandon using the pipeline until some future emergency again called for its use. Midwestern refiners joined them in this proposal for they feared that, with the war over, the flow on the Little Big Inch would be reversed to bring competing gasoline from the East Coast refineries. Finally all parties were satisfied when the government sold the pipelines to transport natural gas from Texas.

With reconversion returning the oil industry to its prewar situation the Truman Administration reorganized the Interior Department. One change was to remove responsibility for petroleum from the Bureau of Mines. Henceforth it was to be the concern of the independent Oil and Gas Division. Another change was to create the National Petroleum Council. This was an advisory body of nearly 100, whose numbers included the presidents of most of the major oil companies as well as representatives from trade associations and industry producers and refiners. It was the logical outgrowth of the relationship between business and the federal government that had developed prior to the war. The National Recovery Administration had served a similar function of coordination. After the Supreme Court declared the NRA to be unconstitutional in 1935 the Interior Department hesitated to create a replacement for fear of violating the Sherman Antitrust Act. But with the recent experience of wartime cooperation Interior wanted to continue the pattern. The Attorney General advised that the N.P.C. would not be a conspiracy provided that the initiative came from the government rather than private business. Thus the cozy relationship between the oil companies and Interior gained a permanent avenue of communication.

The chief issue to stir up the otherwise calm oil politics of the Truman Administration was the ownership of offshore oil. At issue was whether the state governments (or the federal government) had the right to lease the ocean bottom off their coastlines to oil prospectors. The states' rights advocates won the first round by getting their areas referred to as "tidelands," though the lowest tide never came close to uncovering any of them. In fact the oil rich continental shelf slopes gradually downward for 70 to 140 miles along the Atlantic and Gulf coasts until it reaches a depth of about 600 feet after which it drops sharply. Along the Pacific Coast the continental shelf is much narrower, limiting oil drilling to within approximately 20 miles of the coast.[12]

Little drilling had actually been done in these so-called tidelands prior to the war, but by the late 1940's the oil producers had improved their equipment and technology to the point that the exploitation was possible. In the past no one had questioned the states' traditional jurisdiction to lease these lands, but in 1945 President Truman proclaimed that the entire continental shelf was subject to federal control. In spite of this challenge to their right to do so, California, Louisiana, and Texas proceeded to lease the offshore oil fields to producers. The controversy defied resolution. Congress passed two bills renouncing federal claims but President Truman vetoed both. The courts ruled on a series of cases without resolving the underlying issue. The oil companies cared little whether the state or federal government leased them the ocean bottom so long as their rights to it were clear.

The controversy became a major issue of the 1952 presidential election. Though petroleum interests had been involved intimately in the highest levels of national politics since World War I, this was the first time oil politics had become so open. Oil now became an issue to be decided by the entire electorate. The two parties divided sharply. The Democrats supported Truman's position that the offshore lands should go to the national government. The Republicans advocated that the states retain them.

Why did oil so suddenly leap from the shadowy, lobbyist-crowded halls of Washington into the bright glare of the partisan election platforms? The reasons relate to the fate of the New Deal. After 20 years of Democratic rule, the Republicans believed that their best chance of ousting their rivals lay in attacking the growing power of the federal government. The "tidelands" oil controversy seemed a perfect issue with which to draw support. The inability of Congress or the courts to come to a clear decision indicated that it was ripe for debate in the presidential campaign. In an election speech in Louisiana, General Eisenhower argued that the Republicans' position would undo the wrongs of the Washington "powermongers." The Democrats saw this as an attack on the entire range of federal projects including national forests, irrigation projects, waterpower, and mineral lands in the public domain.

Eisenhower's 1952 victory settled the issue. The new President promptly submitted to Congress two bills. The Submerged Lands Act of 1953 gave the states clear title to all lands within three miles on the Atlantic and Pacific coasts and within three leagues (10.5 miles) on the Gulf Coast. The legal rationale behind the larger distance for the Gulf states was that this represented the "historic limits" based on Spanish law, which was recognized at the time these states entered the union. If this were not an abuse at the time the act was passed, it soon became one. The Gulf states redrew their boundary claims to include more territory. This was to some extent encouraged by the White House for it gave a political stake that could be bargained for. When a Texas oilman who was also a member of the Republican National Committee complained that the Justice Department was challenging Texas' claim to the 10.5 mile limit, President Eisenhower backed up the Lone Star State's claim to its historic boundary.

As this vignette illustrates, however, the Republican administration was not totally sympathetic to the states' rights position. The companion to the Submerged Lands Act was the Outer Continental Shelf Act of 1953 which gave the federal government exclusive jurisdiction over the ocean bottom beyond the three-mile (or three-league) boundary. The Interior Department then proceeded to lease these submerged lands to the oil companies.

In passing the Outer Continental Shelf Act, Congress avoided facing its implications for international law. Traditional views, focusing on navigation, held that a nation controls only a limited distance out from its coasts. The old standard was three miles. Now twelve miles is widely accepted. Beyond that are the high seas, open to any nation. On one hand, the United States has supported this, opposing, for example, attempts by Peru to claim jurisdiction 200 miles seaward. The United States has even been reluctant to see the three-mile limit extended to twelve. This is logical for a nation with a strong navy. Protecting its own coast is no problem; close access to another coast confers a military advantage. Among other things it makes easier electronic surveillance for military purposes. On the other hand, the United States has extended its claim to the entire continental shelf, often extending more than 100 miles seaward, in order to exploit the shelf's wealth. The tension between freedom of the seas and the desire to exploit the seabed was resolved in 1958 when the State Department negotiated two treaties in Geneva. The treaties provided that the right to free navigation and fishing would be maintained but that adjacent nations would have the right to exploit the seabed of the continental shelf.

During the Eisenhower Administration a gradual shift in the oil industry brought a new issue to the political vanguard. America had traditionally been an exporter of petroleum. After World War I, the British government thanked the American producers, claiming that "the Allies had floated to victory on a sea of oil." The American producers' contribution to victory in World War II was even greater, as they supplied scores of armies, navies, and air forces around the globe. Yet a subtle shift was underway. Domestic consumption was edging up on production. In 1947 the United States became a net importer. Foreign oil made up 0.3 percent of domestic consumption. By 1953, the year in which Eisenhower took office, the figure was up to 10 percent. The producers' concern increased. Foreign oil was a threat. Venezuelan crude could be delivered to East Coast refineries more cheaply than Texas oil. Eventually, even cheaper crude from the Middle East began finding its way to American markets. Already used to the protection of the federal government, the producers turned once more to Washington to guard their profits. The elaborate prorationing schemes of the Interstate Oil Compact would be worthless if foreign oil could compete freely.

To satisfy the complaints of the producers, President Eisenhower appointed a Cabinet-level committee. Its proposal was a compromise. The oil companies would voluntarily limit their imports to the 1954 level of 12 percent. When these voluntary restrictions failed, the President appointed a second committee. This time the committee recommended that the President make the limit mandatory under authority Congress granted him in the Reciprocal Trade Agreements Act of 1955. The economic self-interest of the oil producers was not the only argument put forth for the import quotas this time. National defense was now considered a salient reason since the 1956 war between Israel and Egypt had shown the United States' vulnerability to having its oil supply cut off. If the United States was to remain invulnerable it had to have a viable petroleum industry. This was a more sophisticated argument than the older one that the Navy needed reserves. First the Teapot Dome scandal had shown the abuse possible with a system of naval reserves. Second, crude oil in the ground is far from the refined fuels that the military need to have instantly available in a war. If crude oil in the ground was the goal, the United States should encourage imports to the end that its domestic supplies might be conserved. But the national security logic ignores the problems of transportation. Gulf oil is shipped to the East and West coasts by tanker. World War II had shown the vulnerability of this means. For domestic production to be secure the Big Inch and Little Big Inch pipelines would have to be reconverted from natural gas to oil, leaving the East without adequate supplies of gas. Furthermore, Venezuelan oil is really no more vulnerable than Gulf oil since the Caribbean can be protected from submarines much more easily than the Atlantic or Pacific. (Oil coming overland from Canada, either Canadian or Alaskan, was not an alternative in the mid-1950's, since this was prior to the great oil discoveries there.)

President Eisenhower hesitated to accept his committee's recommendations for mandatory import restrictions, perhaps because he saw that the goal was greed rather than national security. But pressure from the industry grew, and in 1959 he imposed the quotas. The effect was predictable. According to some estimates the price rise cost the American consumer $4 to $7 billion annually. The armed forces paid much of it to buy the petroleum products they needed to maintain the national security. Venezuela and the Arab states were offended that the U.S. government had limited their access to the American market.[13]

The impact of the quota system was unevenly distributed. It

affected only the states east of the Rocky Mountains. The Pacific Coast states were exempted because production was too low to supply all the needs of that rapidly growing area. East of the Rockies imports were limited to 12 percent of the oil produced in those states. The chief victims were the northeastern states, particularly New England, which would have done better to buy cheap Middle Eastern oil than the costly Gulf oil. A barrel of imported crude cost $1.50 less in New York than a barrel of domestic crude. The American refiner paid $3.00, while his Japanese competitor paid $1.50.

The oil companies were not the only ones to benefit from the imposition of the quotas. The politicians in control of the Interior Department gained as well. Just as with the jurisdiction of the states over the offshore oil lands, the government had created a new commodity which it controlled. In that case the stake over which to bargain was the number of square miles a state could add to its "historic limits." In this case the stake was the right to import oil. No oil could be brought in without a license from the Interior Department. In the old free-market system companies imported crude until the marginal cost was equal to that for domestic crude. The government had no role to play. In the new system the companies would exceed the quota before reaching the point where domestic crude was cheaper. Therefore since foreign oil was always cheaper the problem became how to obtain a license to import as much as possible. Since it paid the companies to get a license, the companies paid to get a license. These payments took many forms. Seldom was it ever a direct bribe of a Department of Interior official. More often it was a political contribution to a congressman or senator with influence at Interior. It might also be a contribution to a presidential candidate or to his party.

But the risk of abuse fostered in securing the specific quotas paled before the abuses of maintaining the system. The domestic producers knew that they had a windfall and devoted their resources to maintaining it. From 1959 through 1973 the import quota was the chief jewel in their crown of privilege. The main technique used to hold on securely to their position was political campaign donations. More than any other industry, petroleum aimed for the top. It focused its efforts on the Presidency and the

Senate. In comparison to other industries it ignored the House of Representatives and the bureaucracy.

Petroleum's nucleus in the Senate starts, naturally enough, with senators from oil-producing states. This reflects the tendency in oil politics toward producer domination over refiners or distributors. Production is concentrated in a few, chiefly Gulf Coast, states, giving the producers about a dozen senators with a major commitment. Refining and distribution are much more geographically dispersed. Refining dominates few states the way producing dominates Texas, Louisiana, and Oklahoma. Indeed there is often an overlap. Distribution dominates no state, although in the mid-1960's some New England senators began to view their states as consumers, and very disadvantaged ones at that. From this nucleus of producer-state senators, the industry extends its influence by means of campaign contributions to other senators willing to vote for the producers' interests. Since this money is channeled via the oil state senators it enhances their power within the Senate as well as the industry's and has helped to give them positions of leadership within the Senate. The one-party structure of the South has reinforced their rise to power. Because the Gulf states are solidly Democratic, a senator, once elected, has little fear of defeat and can concentrate on his job in Washington without worrying about re-election. Since seniority determines committee rank and aids in winning positions of party responsibility, the southern senator can bide his time, knowing he eventually will reach a position of great power. With this in mind, the southern Democratic parties traditionally have nominated young and capable men who can grow old and powerful in Washington. Some examples were Lyndon Johnson of Texas, Russell Long of Louisiana, and Robert Kerr of Oklahoma. All three occupied important party leadership posts.

Gaining the support of the President is a more difficult procedure, but the oilmen have succeeded admirably. Here they lack the natural advantages of a senator's obvious desire to boost his home state's industry, the southern one-party system, and the longstanding relationship spanning many years. Perhaps more serious, the President is much more powerful than a single senator. He commands far greater resources. To cope with this the producers make their primary deal with the President before he becomes President. As a candidate he is vulnerable. He is more than willing to bargain; he is eager. Indeed, this is exactly the role of a presidential candidate: to tour the country making deals with various interests in the various states in order to put together a coalition to win first the party nomination and then the Presidency. The candidate is looking for votes and for money that can be translated into votes. Oil offers the money. Although the exact amount is elaborately hidden, the petroleum industry is generally recognized as being by far the largest contributor to presidential campaigns.

The typical sequence involves inviting the candidate to Houston to address the Petroleum Club. There in front of the oil company executives, television, and the newspapers he outlines his program for oil, which has generally included pledges to maintain the import quotas, the 27½ percent depletion allowance, and drilling write-offs. The ritual may go unnoticed outside of the oil-producing states. This is fine because the rest of the country might be disgruntled if it were to realize the bargain being struck. If the candidate's proposals seem satisfactory (and no one makes a special trip to Houston to offend the industry), the contributions begin to flow. The petroleum interests are often surprising in the catholicity of their taste. All candidates of both parties are welcome providing that their position on oil is right. Eisenhower made the trip to Texas. Kennedy and Nixon both did in 1960. Goldwater was happy to do so in 1964. Johnson was already committed to oil. Oilmen may strike bargains with unlikely candidates. In 1968 Eugene McCarthy felt an alliance with the petroleum industry was compatible with his otherwise radical quest for the Democratic nomination, and the industry, wanting to be on the safe side in the unlikely event he won, agreed. Though the Petroleum Club failed to pick a presidential winner in McCarthy, it did pick up a vote in the Senate. The Minnesota senator shifted from opposing the industry to supporting it even though his constituents gained nothing. McCarthy raised $40,000 in one day at the Petroleum Club. His colleague from Minnesota and the eventual Democratic nominee in 1968 was one of the few candidates to refuse to go to Houston. Hubert Humphrey declined the invitation, stating that the privileged position of the petroleum industry was one of the greatest abuses of the American political system. In 1972 George McGovern likewise declined, but Richard Nixon gladly made the pilgrimage. His ties to petroleum go back to his early campaigns in California. This is not surprising since the state is a leading producer of oil. In 1952 the Checkers scandal revealed that oilmen had contributed to the personal slush fund that nearly cost him his vice-presidential nomination. In the Senate he had been a staunch supporter of giving the states jurisdiction over the offshore oil.

During the 1972 campaign oil company officials and principal stockholders contributed a total of $5 million to President Nixon's re-election, approximately 10 percent of the Nixon campaign budget. Some of this came directly from the corporation (which is illegal) rather than from individuals. After pleading guilty to donating $100,000 of the Phillips Corporation's funds, its board chairman had to pay the maximum fine of $5,000, a trifling sum indicating the degree of seriousness Congress attaches to such crimes. Of the 125 members of the National Petroleum Council, 70 contributed a total of $1.2 million toward the President's re-election.

The petroleum industry's focus on the President and key senators does not mean that it neglects lesser centers of power in Washington. It cultivates a core of supporters in the House of Representatives. Until his death in 1962, Speaker of the House Sam Rayburn was the kingpin. His power had much the same sources as that of the industry's Senate friends. Oil was a major industry in Texas. Oil was willing to support him and channel money through him to congressmen of his picking. The one-party system allowed him to build the seniority he needed. Yet petroleum's power has never been as great in the House. In part this is because influence with the President and in the Senate makes a major effort in the House unnecessary. But it is also due to certain characteristics of the House. It is bigger: 435 compared to 100. Hence it is harder for any single interest to influence. Representation by population decreases the voting power of the oil-producing states. The House is more segmented; each committee is a world unto itself. Hence petroleum interests come up against many more barriers there than in the more fluid Senate. Furthermore, segmentation means more rival interests are at work there than in the Senate. In the upper chamber oil has few peers, whereas in the lower chamber it has many. It must compete with the highway lobby, the banking lobby, and the shipping lobby. The oil interests gain less from the solid South. In the Senate the only safe seats are in the South, and many of these are in oil-producing states. In the House many nonsoutherners come from safe seats in the Democratic cities or the Republican hinterland. What is a competitive two-party state for a senator is often a series of safe one-party districts for the representatives. It is not only Southern congressmen, therefore, who enjoy the benefits of seniority.

In the late 1960's petroleum's privileged position began to erode slightly. In Congress many of the old stalwarts were gone. Death had claimed Speaker Sam Rayburn, Senator Robert Kerr, and Republican leader Everett McKinley Dirksen of Illinois, senator from a northern producing state and firm friend of oil. Lyndon Johnson was first Vice President, then in the White House. As President he could not openly represent the industry the way he could as a senator from Texas, and in fact his administration became somewhat concerned with the favorable treatment it was getting. Just prior to leaving office in January 1969, the Johnson Administration proposed that the 27½ percent depletion allowance be cut. This figure had stood sacred since 1926. Now the Treasury proposed that it be reduced along with a number of other reforms in a bill that eventually became the Tax Reform Act of 1969. The Senate split along predictable lines. Those from the producing states argued that the allowance encouraged exploration and gave no undue advantage to the oil industry. Those from the non-producing states argued that it was nothing but a tax loophole that deprived the Treasury of $7 billion each year. The American tax-payer was subsidizing the oil industry. The reformers managed to split the petroleum lobbyists by proposing that the smaller, in-dependent companies be entitled to a higher allowance than the bigger, major companies. The American Petroleum Institute represents chiefly the majors (Jersey Standard, Mobil, Shell, In-diana Standard, Texaco, Gulf, and California Standard) even though many of the independents are members. The independents are represented again, less powerfully but more in line with their specific goals, by the Independent Petroleum Association of America. Both the A.P.I. and the I.P.A.A. supported retaining the 27½ percent level, but a regional organization made up only of small independents broke ranks. The Kansas Independent Oil and Gas Association supported a sliding scale. Firms grossing less than $1 million would get 27½ percent; firms with less than $5 million would get 21 percent; and firms with over $5 million would get only 15 percent. Although this proposal was not adopted, the 43-year reign of 27½ percent was broken. The final version of the bill cut the allowance to 22 percent. The industry, however, hardly suffered a crippling blow. Even after the 1969 reforms the industry was still allowed to deduct many of its intangible costs for exploration, drilling, and development—and to deduct them even if they occur offshore or abroad. In addition, payments paid to foreign governments are conveniently called "taxes" rather than royalties, so the companies can deduct them against American taxes. The Treasury estimates that these tax loopholes enable the producers to save 19 times their original investment in a well.

The international oil corporations' right to deduct foreign "taxes" from American taxes dollar for dollar results not from Treasury naiveté but from a deliberate decision made in 1950. At that time the State Department feared that the United States' support of Israel would drive the Arab states into the Communist bloc. While direct foreign aid to the Arabs would offend Americans who supported Israel, the oil companies could serve as a conduit for indirect aid. In response to a decision of the President's National Security Council, the Treasury secretly ruled that the oil producers could fully deduct "taxes" paid to the Arabs. The tax provision became known as the "golden gimmick." In 1950 Aramco, a consortium of four American companies, paid the United States $50 million in taxes and paid Saudi Arabia $66 million. The next year it paid the United States $6 million and Saudi Arabia $100 million. In effect the United States gave $44 million to the Arabs. The amount has since grown; by 1974 the five biggest corporations had piled up tax credits of over $2 billion. Since 1962 the petroleum companies' foreign tax credits have exceeded their American tax liabilities every year. At the same time that "taxes" paid to the Arabs cost the companies nothing, high prices for imported oil drive up the value of any crude the company produces domestically.

While the oil industry emerged from its battle with the tax reformers with only a slight dent in its armor of privilege, it faced attack from another virtuous band: the environmentalists. Besides a mild tax reform, 1969 brought a dramatic confrontation between exploitation and nature. A Union Oil Company well six miles off the coast of Santa Barbara exploded, releasing 235,000 gallons of crude oil, which spread out into an oil slick of 800 square miles. The slick washed up on the city's beaches, killing birds, fish, and plant life. The gross pollution of a beautiful and well-known shoreline, coming on top of a series of lesser spills, mobilized environmentalists across the nation. Congressional hearings revealed confusion in the Interior Department over which goals to pursue. Former secretary Stewart Udall, who had approved the leases, testified that he had done so under pressure from the Bureau of the Budget. He described the ill-fated decision as a "sort of conservation Bay of Pigs." The incumbent secretary, Walter Hickel, displayed equal equivocation. A week after the blowout he suspended all drilling in the Santa Barbara Channel, then three weeks later reversed the order. Confronted with conflicting demands from all sides, the President chose to follow the time-tested course. He appointed a special commission to investigate the problem. The commission recommended pumping the field dry as the only way to end permanently the risk of oil leakage in the channel. On this basis the secretary allowed unlimited drilling to resume, a move that outraged the conservationists.

One effect of the Santa Barbara oil spill was to spur the passage of the National Environmental Policy Act of 1969. This landmark legislation established a new federal office specifically charged with protecting the environment. In addition to establishing the Council on Environmental Quality in the Executive Office of the President, the 1969 act required that the government file a special statement any time a federal action would have a significant impact on the environment. This gave concerned citizens a weapon with which to do battle with the government. For example, in 1971 a citizens' group successfully blocked Interior's lease of oil lands off the Louisiana coast on the basis that the department had failed to file a proper environmental impact statement.

Yet in a single day in January 1974, when talk of an oil crisis made environmental protection seem less important, the Department of the Interior approved 87 bids totaling $1.4 billion to begin drilling for the first time off the Florida, Alabama, and Mississippi coasts. This scramble for new fields offshore followed the discovery of the Jay field in the Florida panhandle and stepped up drilling in the Big Cypress Swamp in southwest Florida, the area that furnishes the water for the Everglades.

Along the Atlantic Coast attention has centered on the Georges Bank (off Cape Cod), the Baltimore Canyon (Long Island to Virginia), and the Southeast Georgia Embayment as the most easily exploited petroleum deposits on the Outer Continental Shelf (OCS). The Interior Department proposal to open these areas to drilling set off immediate protests from environmentalists who conjured up memories of the 1969 Santa Barbara oil spills.

Offshore drilling promises to remain a source of controversy as these new areas are opened. Production in the Atlantic continental shelf may radically alter the industry's pattern. Wells 50 miles off the New Jersey coast can pump crude directly to that state's massive refinery complex. The economic effect will be to lower petroleum prices in the Northeast. The political effect will be to put the Atlantic states into the producers' camp in Congress. Massachusetts, New Jersey, and Virginia might join Louisiana, Texas, and California in a petroleum bloc in the Senate. Conceivably the coastal states would be arrayed against the inland states when voting on oil issues.

Such sudden and unpredicted shifts in the geographic location of new production sites have always had a profound impact on politics. Discoveries offshore are perhaps easier to adjust to than those on land. As previously noted the boom and bust cycles of the 1920's were based on new discoveries: Spindletop, Seminole, Oklahoma City, east Texas. Discovery of a major pool on the North Slope of Alaska in 1968 had a similar effect. At first flush the find seemed to be a panacea. It came at a time when reserves in the "lower 48" seemed to be declining ominously and Middle Eastern sources seemed uncertain due to the frenzied politics of the region. While the physical difficulties of transporting the crude from the Arctic were immense, they were economically surmountable. The producers could sell at competitive prices on the world market. Domestically the picture was even better since the import quota system kept the price higher than the world price. The state of Alaska joyfully auctioned leases in 1969 bringing the state $900 million of badly needed revenue.

The oil companies had not reckoned with the opposition that soon emerged. Their desire to exploit the Alaskan oil field soon clashed head on with the new environmental movement. The environmentalists argued that a pipeline from the North Slope to the port of Valdez on the south coast would ruin the state's delicate ecological balance. To block the pipeline the ecologists successfully sued to enjoin the oil companies from beginning construction, using the argument that the pipeline violated legislation protecting the environment. Thousands of lengths of pipe sat rusting in the northern cold as the courts heard arguments pro and con. The Nixon Administration pushed for construction to begin. Only court action blocked the Interior Department's approval. Congress resolved the impasse by passing a law specifically stating that the pipeline met the criteria of environmental protection required by the 1969 National Environmental Policy Act.

The long delay in constructing the Alaskan route brought forth serious consideration of an alternative. Rather than build a pipeline to the south coast of Alaska whence the crude would be shipped by tanker to the West Coast or to Japan, the oil companies considered building a longer one across Canada to Chicago. This route offered several advantages. It would do less damage to the Alaskan environment (though perhaps more to the Canadian). The pipeline, while longer, would actually carry the oil more cheaply than the combination of the shorter pipeline and shipment by sea. The third advantage was that the Canadian route would deliver the oil to the Middle West, where it is needed more than on the West Coast. Why then did the oil companies favor the trans-Alaskan pipeline? Speed was one reason. The shorter route could be finished a year earlier. Less concern with the environment was another. Ecological damage weighed little against industrial profits. A more subtle reason was political. Under the import quota system a company could ship Alaskan oil to Japan, then under the provisions of the quota be entitled to import the equivalent amount from Venezuela to New York, thereby making two sales rather than one. Of further benefit was the fact that the companies would thus evade the provisions of the Jones Act, which requires that shipments between two U.S. ports be via American carriers. Since American ships are much more costly than foreign ones, the companies profit again.

In April 1973, President Nixon suddenly altered one of the two assumptions on which these calculations were made. After 14 years he ended the import quota system. The move came in the context of increasing public concern with oil shortages. The term "energy crisis" crept into the rhetoric of public discussion. Consumers wakened at least partially to the degree to which the quota system distorted the market. Political leaders from the Northeast and Midwest took up the cause. The system forced the average family in New York to pay an extra $102 per year for gasoline and fuel oil. A Vermont family paid $196 and a Wyoming family paid a $258 premium. While the case for the consumer had strengthened, the old rationale of national defense had weakened. The public was beginning to give up the illusion that domestic oil was secure and foreign oil subject to torpedoing; the nation was becoming further and further removed from the mentality of World War II. In nuclear war a nation's petroleum industry made little difference. If a thousand ICBM's could blast a nation's cities to radioactive ashes in 15 minutes, it made little difference whether the refineries the missiles destroyed were processing crude from Texas or Venezuela. The war of the future would be either limited or nuclear. American logistics in Vietnam serve as a model for the limited war. Procurement of petroleum was along basically civilian lines. The military purchased its fuel for southeast Asia on an open world market from refiners in Singapore, who in turn purchased the crude on the open market in Indonesia and Iran.

President Nixon, in abandoning the quota system, did not abandon his friends in the petroleum industry. To cushion the blows of a transition from protectionism to free enterprise the Republican President substituted an import fee of 1 cent per gallon of crude. Combined with the existing tariff this amounts to a total of 52½ cents per barrel. Economists considered the new fee a slight improvement. It is less distorting than the quotas. For politicians with special access to the federal bureaucracy it is a loss, since they have lost a political commodity. They can no longer claim to exert their influence on behalf of importers who wish to obtain a license in return for whatever favors the importer might wish to bestow on the politician. Yet the move is not without precedent. In the 1930's Congress became so overwhelmed by trying to offer special favors to businessmen seeking tariff protection that it turned the responsibility over to the Tariff Commission. Congress at least removed itself from the direct line of fire, though the attempts to exert influence merely shifted from Congress to the commission.

President Nixon abolished the quota system because of America's steadily increasing need for foreign oil. This has been a long-term trend. In 1959 it prompted the oil producers to prevail on Eisenhower to impose the quota. Within a decade the quota had become so effective that the distortions were creating pressure to ease it. Following a middle course, Nixon did so in 1970 and again in 1972 by making slight increases in the amount of oil that could be imported. This was insufficient and so in 1973 he abandoned quotas altogether. The increasing use of foreign oil has had serious ramifications for American foreign policy. In the 1950's the United States' chief foreign supplier was Venezuela. Today it is the Middle Eastern countries. In the 1950's weak demand and abundant supplies pegged the world price low. Today the opposite condition has raised the price. In the 1950's the producing countries were divided. Today they are united.

The vehicle of their unity is the Organization of Petroleum Exporting Countries. It is composed of seven Arab states—Kuwait, Saudi Arabia, Iraq, Abu Dhabi, Qatar, Libya, and Algeria—and six non-Arab states—Iran, Venezuela, Indonesia, Nigeria, Gabon, and Ecuador. Since its founding in the cheap oil days of the late 1950's, OPEC has emerged as an economic giant. A virtual monopoly of all oil produced for the world market enables it to wring concessions from the biggest oil companies in the world. Jersey Standard (now Exxon), Shell, British Petroleum, and all the rest must accept its terms. The heart of OPEC is the seven Arab countries. They have maintained remarkable solidarity in the face of incentive for one to profit at the expense of the others. In 1967 the Six Day War between Israel and the Arabs blocked the Suez Canal. The price of oil rose because of the expense of sending tankers around Africa.

Libya restrained its greed for the profits that its location west of the canal could have given it. It actually reduced production, then negotiated higher prices which the other Arab states then adopted. The western companies had little choice. Europe was absolutely vulnerable. It had no sources of its own. The United States is vulnerable only in a marginal fashion, but because it is economically and politically so tied to Europe it shares its vulnerability. First the major oil companies are truly international. Exxon and Gulf have extensive refineries and distribution in Europe. Royal Dutch-Shell and B.P. are in fact European companies with extensive investment in the United States. Hence the major companies are so involved on both sides of the Atlantic that Europe's vulnerability becomes America's. OPEC's monopolistic position and its willingness to use it in bargaining has prompted the oil companies to seek the help of their own governments in countering it. Though the major buyers bargain collectively, OPEC has been able to get almost any concession it demands. At first the western companies merely could not force a reduction in the price as they had done in 1958. Then as the producers' consortium grew stronger and western appetite for petroleum grew bigger, the demand was for higher prices and larger royalties. Next the OPEC countries began to demand part ownership of the drilling companies that the western companies established in the producing countries. By the early 1970's some of these demands were for 51 percent control. The trend points toward increased ownership of the "downstream" sector—i.e., refining and distribution. Arab sheiks would own not only the production facilities in their own country, but the tankers that carry the crude, the refineries in New Jersey, and the service stations along the turnpikes and highways.

Many of these fears lay in the background when the two sides met in Teheran for a major bargaining session in 1971. In preparation the American companies received the Justice Department's assurance that a joint bargaining position would not be considered to be restraining trade (i.e., the companies would not be liable to an antitrust prosecution). The State Department sent its under secretary to visit Iran, Saudi Arabia, and Kuwait to apply diplomatic pressure on the shah, the king, and the emir. For their part the OPEC countries hinted that they would cut off supplies if their demands were not met. From this critical meeting the two sides both emerged with what appeared to be a satisfactory settlement. OPEC got a price rise of 45 cents to 80 cents with further rises until 1975. Though high, the oil companies could manage with the new prices. The American companies had another set of price rises in the wake of the 1971 and 1973 devaluations and the floating exchange rates. According to a June agreement negotiated in Geneva, the prices would be raised to compensate for the lower value of the dollar. Then three months later OPEC summoned the oil companies to Vienna to hear the details of a still further price rise.[14]

Thus the upward price spiral was well underway prior to the Arab attack against Israel launched on Yom Kippur, 1973. In retaliation for their support of Israel, the Arabs cut off all petroleum supplies to the United States and the Netherlands. In addition the Arabs decreed that they would reduce production overall in order to pressure neutral nations to give more support to their side. Japan was the first to yield to this blackmail. As the world's largest petroleum importer Japan depends on the Arabs for 40 percent of its supplies. The boycott threatened to bring its economy to an abrupt halt. The Japanese capitulation began with a call for Israeli withdrawal from captured territory, a fivefold increase in its donation to the United Nations fund for Palestinian refugees, and the offer of $50 million in loans to Egypt and Syria. In return the Arabs reclassified Japan as a "friendly" nation thereby entitled to exemption from the boycott. The European nations (except for the Netherlands) came to similar agreements. The OPEC countries, including the non-Arab members, took advantage of the boycott to raise prices. The net result was that Persian Gulf oil, which sold for approximately $1.50 per barrel during the 1960's, sold for eight times that amount after the Yom Kippur War. In comparison, domestically produced crude, protected by the import quota system, which sold for approximately $3.00 during the 1960's, rose to $9.00 in the free market.

From the beginning, however, the boycott was unstable. Market forces and Arab disunity worked against its complete effectiveness. As much as 700,000 barrels a day leaked into the United States. Much came as gasoline and heating oil from Caribbean refineries, which refused to divulge their sources. The evidence, though, pointed chiefly toward Libya. Its political quarrel with Egypt suggested a motive for sabotaging the boycott. Profit was enough motive for others. Though officially beyond the pale, tankers mysteriously continued to arrive at the huge Dutch refinery complex at Rotterdam from undisclosed Arab and European sources.

The Arab nations' accusation that the United States favors Israel at their expense is not paranoia but an accurate observation. Support for Israel derives from the large number of American Jews, from post-World War II concern with the plight of European Jews, and from sympathy for an experiment in democratic nation building. In 1948 President Truman gave immediate support to the Israeli declaration of statehood. Aside from humanitarian concerns, he knew that several million Jewish voters would be going to the polls in the presidential election that fall in swing states like New York, New Jersey, and Illinois. That electoral logic has kept subsequent Presidents solidly in the pro-Israeli camp. For similar reasons many congressmen have adopted a like stance. Senators and representatives from states with large Jewish populations have an obvious reason to support Israel, but so do others. One senator from a western state with only a few thousand Jews reported that "they all contribute to my campaign." Typically, Democratic congressmen are more pro-Israel since Jews favor that party four to one. This gives Republicans more freedom to favor the Arabs', and hence the oil importers', cause. In fact few choose to do so since the Arabs have few supporters among anyone's constituents. Backing the 2 million Israelis against the 125 million Arabs is like cheering for David over Goliath.

The embassies of the two sides actively promote their respective causes. The United States is unique in the extent to which such domestic lobbying by foreign governments is an accepted part of the political system. In most other nations a diplomat would approach only the foreign ministry openly. If he tried to influence its parliament or citizens he would do so secretly. In the United States such lobbying or appeal to public opinion is acceptable. Yet in doing so, the Arabs were long ineffectual. In contrast, the Israeli embassy spearheads a massive program including free trips to Israel for congressmen and government officials, speeches by the ambassador, and close ties to the American Jewish community. It is these ties that excite the most controversy. *The New York Times* outlined the process by which the Israeli embassy coordinated demonstrations against President Georges Pompidou during his 1970 visit to show opposition to the French leader's pro-Arab policies. When the angry mobs became so disruptive that Pompidou threatened to break off the visit, the White House called the Israeli embassy for help. The demonstrations were subdued, and President Nixon was able to mollify the offended Frenchman. When a reporter later questioned whether it was not strange for the White House to call on a foreign embassy to help restrain American citizens, the administration spokesman replied that "the question is naive."

The political instability of the Middle East has encouraged American importers to develop non-Arab oil. Iran has been a prime source. Though Moslems, the Iranians are not Arabs and have remained neutral on the Israel issue. Iranian oil is shipped to the Israeli port of Elat on the Red Sea, thence piped to the Mediterranean, where it is again pumped aboard tankers and shipped to Europe. During the brief 1967 boycott Iran diverted crude for Japan to the boycotted nations. In turn the noninvolved Japanese easily substituted Arab oil. Iran was long an exclusive province of the British. In 1951 an ardent nationalist prime minister, Mossadegh, seized the oil fields and expelled the British company, Anglo-Iranian (now British Petroleum). The British managed for two years to keep the "stolen oil" from Iran off the world market but were unable to reclaim their oil fields. In 1953 a coup d'état ousted Mossadegh in favor of a conservative regime personally loyal to the shah, whom the prime minister had sent into exile. The royalist coup supposedly was sponsored by the U.S. Central Intelligence Agency. The CIA furnished the money and possibly the plan. The American rationale was to assist the British and to end the risk of a communist takeover of the unstable nation. With the government safely in conservative hands the Anglo-Iranian Company returned, but not alone, for the United States was now entitled to a share of the wealth. Anglo-Iranian got 40 percent. Royal Dutch-Shell got 14 percent, and Compagnie Française des Pétroles got 6 percent. The Americans got 40 percent: 7 percent each for Jersey Standard, Mobil, Gulf, Standard of California, and Texaco and 5 percent for the independents. Since then the exporters have gotten along more or less smoothly with the shah's conservative regime. After the British military withdrawal from the Persian Gulf region from 1967 onward, the U.S. Department of Defense viewed Iran as the logical policeman. It has been supplying the Iranian military with aircraft and boats with which to patrol the Persian Gulf.

Closer to home the United States has continued to buy heavily from Venezuela. Venezuelan reserves are nearly one-half the size of U.S. domestic reserves. American companies own two-thirds interest and are the largest buyer of the production. The Venezuelan government was for a long time favorable to American purchase of the oil. For their part the companies have treated Venezuela better than other exporters. In the late 1940's they took the then unprecedented step of splitting the revenues 50-50 with the South American country. They also agreed that beginning in 1983 foreign-owned facilities would revert to Venezuelan ownership. Now as 1983 approaches the situation looks more uncertain. The Venezuelan government fully intends to see that the reversion occurs on schedule. Furthermore it has supported the Arab strengthening of OPEC. It has raised its export prices to keep pace with the Middle East. At the same time it seems little disposed to help the United States. Much Venezuelan oil now goes to eastern Canada. While this would be available for American purchase when the Canadians finished construction of the Calgary to Montreal pipeline, the Venezuelans show little inclination to sell it to the United States.

Venezuela's neighbor, Ecuador, recently struck oil. In 1967 a Gulf-Texaco consortium discovered high grade crude in the Amazon jungles. By 1972 a pipeline across the Andes began pumping it to a Pacific port. Noting the mistakes of Venezuela and other oil exporters, the Ecuadorian government carefully outlined an economic development plan that promised to bring the benefits of the new wealth to all people and not just to the producers and a small elite. But one of the first effects was inflation. The cost of living increased 15 percent according to an official report and 30 percent according to an unofficial one.

The United States imports little from directly south of the border. This is partly the result of bad relations engendered in the 1939 nationalization of the American producers in Mexico. As this was the Americans' first experience with a leftist government threatening nationalization they were unprepared for the government actually to carry out its threat. They treated the Mexican officials with contempt even though they treated their Mexican employees well. Once nationalization came they were left with nothing except ill will and the lesson for future dealings with other governments that threatened nationalization. Perhaps more important, Mexican production is small for the present, and not much oil is available for export. Some enters the United States and is entitled to preferential treatment if it comes in overland, but the quantity is small.

Imports from Canada are much larger. They come from fields recently discovered in the western prairies. When American capital began flowing into Calgary to develop the discoveries it provoked an outcry from nationalistic Canadians fearful of an American takeover of their economy. The government responded with a series of laws restricting the amount of American capital that could be invested north of the border. The discovery also demonstrated the insincerity of the national defense argument used to justify the import quota system imposed in 1959. Though Canadian oil could be piped overland safe from the dangers tankers faced from submarines supposedly lurking offshore, it was denied entry free of the quota. Carrying the argument to its ludicrous extreme one senator justified this denial by warning of the danger of war between Canada and the United States.

The pipeline from Calgary to Montreal, now nearly finished, will divert half a million barrels per day from the midwestern United States to eastern Canada. This is part of Prime Minister Pierre Elliott Trudeau's decision to make Canada self-sufficient in energy by 1980. In addition to reducing exports to the United States, this Canadian commitment to autarky involves establishing a government-owned oil corporation.

The gradual changes in the oil industry during the 1960's began to be noticed well before international crises thrust them into the headlines. It was apparent that foreign oil was more and more in demand. The 1959 import system was protecting domestic procedures so well that crude oil was desperately scarce. The Middle Eastern situation kept importers under constant tension. The new concern with the quality of the environment demanded low sulfur fuels that would not pollute. To respond to environmental concern, the Department of the Interior directed the National Petroleum Council, its industry advisory body, to study the situation and report. What began as a study confined to oil and gas, as befitted the Petroleum Council, was soon expanded officially to include all forms of energy.

The membership of the N.P.C. represents the industry establishment. The government, which officially sponsors the council, is hardly represented. An Interior Department assistant secretary serves as co-chairman, not chairman. He is the only government representative on the full council. Consumers are not represented at all. The remaining 29 members are drawn exclusively from private industry. All of the seven majors have at least one member; a few have two. About half are from the independent companies, though these may include businesses as large as Standard of Ohio and Atlantic-Richfield. Two industry associations have members on the council: the A.P.I., which the majors dominate, and the I.P.A.A., which the independents dominate. Frank N. Ikard represents the A.P.I. here as well as on Capitol Hill, where he is the institute's chief lobbyist. From 1952 to 1961 Ikard was a Texas congressman and protégé of Speaker Sam Rayburn. Since he left office, his congressional contacts and reputation have helped him to promote the industry's position.

The council has a series of subcommittees staffed by the experts who do the actual work. In terms of representation the subcommittees are miniatures of the full council. The chairmen are from private industry; the Interior Department co-chairmen are the government's only representatives. The majors and the independents divide the committee places with a sprinkling of personnel from the trade associations. Since the N.P.C.'s assigned task includes other forms of energy, the staff includes a few experts on coal, electricity, and nuclear energy.

With a membership such as this, the policy recommendations of the N.P.C. come as no surprise. Its report, *U.S. Energy Outlook,* concluded that the status quo should continue. The petroleum industry surveyed the cozy relationship it has with the federal government and found it satisfactory; the situation established in the 1920's and 1930's should continue unchanged. The report echoed the old arguments the industry has used to rationalize its privileges. The import quota system should continue for reasons of national security. The tax depletion allowance should continue. The cut from 27½ percent to 22 percent cost the industry $500 million per annum (or, turned around, saved the American taxpayer the same amount). The federal government should continue leasing offshore oil lands. It should continue to encourage the domestic industry and support American companies producing overseas. Suggestions for change were chiefly for more of the same. Offshore leases should be more easily available. Producers should have greater access to public lands. A few of the recommendations were contradictory, presumably reflecting the conflicting interests of various companies—e.g., while imports should be restricted, refiners should have adequate supplies from overseas. The report dealt with the conflict between oil and the environment both by minimizing the problem and by favoring the needs of the industry. This is called achieving a "rational balance." The government should minimize delays in oil exploration, laying pipelines, and constructing deepwater terminals and refineries. It should establish standards so the companies will know how much pollution will be legal. In sum, the report expressed general happiness with the relationship between the petroleum industry and the government and sought more of the same in the future.

The happy future toward which the N.P.C. looked proved short, and the warmth of the relationship cooled off a few degrees. Despite the extensive research and consensus-building that the N.P.C. devoted to arriving at its vague recommendations, the White House was not paying attention. Though dated December 1972, the report did not actually appear until the spring of 1973. Literally within days of its publication President Nixon announced a policy the opposite of the N.P.C.'s recommendation when he ended 14 years of import quotas. This hardly meant that the President had turned against the oilmen. He softened the blow with a fee of 1 cent per gallon on imported crude, which served to hold back any flood of the foreign product. But it did mean that the domestic producers had lost a major bulwark of protection.

President Nixon turned on the industry in this mild fashion in order to counter the petroleum shortage that afflicted the country in the early 1970's. This shortage derived first of all from regulation. The government has long intervened in the market, causing distortions. If the distortions result in an artificially high price the consumers tend to suffer in relative silence. If the distortions result in an artificially low price, the consumer soon comes up against a shortage and complains. In this case he will express his dissatisfaction politically by writing his congressmen or voting against the party in power. The wage-price freeze President Nixon imposed in August 1971 as Phase I of his New Economic Policy brought about one distortion. Since prices were frozen at their summer levels, gasoline was high and heating oil low. Thus even when winter came refiners could make more profit producing gasoline than heating oil and so oriented their output. Ending the freeze helped to remedy the distortion. A year and a half later the nation faced the reverse problem in the summer of 1973. This time gasoline was in short supply. The petroleum industry blamed the federal government. It pointed to continuing price controls, the cut in the tax depletion allowance, the import quota (and its successor, the import fee), and antipollution devices on automobiles. It called on government assistance to end the crisis.

Critics of the oil companies labeled the crisis as phony. Congressman Charles A. Vanik (Dem., Ohio) charged that: "Contrary to the barrage of the industry's media propaganda, the energy crisis is not, fundamentally, a crisis of supply. What is really at stake in this 'crisis' is the profit margin of the petroleum industry."[15] The congressman's view is supported by the remark of an oil company executive to a government official: "You give us the profits and we'll give you the oil."

This did not, however, prove to be the case. The major distributors at first refrained from increasing their profits by raising their prices. Rather than simply upping the price of a gallon of gasoline at the pump, the big companies took other tacks. One was to ration the amount delivered to service stations. An economist would recommend rationing a scarce commodity by raising the price until the marginal buyers dropped out. Those who wanted the goods would be willing to pay the higher price. Those unwilling to pay the higher price did not want the goods as much. For some, gasoline is worth buying at a dollar a gallon; for others it is not. This is the standard market-clearing process. In spite of their frequent appeals to the free enterprise system and calls to restore competition in the N.P.C. report, the distributors hesitated to use this classical economic approach. One reason was that the companies had certain nonmonetary goals. The large brand name companies distributed through three types of dealers: company-owned stations; privately owned but brand name stations; and nonowned, nonbrand discount stations. The shortage gave the distributor an opportunity to squeeze the last two. Discount competitors could be forced to close, at least temporarily, which would drive customers to the brand name stations. To a lesser extent the distributors could also squeeze the privately owned brand name stations. Some would be willing to sell to the company. Others would lose regular customers to the company-owned stations. Thus before raising prices the distributors rationed supplies on a nonprice basis. To the extent to which this is true it supports an observation of some economists that the goal of big business is not so much to maximize profit as to achieve survival, stability, or aggrandizement. In this businesses behave much like government bureaucracies. It is no wonder that industry finds cooperation with the Department of Interior so congenial.

A second reason for the distributors' initial reluctance to raise prices relates to the high visibility of the method. Increasing a cost to the consumer directly is conspicuous. He is likely to complain and bring political pressure to bear. Indeed this happened, for when President Nixon decreed a 60-day freeze on prices in June 1973, he specifically singled out gasoline. It is better to increase profits where they are less visible to the public. Hence the shortage of gasoline furnished a golden opportunity for the industry to push some of its schemes for making invisible profits. These included increasing drilling on public lands and offshore, shifting the cost of research from the private companies to the government, and securing federal funds to build supertankers and superports to unload them. Some even hoped to restore the tax depletion allowance to 27½ percent.

The distributors' initial caution about raising the price at the pump disappeared after the Arab boycott began. By then the political environment had changed radically and continued to change almost from day to day. Many of these changes were institutional. The actors in the arena changed with unpredictable suddenness as the government created new agencies and abandoned old ones, hired new czars and fired old ones, proclaimed new rules and forgot old ones.

The physical properties of crude oil that structured its early development are now less important. In comparison to coal, oil production, transportation, refining, and distribution require an advanced technology and large amounts of capital. Fifty or a hundred years ago these requirements caused the industry to develop in a pattern of massive private corporations enjoying a cozy relationship with government. Today drilling a well and putting the refined product on the market presents few engineering or business difficulties. The key factor is not the crude oil's characteristics but its location. Geography now overshadows technology. Within the United States, this means oil has dominated the politics of Louisiana and Texas to the same degree coal has dominated Pennsylvania and West Virginia. The style, however, differs. Privileged access and campaign donations are characteristic of an oil state, while violence and labor-management conflict are characteristic of a coal state. The geographical dichotomy between onshore and offshore drilling sites generated state-federal conflict during the 1950's because the dichotomy paralleled the jurisdiction of the two levels of government. Legally defining the physical boundaries of a state as extending three miles or three leagues or some other distance from the shore determined which level of government was to have jurisdiction and, hence, structured the politics that would determine the fuel's exploitation. Today these geographical determinants of oil politics are comparatively quiescent. The conflicts over control of domestically produced onshore oil were settled by the mid 1930's and those over offshore oil were settled in the 1950's. The geographical issue now dominant is international. Worldwide deposits of easily exploited crude do not lie randomly about the globe but are concentrated in a few countries. Since the most vast and cheaply produced oil fields are in the Middle East, the Arab states suddenly are able to manipulate the supply to the West to further their political aims, chief of which is to subdue Israel. Until peace comes to the Middle East or extensive, inexpensive reserves are discovered elsewhere the Arab nations will be able to use their control of oil to wring concessions from the United States, Europe, and Japan.

The market forces governing the petroleum industry have reflected the extremes both of declining demand and of declining supply. Oil was often a "sick industry" during the 1920's and early 1930's as the unpredictable discoveries of massive new fields destabilized the industry. While oil (unlike coal) has enjoyed long-term growth, the short-term price collapses led to governmental intervention to stabilize the market. The result of these governmental rescues is the privileged position of petroleum illustrated by prorationing (a program at the state level to allocate a special amount to be pumped at each well), depletion allowances, import controls, and so on. The price the oil barons gladly pay for this comfortable arrangement is the campaign donation system focusing primarily on the Presidency and the Senate. On the other hand, (and again unlike coal) oil has suffered declines in supply as well as declines in demand. The crisis of 1919 was an early example. The 1973–74 crisis is a recent one. Having learned the benefits of governmental intervention in the former, the industry chose the same strategy in the latter. Indeed the American people did enjoy some benefits from the years of government distortion at the time of the Arab boycott. The net effect of federal and state manipulation from the 1930's to the 1970's was to favor domestic production over foreign. This was exactly what the United States needed in 1973–74. The United States was better able to survive the Arab boycott because it imported only a small amount from the Middle East. In the balance, however, the American people paid dearly for the brief benefit they gained. Furthermore much of the benefit consisted of timing. Since Persian Gulf crude is so much cheaper and more plentiful than any other supply, the Arab rise to power was inevitable. Governmental favoritism merely delayed the day of reckoning a few years. Given that fundamental economic adjustments needed to be made, an earlier time might have been better.

Like coal, oil emerged over a long time span, thus mitigating the impact on its development of any single general political environment. Its nineteenth-century origins decreed private ownership, but its need for comparatively greater concentrations of capital led to confrontations with the trust-busting of the Progressive era. When the Supreme Court split up the old Standard Oil Company in 1911 it unwittingly created successor corporations that dominate the field to this day. Four of the present big seven (Exxon, Mobil, California Standard, and Indiana Standard) and several smaller companies derive from John D. Rockefeller's original company. The federal policy of fostering competition reversed itself in the World War I mobilization aiming the industry toward cooperation. Henceforth the industry was to establish an increasingly intimate relationship with federal and state governments. Politics offered a refuge from the uncertainties of the marketplace. The industry found the New Deal propensity to intervene in the economy compatible with its own quest for privilege. Since then the oil industry's web of relationships with government has been embellished.

The anti-Communism that dominated American politics during the 1950's furnished a convenient rationale for import quotas. National defense against the Communist menace demanded self-sufficiency. Yet the American military fought Communism in Vietnam with Persian Gulf and Indonesian crude refined in Singapore. The issue of protecting the environment, too, influenced oil politics peripherally. Public outrage with oil spilled from offshore wells, tanker accidents, and refineries caused the industry to invest more money in spill prevention and cleanup. While concern for the environment hurt oil's public image, it did not hurt its profits. When Congress required automobile manufacturers to install antipollution devices, it threatened Detroit's profits but not Houston's. Fewer miles to the gallon meant more gallons purchased.

In the early 1970's energy itself became a transcending political issue, helped along by the oil corporations' heavy advertising. The thrust of the public relations campaign was that the "crisis" demanded more government help: The Interior Department should open leasing on public lands and offshore. Congress should lessen the environmental safeguards that were blocking construction of the Alaskan pipeline. The Cost of Living Council should approve higher prices for gasoline and heating oil. Industry demands this time produced backlash. President Nixon proposed a tax on "excess profits." Congressional committees launched a series of investigations exposing petroleum's privileges and profits. The channels of cooperation, flowing smoothly since World War I, finally came under intense critical scrutiny.

Notes

1. Sam H. Schurr and Bruce C. Netschert, *Energy in the American Economy* (Baltimore: Johns Hopkins, Resources for the Future, 1960), p. 36; Executive Office of the President, Office of Science and Technology, *Patterns of Energy Consumption in the United States,* 1972, p. 22.

2. Harold F. Williamson *et al.,The American Petroleum Industry* (Evanston, Ill.: Northwestern, 1963), pp. 4–14.

3. *Ibid.,* pp. 299–335.

4. Robert Engler, *The Politics of Oil* (New York: Macmillan, 1961), pp. 132–33.

5. *Ibid.,* pp. 261–95; Gerald D. Nash, *United States Oil Policy 1890–1964* (Pittsburgh: University of Pittsburgh, 1968), pp. 23–48.

6. Nash, *op. cit.,* pp. 29–38.

7. Williamson *et al., op. cit.,* pp. 316–21.

8. *Ibid.,* pp. 308–10; Engler, *op. cit.,* pp. 83–85; Nash, *op. cit.,* pp. 73–81; Richard O'Connor, *The Oil Barons* (Boston: Little, Brown, 1971), pp. 244–48, 260–62.

9. Nash, *op. cit.,* pp. 72–127; Williamson *et al., op. cit.,* pp. 238–99, 466–535; Engler, *op. cit., passim.*

10. Herbert Werner, "Labor Organizations in the American Petroleum Industry," in Williamson *et al., op. cit.,* pp. 827–45.

11. Williamson *et al., op. cit.,* pp. 764–66; Engler, *op. cit.,* p. 170.

12. Engler, *op. cit., passim.*

13. Engler, *op. cit.,* pp. 230–66; O'Connor, *op. cit.,* pp. 416–21.

14. "OPEC Signals Another Crude Price Boost," *Oil and Gas Journal,* September 24, 1973, p. 80.

15. David Hess, "Is Energy Crisis a Myth to Enrich Oil and Auto Tycoons?" *The Philadelphia Inquirer,* April 18, 1973.

4

Natural Gas

Oil and gas are twins. The same companies pump them from the same wells. To an extent not duplicated by any other two sources of energy, these two share the same political arena. Yet the twins are separated at birth: each goes its own way politically as well as physically. Oil, for all its close ties with federal and state governments, is not officially a regulated industry. Gas is. Oil's chief federal protagonist is the same as coal's, the Department of the Interior. For gas, it is the Federal Power Commission. While the oil companies produce the gas, they are soon forced to give the child up for adoption. Federal law requires transportation and distribution be done by different companies.

The political status of the gas industry derives from its physical characteristics and the general political milieu of the era in which it rose to prominence. Unlike coal and oil, market forces explain little of the fuel's politics. Natural gas typically is found together with crude oil deposits. Oil drillers have a high probability of finding gas, though it can also be found alone. The oil forces the light vapor up against the underground rock dome that has trapped it since the earth was young. Below the oil lies the heavier water. Early drillers considered the gas a nuisance. True, it could be used for lighting and powering on-site machinery, but it was difficult to transport and impossible to store. No one outside the immediate vicinity would buy it. Furthermore, the gas was dangerous. It was poisonous and explosive. The solution for the producer was to vent it into the air or to pipe it a safe distance from the well head and burn it. At night the sky over the oil fields was red with the gas flares. In time the producers learned the dysfunction of doing this. The gas was needed to conserve the oil; its pressure made the crude oil flow from the well. If the gas escaped, the oil stopped flowing. The solution was to cap the wells and even pump gas back into dry wells to make them flow again.[1]

After conservation, petroleum technology made a second stride forward that promoted the natural gas industry. In the 1920's electrical welding techniques were perfected sufficiently to permit the laying of a leak-proof pipeline. Early attempts to transmit gas through old-fashioned screw-thread jointed pipes resulted in loss of up to 40 percent. Until very recently there was no alternative to a pipeline for distributing gas. Since the fuel is gaseous, it is extremely bulky for the amount of energy it yields. It could not be compressed. A railroad tank car could not carry nearly enough to make even the shortest trip worthwhile. But the high pressure welded pipelines developed during the 1920's could. Suddenly gas had a market as the pipelines connected the wells to cities hundreds and thousands of miles away.

At the same time the industry was undergoing a shift comparable to that experienced by both oil and coal. The center of production was moving west from the Appalachian mountains that bore it. Oil began in Pennsylvania, then moved to the Midwest; and then, as the old wells ran dry, shifted to the Great Plains and the states bordering the Gulf of Mexico. The gas industry followed. Since the gas fields were not depleted as quickly and since the earlier pipelines could transport only short distances, it lingered longer to take advantage of its nearness to the northeastern cities. Indeed, the industry still exists in its original Appalachian birthplace even though belittled by the great volume sent from the West. Coal, too, partook of this shift westward, at first because of the general population migration and today because of the demand for low sulfur fuel. The consequence of these shifts has been to dislocate political arrangements in the states affected at the same time as it dislocates the economic ones. Pennsylvania and West Virginia have been through a series of booms and busts with successive waves scrambling to exploit the states' buried treasures. Texas, California, and Louisiana have had to face fewer of the busts so far.

The physical characteristics of gas have influenced its political constituency in terms of manpower as well as geography. Gas is almost ready to use as it flows out of the well. It needs no digging or refining and hence virtually no workers. Traditional coal mining required a large labor force, and the politics of coal was primarily labor politics. Oil required many fewer workers. The refineries were the only sites at which a large enough number of workers came together to make trade unions likely. High wages and company unions blunted the thrust of the union movement. Gas has no centers of labor activity. The jobs in the industry are drilling wells and laying pipelines. For both, the workers are dispersed and mobile. Most gas workers were included in the scope of the Oil Workers International Union, formerly known as the International Association of Oil Field, Gas Well, and Refinery Workers. The union's little success came in the oil refineries, not in the fields or on the pipelines where the gas workers were. Even in the refineries the union could recruit few members in spite of a series of major C.I.O.-sponsored organizing drives between 1935 and 1941. A few unions of New England gas workers in the city systems affiliated with the United Mine Workers after the A.F.L. refused to grant them charters in 1936. Since most of these cities had not yet converted to natural gas from coal gas, the affiliation had an inherent logic. John L. Lewis was always happy to better his A.F.L. nemesis. These were the exceptions, however, for the trade unions never played a major part in the gas industry's affairs.[2]

The desire to conserve oil caused the producing states to regulate gas. Wasting gas could result in wasting oil. At the other end of the distribution chain was also a tradition of government regulation. The consuming cities had long regulated the distribution of gas as a public utility. Their rationale was that the structure of the market made it a natural monopoly. A number of firms cannot compete. A distribution system requires digging up the city streets, laying mains, and installing meters. The householder cannot go to a rival company if the price is too high or the service poor. One company must get the exclusive franchise, then be closely supervised. The gas in the early days was not natural but manufactured locally from coal. But the distribution system was the same. When improved pipelines permitted long distance transportation the cities eagerly signed up for the cheaper, cleaner, odor-free product that burned with twice the energy.

Thus as the natural gas industry began its great expansion in the 1930's it was regulated at both ends but not in the middle. The cities soon found themselves in an economic squeeze. Large transmission companies could manipulate the price and the quantity to the detriment of the public. The city of Detroit charged that it was being victimized by a monopoly. Interlocking companies controlled by John D. Rockefeller and J. P. Morgan interests conspired to deny the city natural gas because to provide the gas would threaten to undo their monopoly in Ohio and Indiana. The gas barons considered Detroit their territory and blocked attempts by independent companies to raise the financial capital on Wall Street to build a pipeline from the Southwest to Detroit. Other cities raised similar complaints. St. Paul protested that the gas monopoly demanded a 20-year franchise or nothing. Indianapolis grumbled that it could obtain natural gas only by turning the city-owned company over to the private monopoly. Milwaukee complained that there was a conspiracy bent upon stifling competition.[3]

The cities had a valid point. The long-distance pipeline system was monopolistic—for much the same reasons that local distribution was a natural monopoly. First, there was no alternative to the pipelines for transportation. Neither ships nor rails could compete. Second, the costs of the original investment were high. Building a line demanded huge amounts of capital. Once it was committed, there was little flexibility. A company could not move its pipeline from a city if it lost a contract. Third, the great scope of the enterprise gave many points of risk. Eliminating the risk led the companies to try to integrate vertically. Controlling both production in the southwestern fields and sales in the northern cities eliminated the risk.[4]

The instrument of vertical economic integration was the holding company. The holding company allowed a limited group of investors to extend its control over a larger number of companies. This was the conspiracy which built the monopolies which so angered the northern cities. The scheme was much like a pyramid, but a pyramid of economic power. A holding company would be formed to buy controlling interest in a pipeline company. Twenty percent might be sufficient. Then a second holding company could buy controlling interest in the first holding company. Again 20 percent might be sufficient. Thus a pipeline could be controlled by those investing only 4 percent of its value (20% of 20% = 4%). The basic plan was embellished. Companies would issue various securites: nonvoting bonds and preferred shares for others; voting common stock for themselves. Fraud crept in. A holding company would charge exorbitant fees for valueless financial and management services. For the parent company to exploit its subsidiaries was routine. Even when run honestly, the system fostered extensive concentrations of economic power that tempted the owners to demand usurious prices from their customers—in this case, cities wishing to purchase gas.

The big four of the natural gas industry were Standard of New Jersey, Columbia Gas and Electric, Cities Service, and Electric Bond and Share. Together they controlled 18 percent of gas production, 56 percent of the pipelines, and 60 percent of the interstate movement. With six others they controlled 86 percent of the interstate transmission.[5]

Congress' first attack on the monopolistic control of natural gas focused on the holding company device. After extensive investigation by its own committees and by the Federal Trade Commission it passed the Public Utility Holding Company Act of 1935. The act required such companies to register with the then newly created Securities and Exchange Commission. The SEC was to require the companies to simplify their organization. They had to be confined to a single geographic region. Pyramiding could extend only to the second level. That is, a holding company could own an operating company but not another holding company.

The act presents a novel concept in law enforcement: complexity may hide wrongdoing; therefore the company must simplify itself. Since the intricate interrelationships among the various members of a financial family are so complicated, hidden evasion of the law becomes possible. The remedy is for the government to decree that the relationships be made less complicated. Exposure to scrutiny will expose the evil. The act did not contemplate that the offending companies would reorganize themselves spontaneously. The SEC was to supervise. In giving the commission the power to involve itself so deeply in the affairs of a private business, the act broke new ground. Previous laws had ordered businesses to reorganize.

The Sherman Antitrust Act often led to that. But the Holding Company Act was unique in the degree to which it contemplated the SEC would superintend a company. It could bring in accountants, economists, engineers, and lawyers. The burden was on the company to disprove the correctness of an SEC order. Prior laws had kept the government outside a company and required the government to prove in court that what it ordered was justified.

From the SEC's viewpoint the administration of the Holding Company Act was a success. The Supreme Court upheld the SEC's right to intervene so deeply into a business. The SEC regionalized the utilities into geographic unities. It ended the abuses that the pyramiding had perpetuated on consumers and small investors. Administratively the SEC justified the new type of responsibility Congress gave it and in so doing built a pattern for more detailed supervision by other regulatory agencies.[6]

From the gas industry's viewpoint the impact was revolutionary. The companies lost their autonomy and came under the jurisdiction of the SEC, where they remained for between 10 and 20 years. By the end of this period little of the former financial system remained. Three of the natural gas Big Four were gone. The fourth remained as an integrated regional system in the Appalachian area. Oil companies were eliminated as public utility holding companies. Standard Oil retired from the business. The major gas companies split from the major electrical companies. In short, the great gas empires of the 1930's, which had emerged so suddenly with the development of electric welding, fell nearly as suddenly with the passage of the Holding Company Act. The pipelines were still there, but the companies that built them were gone.

While the Holding Company Act of 1935 eventually revolutionized the industry, it did little for the consumer. New Deal innovations in the way the SEC so specifically administered the finances of the holding companies brought no relief to the cities, which continued to pay high prices to the companies now made more honest. The reformed companies still charged dearly for their gas. The consuming states sought to remedy the situation. To protect the consumer they regulated the price he paid. At the other end the producing states regulated the gas at the well head. The problem lay in between. No one state could regulate the interstate movement. The U.S. Supreme Court had spoken clearly on this point.

Pressure built up for Congress to fill this gap in regulation. The vacuum allowed the transmission companies to demand exorbitant prices and left the cities and states powerless. Lack of interstate regulation undercut attempts at intrastate regulation, for any company threatened by state control could easily deny the gas to that state, thereby depriving it of vital energy. The state was powerless to prevent the company from spiriting away its fuel. When the states faced a similar problem of interstate cooperation with respect to oil production after the Supreme Court declared the NRA unconstitutional, their solution was to form the Interstate Oil and Gas Compact. This case was different, however, for those affected were consumers rather than producers. A small group with a specific interest finds it easier to organize for political action than does a large group with a diffuse interest. A few hundred producers have a greater incentive to organize than do a few million gas consumers. For the former the rewards are millions of dollars, while for the latter they are a few dollars each. The cities themselves were the chief proponents of action. Detroit organized the Cities Alliance to work for regulation of interstate transmission. The U.S. Conference of Mayors lobbied for federal control.

The cities' efforts paid off in 1938, when Congress passed the Natural Gas Act. The act made no attempt to regulate the production at one end or the distribution at the other; its sole purpose was to fill the gap in between, to occupy the area in which the Supreme Court said the states could not act. The responsibility for regulation went to the Federal Power Commission as a logical extension of its responsibility for regulating electrical public utilities.

The FPC was to regulate the pipelines in two ways commonly found in public utility legislation: controlling rates and controlling facilities. Of the two the latter was more straightforward. The FPC issued certificates permitting a company to build a new pipeline, sell to a new customer, or expand its facilities. Before it could expand its services it had to persuade the FPC that what it proposed was beneficial. The effect was to give to the federal government some of the power that was so misused by the holding companies. If a holding company decided to withhold service from a certain city, that was a supercilious exercise of raw economic power. If the FPC decided to withhold service from a certain city, that was a thoughtful exercise of administrative judgment. Presumably the advantage in the government's making the decision was that it had the people's interests at heart whereas the holding company did not. In fact, the FPC balanced a number of conflicting interests just as the company did, only in this case the interests were different. The FPC did not confine itself to the interests of the various consumers but spent some time considering politically powerful representatives of other forms of energy. Coal interests frequently intervened in commission hearings. The operators feared losing sales if gas moved into their territory. Workers feared losing jobs. Railroads feared losing freight.

Issuing certificates for new development, difficult as it was, seemed a pleasure compared to the legalistic problems the FPC encountered in attempting to set rates. The commission's first problem was to set a standard on which to base the price the companies could charge for the gas. The traditional standard was based on *Smyth* v. *Ames*, an 1898 case which established that the Supreme Court could determine the fairness of rates. The court was to determine a fair return on a fair value of the company's property. The criteria included (1) the original cost of construction, (2) the amount expended on improvements, and (3) the cost of reproducing the facilities. Since the Supreme Court never made clear how much emphasis a judge was to put on original cost and how much on reproduction cost, the utility had a great incentive to challenge an unfavorable ruling. The result was endless litigation. For the Supreme Court this was an advantage, for it preserved its dominance in the arena. During most of the years after handing down the *Smyth* v. *Ames* decision in 1898 the high court used this power to favor the utilities, but with the reordering of American politics in the Great Depression new justices came to the Court who wished to shift to favoring the consumers. To do so required strengthening the regulatory agencies. For natural gas this meant the FPC. In *FPC* v. *Hope Natural Gas Company*, the court overruled *Smyth* v. *Ames*. Its vague standards provided no firm foundation for regulation. The new standard was based on "prudent investment" or "actual legitimate cost." It consisted of an actuarial formula starting with the original cost, deducting depreciation, and adding an allowance for working capital. The chief advantage was that it was easy to apply. It was mechanical. There was little room for disagreement since all parties in the industry accepted a uniform system of accounts. Under the new procedures after the *Hope* case lengthy litigation declined. The parties frequently agreed on price privately without resort to formal FPC hearings. The simplicity of the new method was part of the reason prices were more easily agreed to. The other was that the courts now backed up the commission. A challenge to an FPC ruling now had little chance of success.[7]

The *Hope* case made clear to the industry that the FPC was free to regulate the interstate transportation of gas without second guessing by the courts. Having established its rights to act autonomously in transmission, the commission next faced the problem of jurisdiction over production. Those who wished to lower the price to the consumer realized that it was not enough to regulate the price of the gas in the pipelines if the price before it entered was not regulated. The producers fought the FPC's attempt to assert its jurisdiction. The problem was a double one, for a pipeline could obtain the gas either from its own wells or from independent producers. Jurisdiction over the first was determined in the *Colorado Interstate* case. The FPC decided that since the Colorado Interstate Company was an integrated company obtaining gas from its own wells, the commission would have the right to determine the price on the basis of a traditional cost of service criterion on the entire system. The producers objected that this gave too low a price. That scheme might be all right for the pipelines themselves, where costs were fixed and easy to estimate, but it was completely unfair in production, where the risks were high. A company might have to drill many dry holes before hitting gas. The FPC method gave the Colorado Interstate Company a return of only 10 cents an acre.

The issue of the FPC's jurisdiction over the second way of obtaining the gas—purchase from independent producers—was not to be so easily settled. The majority of the five commissioners maintained that the Natural Gas Act of 1938 exempted these "arm's length" transactions. But the minority held that Congress had not intended to allow such sales to go unregulated.

In view of its failure to prevail in 1947 in the *Colorado Interstate* case and the disagreement among the five commissioners, the industry took its pleadings to Congress. Oklahoma congressmen obligingly introduced legislation to restrict the FPC's jurisdiction. The industry bill took its name from its chief advocate, Senator Robert Kerr of Oklahoma, a millionaire oil and gas producer.

As Congress debated the Kerr bill, President Truman submitted the name of Leland Olds for a third term on the FPC. In Commissioner Olds the Congress found a scapegoat. His political execution was to be an example to deter future commissioners from opposing the wishes of the natural gas producers. The producers opposed Olds because he had been a leader in the FPC's expansion of its regulatory activities. He believed that the commission could not control prices to the consumer without controlling prices to the pipeline. Furthermore, Olds had been an outspoken critic of the Kerr bill because it would prevent the FPC from doing just that. If Olds's policies were to prevail, it would not only mean regulation of natural gas production but would point the way toward control over crude oil too. The Senate hearings on confirmation became a spree of vilification. The oil and gas interests launched an all out personal attack against the commissioner. The subcommittee, chaired by the new senator from Texas, Lyndon B. Johnson, was unanimously hostile. The witnesses tried to smear Olds as a Communist. They resurrected articles he had written for labor union newspapers during the 1920's and 1930's that expressed admiration for the U.S.S.R. Olds was painted as an enemy of the American system of free enterprise. Olds's position was hopeless. His denials of sympathy for Communism fell on deaf ears. The subcommittee disregarded the pleas of consumer groups that testified in his behalf. President Truman in desperation asked the 48 democratic state chairmen to telegraph their senators urging Olds's reconfirmation. It was to no avail. The Senate rejected the commissioner by a vote of 53 to 15.[8]

The saga of Leland Olds's defeat once again illustrates one of the maxims of public policy analysis: the particular policy often gets tangled in transcending political issues. The United Mine Workers became involved in labor's realignment from the Republican to the Democratic party. The oil industry became involved in the growth of the federal government during the New Deal. So too, the regulation of natural gas became involved in the anti-Communist mania that swept the nation in the late 1940's and early 1950's. Communist treachery offered an easy answer to any problem. If foreign policy went badly it was because, according to Joe McCarthy, 256 Communists had infiltrated the State Department. If the local health department fluoridated the city drinking water it was a Red plot. If the FPC sought to regulate the production of natural gas it was because Commissioner Olds was a Communist. No one dedicated to capitalism would do so. The anti-Communist craze was born of fantasy and fueled by demogoguery, but it swept the country. Republican Senator Joseph McCarthy built a national following that allowed him to dominate the headlines for five years. Millions of fanatic partisans eagerly awaited his wild accusations. President Truman could not counter his mesmerizing attacks. President Eisenhower tried to ignore the problem but in fact aided the Wisconsin demagogue by leading the G.O.P. to control of the Senate, giving McCarthy a committee chairmanship. Leland Olds's defeat was not the only one attributable to the anti-Communist fad. Other government officials were sacrificed. In Olds's case the impact of the 1949 charges may be compared to his previous reappointment. In 1944 the Senate subcommittee similarly heard accusations of his Communist sympathies of 25 years before. Then the senators ignored them. By 1949 national concerns had changed, and the charges proved fatal to Olds's career.

Having won the victory over government regulation by denying Commissioner Olds his reappointment, the natural gas lobby moved to solidify its position by passing the Kerr bill. The industry forces won close votes in the House and Senate against the opposition of members from consuming states. The bill went to the President, who vetoed it. In his veto message Truman cited the monopolistic features of the industry. Because sales required pipelines, competition could never be free. Keeping prices down demanded government regulation. With the votes in Congress so close there was no possibility of overriding the veto. The Kerr bill was dead.

Truman's 1950 veto resolved definitively only the question of FPC regulation of integrated companies. The situation with respect to "arm's length" sales by independent companies remained uncertain. Although the five commissioners divided on the issues, the majority shunned the responsibility, arguing that the FPC lacked the authority under the provisions of the Natural Gas Act. The state of Wisconsin disagreed. As a consuming state it suffered the penalty of the commissioners' nonregulation. Wisconsin challenged the Phillips Petroleum Company, a giant corporation producing one-sixth of the nation's natural gas, contending that the FPC should take jurisdiction. When the FPC denied its own authority, Wisconsin appealed to the Supreme Court. The court supported Wisconsin. The commission did have jurisdiction. Phillips was to be regulated.

The 1954 *Phillips* v. *Wisconsin* decision suddenly confronted a reluctant FPC with a flood of cases. The new responsibility went contrary to the ideology of the Eisenhower appointees. The commission gingerly proceeded to determine the rates. Throughout the 1950's the backlog of rate cases piled up. Few were decided. Even the *Phillips* case itself remained unsettled. The Supreme Court in 1954 only determined that the FPC had the authority to set the price. It had not set the price itself. So the commission sifted through thousands of pages of testimony trying to establish a fair rate for the Wisconsin public to pay.[9]

Even the overburdened and reluctant FPC threatened too much regulation. The industry turned once more to Congress for relief. In 1956 natural gas supporters brought a bill to exempt producers from federal regulation close to a vote in the Senate. At the last moment Senator Francis Case, Republican from South Dakota, dramatically announced that a lobbyist had handed him twenty-five $100 bills in a plain envelope. Ostensibly a contribution for Case's re-election bid that fall, the money was actually a bribe to support the gas bill. Senator Case's candor earned him little thanks in Congress. Lyndon Johnson, by then Democratic majority leader, accused him of sabotaging the work of the Senate. Senator William Fulbright suggested that the bribe actually came from an opponent of the bill who sought to embarrass the natural gas lobby. The senators finally decided to appoint an investigating committee whose members were known to be reliable upholders of congressional mores. Congress was not anxious to expose its inner workings; too many had already been exposed for the sake of the

1956 bill. Though the bill was forced through the Senate in spite of the scandal, President Eisenhower vetoed it. He could not afford to have a bribe or special privilege become an issue in his campaign for re-election even though he favored the bill and had promised to sign it.

The Senate investigation proved to be a whitewash. The $2,500, the committee decided, was not a "bribe" though it had been intended to influence Senator Case's vote. It came (via an intermediary to comply with the law prohibiting direct donations by business) from the Superior Oil Company, which eventually paid a $10,000 fine for failing to register its lobbyists. The committee found virtually no other evidence of wrongdoing. Indeed it found little evidence of lobbying. Most of those representing special interests on Capitol Hill, it seemed, were simply engaged in "educating the public." One of the more skeptical senators on the investigating committee complained:

> It strikes me as a strange situation that the president vetoed the bill because of the arrogant lobbying, but nobody lobbied, nobody saw anybody lobbying, nobody heard anybody who lobbied. It was the best kept secret of the year.[10]

In 1958 the gas interests tried again to deprive the FPC of jurisdiction to regulate the producers but blundered once more through the gaucherie of one of its partisans. Texas Republicans organized a $100 a plate dinner to raise money for the party's leader in the House of Representatives, Joe Martin of Massachusetts. Unfortunately, the letter of invitation stated explicitly the favors Congressman Martin had done for Texas gas and oilmen. The resulting public cry of indignation killed any chance of passing the bill that year.

Lobbyists are generally more discreet. It is not good policy to stuff cash in envelopes or announce the payoff in a dinner invitation. In the Teapot Dome scandal Harry Sinclair was more subtle, paying the Secretary of the Interior with a "loan" that was not to be repaid. Lawyer-congressmen generally remain partners in law firms, which can enjoy the lucrative retainer a business may wish to pay in return for legal services. Others can benefit from inside tips on when to buy a company's stock or earn generous fees for speeches.

In 1960 the FPC decided to crawl out of the regulatory swamp in which it was drowning itself. It had bogged down completely in the flood of rate and certificate cases after the Supreme Court declared in *Phillips* v. *Wisconsin* that the committee's jurisdiction included all wholesales of natural gas. As the first step in reforming its procedures, the FPC terminated its attempts to set rates on the Phillips case, which the Supreme Court had remanded to it back in 1954. The commissioners decided that the data was by then too old to use. Henceforth the FPC would no longer set rates for individual producers; it would now determine rates on an area basis. According to its new "Statement of General Policy" the power commission would set two general prices for each geographic area. The higher price would apply to new production; the lower would apply to existing production. The official intent of the guidelines was not that these prices would be permanent but that they would serve temporarily while the commission made a final decision.[11]

The Federal Power Commission's first major determination under its new area system came in 1965. In the Permian Basin decision the commission rejected using the prices privately negotiated as a guide because the industry was not competitive. Just as in the temporary "freeze" prices, the FPC established two levels. The lower was for old gas wells and for all wells pumping both oil and gas. The higher price was for new wells producing only gas. The rationale was to encourage drilling for new gas wells without unnecessarily rewarding the old wells or the discovery of gas incidental to the search for oil. The drillers who had developed the capacity to find gas by itself therefore would be encouraged to do so by the new price structure. Three years after the Permian Basin decision the FPC issued a similar plan for the southern Louisiana area. Once again the commissioners prematurely congratulated each other for reaching a final solution to the problem of rates.

Setting rates was not the Commission's sole problem during the period. Regulating the pipelines continued to be an issue. A long controversy flared in 1957. The El Paso Natural Gas Company attempted to take over the Pacific Northwest Pipeline Corporation. Under the provisions of the Natural Gas Act of 1938 the FPC had to approve such mergers. It did so in 1959, and the two companies joined. But the Justice Department sought to undo it. It argued that the merger would violate the Clayton Act. In 1962 the Supreme Court ruled that the FPC had acted wrongly. It should have waited until the Justice Department had settled the antitrust issue. In 1964 the high court did settle the antitrust issue, when it ruled that the merger did violate the Clayton Act. The case went back to the lower court for implementation.

At the same time it was fighting off the Justice Department in the courts, El Paso was seeking aid in Congress. In 1962 it persuaded the FPC, which approved the takeover, to propose legislation giving the power commission sole jurisdiction over such mergers. The bill exempted from antitrust prosecution any merger approved by the FPC. When this failed El Paso reintroduced a similar bill in 1967. The Justice Department continued to oppose any proposal that would "forgive" the merger. It feared that such a victory for El Paso in Congress when it had lost in the courts would encourage big corporations to act in defiance of the Clayton Act, believing that they could recoup judicial setbacks with legislative successes. A wealthy business with the resources to conduct extensive litigation would do so. Either it eventually would win its legal case or it would buy enough time to persuade Congress to pass special legislation permitting it to do what the courts forbade. Not only did El Paso play the courts off against Congress, it also played the FPC off against the Justice Department. The two bureaucracies each had their own goals and constituencies. The commission's goal under the Natural Gas Act was to regulate the pipeline companies. The Justice Department's goal under the Clayton Act was to prevent mergers that would limit competition. The two agencies, acting under two laws, had goals which did not contradict each other but also did not mesh. The FPC maintained that it was serving the public interest of furnishing more fuel to the consumers. Justice maintained that it was serving the public interest of preventing undue concentration of economic power in the hands of a few giant corporations.[12] The FPC's constituency on one level is made up of all consumers of natural gas, particularly individuals. On another level its clientele has shifted from the public to the industry. This is a commonly noted malfunction of regulatory bodies. They go through a life cycle. In the early days the agency was oriented toward the consumer. It strived to serve the citizens whose demands brought it into being. As time passed the public lost interest. Popular apathy allowed the industry being regulated to assert itself. The consumers no longer devoted time and attention to seeing that the regulatory agency served their interests, so the agency ceased to do so. It oriented itself toward the industry. The industry lobbied for pro-industry members to be appointed. It argued its cases at length to persuade the agency members and particularly the staff. Eventually the regulated became the regulator.

The tendency results from more than mere apathy brought on by the passage of time. As mentioned earlier, a small group with an intense interest can outweigh politically a large group with a diffuse interest. For the pipeline corporations the decisions of the FPC are critical. An unfavorable ruling can bring loss and even the demise of the company. A favorable ruling can bring millions of dollars. The FPC's approval of El Paso's purchase of Pacific Northwest meant hefty profits. The Justice Department's antitrust suit brought loss for El Paso and the demise of Pacific Northwest. For the average consumer, the decisions of the FPC meant only a few cents more per month on the gas bill. Although the cost was great in the aggregate, it was trivial for any single consumer. Hence no individual had an incentive to intervene in the FPC hearings to argue against the merger. The only consumers for whom it made sense to devote time and money to opposing the merger were the industrial users who purchase thousands of dollars worth of gas. In general these industrial consumers have managed to achieve a very favorable position. The FPC permits them to buy at much lower rates than are set for individuals. The industries may be few but because their interest is intense they have an incentive to act.

The Justice Department has a different political environment. It is not an independent regulatory agency as the FPC is. Its Antitrust Division is insulated from direct pressure by the larger department. Unlike most bureaus it has no clientele standing in relation to it the way the gas industry stands in relation to the FPC. The Antitrust Division's constituency, such as it is, is the President, the courts, and some senators and representatives who believe in trust-busting. There is a long populist tradition dating back to Theodore Roosevelt and earlier for attacking monopolistic businesses. Economic concentration has long been considered an evil. The Sherman and the Clayton acts have furnished a solid legal basis for the Justice Department prosecutions. The Antitrust Division has a reputation for vigorous enforcement against big business that dates back to the New Deal. Thus the different forces motivating the Justice Department gave it an impetus to move in a different direction from the FPC.

The *El Paso* case dragged on for so many years and touched so many levels of government that the issues changed. Early opponents softened their critique. In 1957 California saw the merger as a threat. Unlimited gas was available, but there was only one pipeline to transport it. By 1972 gas was in short supply, but El Paso had two competing pipelines challenging it for the California market. In 1957 the public seldom worried about the environmental impact of fuel. By the mid-1960's smog threatened southern California, and the oil spills in the Santa Barbara channel showed the ugly side of oil. Natural gas became increasingly desirable as an environmentally clean energy source. West Coast consumers were eager to buy El Paso's gas at a higher price.

March 5, 1973, the Supreme Court handed down its fifth and presumably final decision on the El Paso merger. It affirmed a lower court ruling on exactly how to break up the El Paso-Pacific Northwest combination. The Pacific Northwest pipeline went to a separate company. The decision undercut El Paso's efforts to persuade Congress to legalize the takeover. In a recent year these efforts cost the company nearly a million dollars for lobbying.[13]

Federal leasing policy has an effect on the supply of natural gas just as on that of coal and oil. For the future the chief area of development is off shore. Under the provisions of the Outer Continental Shelf Act of 1953, the same law regulating oil drilling, the Secretary of the Interior controls the leasing. As the law is administered, it provides nearly total freedom for the producing companies. The U.S. Geological Survey and the Bureau of Mines, which are supposed to provide the scientific knowledge of the continental shelf, have extremely limited capabilities to perform the required surveys. As a consequence, the Interior Department must rely primarily on the drilling companies themselves for information. Naturally enough, this often proves to be self-serving.

The royalties from the leases present a different sort of a problem. The need to increase revenues for the federal budget has generally encouraged the Interior Department to lease drilling territory prematurely and without regard to conservation or any overall plan. Although the leases are designed to encourage rapid development of natural gas, the producing companies tend to hoard their wealth. This they can easily do by fulfilling the minimum terms of the lease. The companies believe that the gas reserves will be worth more in the future than in the present, even with the costs of maintenance. Interior, for its part, does not put pressure on the lessees to produce.

As the desire for the cleanliness and convenience of gas has increased demand, the United States has sought to import natural gas. Canada has long exported a major part of its production to its southern neighbor. In recent years Canada piped 40 percent to the United States. The Federal Power Commission has attempted to use its authority to regulate the price of transmission as a means of extending its power over Canadian supplies. It has used its power to disapprove importation as a lever to force the Canadian producers to lower their prices. In 1967 this unwarranted meddling brought it into conflict with the Canadian Natural Energy Board. The Canadian board refused the producer permission to export under the American commission's restrictions. The two companies involved finally worked out a compromise price that the two nations' regulatory agencies approved. The Americans got their gas, while the Canadians made clear their unwillingness to be regulated by a foreign power commission.[14]

Importation of natural gas except from Canada was impractical until recently because of the physical characteristics of the fuel. Since it was extremely bulky it could be transported only via pipelines. This feature shaped the domestic development of the industry, giving it its monopolistic nature, which in turn led to its regulation as a public utility. But in the 1960's the industry developed the technology to liquify the gas.[15] Now it can be economically transported long distances by ship. Foreign sources can supply the American market. The technology of liquification is costly. The gas must be cooled to −259 degrees Fahrenheit then carried in special ships and stored in special tanks. Costly as the process is, it is an efficient way to supply the East Coast cities. In 1968 Boston became the first city to import liquified natural gas (LNG). The chief source of LNG is Algeria. France, Italy, Spain, and Britain have imported substantial quantities. Algeria's radical politics have worried potential buyers. In view of its fanatical hostility to Israel, American companies fear that it may cut off supplies as a means of pressuring the United States to weaken its support for the Jewish state. On the other hand, Algeria has generally acted in a businesslike manner when it has come to gas exports. Radical politics has not prevented earning a profit.

Once the LNG reaches the United States aboard the specially constructed cryogenic tankers, it faces political opposition in many communities from citizens concerned with safety. The gas is highly explosive, and few residents want a storage facility in their neighborhood. The 1973 explosion of an LNG tank under construction in New York City killed most of the work crew. The resulting citizen outcry brought the development of LNG facilities in the city to a halt.

In the Pacific LNG development may follow several lines. Alaskan gas may be liquified, then transported to California. But the price will be competitive only if the tankers can be of foreign registry. Labor laws make American ships too expensive, yet the Jones Act forbids using foreign registered ships between two American ports. If the Jones Act cannot be circumvented the Alaskan LNG will have to be sold to Japan. A second pattern may be to buy Russian gas from Siberia and ship it to the West Coast. The ultimate irony of the Jones Act might be to send Alaskan LNG to Japan while bringing Siberian LNG to California. The first steps in establishing that commerce came in June 1973, when the El Paso Natural Gas Company and Occidental Petroleum Corporation signed a letter of intent with the Soviet foreign trade ministry committing the parties to a $10 billion project. A companion deal would pipe Russian gas to an Arctic Ocean port for liquification then shipment to the East Coast of the United States. Financing the El Paso-Occidental deal involves a consortium of commercial banks plus the backing of the U.S. Export-Import Bank. The Export-Import Bank is a government bank whose purpose is to stimulate exports by offering generous financing to foreign buyers. It seeks borrowers who are too risky for the commercial banks. The Export-Import Bank backed El Paso's purchase of LNG from Algeria.[16]

The Russian LNG agreement is deeply enmeshed in the intricacies of American-Soviet politics. The deal itself is indicative of a changed attitude between the two superpowers. Many observers hail it as a symbol that the Cold War is ending. Indeed, the key negotiations took place at the height of the American-Soviet tension accompanying the October 1973 war between Israel and the Arabs. Russian willingness to sell the gas where it brings the best price rather than where it will re-enforce geopolitical strategy represents a relaxation in hostility toward capitalism. Formerly Russia would try to hold its resources within the Communist bloc even if that meant accepting a lower return. More specifically the El Paso-Occidental deal with the Russians was tied to President Nixon's diplomacy. The President used the initial June agreement to embellish his summit meeting with Communist Party Chairman Leonid Brezhnev later that same month. In conjunction with the private business agreement the two governments signed an official protocol complementing the former at the diplomatic level. On a more practical level the sale of Soviet gas to Americans was long held up because the Soviets would not allow the American companies to send geologists to Siberia to inspect the gas fields. The Russians have traditionally forbidden westerners to travel about the U.S.S.R. outside of tourist sites. This has been an obstacle to agreement on disarmament. Soviet willingness to allow western geologists to explore for natural gas bodes well for those hopeful of extending the 1963 nuclear test ban to include underground explosions.

Peaceful uses of nuclear power promise an increased supply of natural gas at home. Rich deposits of gas beneath the Rocky Mountains cannot be tapped economically because gas is trapped molecule by molecule in the sandstone. The problem essentially is the same as that of extracting oil from the shale in which it is deposited. When a nuclear bomb explodes in the midst of the rock the gas is freed and collects at the top of the cavity that the bomb blasts inside the earth. To determine whether this plan could be used commercially the Atomic Energy Commission, the Bureau of Mines and the ubiquitous El Paso Corporation exploded an atomic bomb 4,200 feet beneath a Colorado site in 1967. The code name was Operation Gasbuggy. After waiting two years for the most dangerous radiation to decay they drilled a well down to the blast cavity to tap the gas. Three-month-long production runs yielded 109 million cubic feet. In comparison a nearby well using conventional techniques produced 85 million cubic feet in nine years. The AEC graduated to bigger blasts. Three hydrogen bombs exploded a mile underground in the continuing series of experiments. To fully develop the gas field will require 140 to 280 more such explosions. So far the local residents have supported the program. They have been willing to tolerate having their houses, barns, and stores shake from the explosions as the price to be paid for the jobs and income the gas industry promises to bring.[17]

A jolt from blasting is not the only price to be paid. Locally the penalty is a series of artificial earthquakes in the months that follow a nuclear explosion as the earth partially sinks back into the gaseous cavity. Nationally the penalty may be the destruction of the much more valuable shale oil that lies far above the gas-bearing sandstone and just below the surface. If the blasting for gas contaminates the shale or allows the crude oil to drain away, the country will lose a hundred times as much energy. Other penalties may be nuclear pollution of the water table or the atmosphere as radioactive particles seep upward, perhaps not until a century hence. A more immediate problem is whether the gas obtained will be safe for consumption. The gas blasted from the sandstone is radioactive. This irradiated fuel will be piped into millions of California homes for cooking and heating. The AEC claims the level of radioactivity will be low enough to be harmless. Not all agree.

The coal industry proposes that the logical alternative to radioactivity, high prices, and foreign dependency is synthetic gas. This would bring the process back full circle, for prior to the switch to natural gas the cities used coal gas. The synthetic product gave way to the natural because natural gas could produce twice the energy. Now modern techniques of gasification can achieve coal gas with comparable energy. The conversion cost is still much higher, but the location of the coal regions near the northern cities may equalize the difference, particularly as the price of natural gas rises. The emergence of synthetic gas poses a problem for the Federal Power Commission. The Natural Gas Act gives it power to regulate natural gas or a mixture of natural and synthetic gas but not pure synthetic gas. The new product may escape regulation. In the old days this was not a problem since the coal was gasified at the cities where it was consumed. It never traveled between states. The new technology, however, will convert the coal at plants near the mines, then ship it interstate via pipelines. Just as prior to the 1938 act, the industry will be exempt from regulation in the transmission link of the process. If and when the FPC goes to Congress to get new legislation expanding its authority, it can expect opposition from the synthetic gas producers eager to maintain their freedom from regulation.

The urgent desire to develop coal gasification, blast with hydrogen bombs, sign deals with the Russians and Algerians, and drill beneath the sea stems from the critical gas shortage that first appeared in the 1960's. According to the figures of the American Gas Association, production (and of course consumption) rose from 13 trillion cubic feet to 21 t.c.f. at the end of the decade. Reserves scarcely rose at all. They were 262 t.c.f. in 1960 and 275 t.c.f. in 1969. The industry uses a ratio of reserves to production as a measure of the long-term supply. Thus the reserves-to-production ratio fell from 20:1 to 13:1. Stated another way the United States had a 20-year supply in 1960 and only a 13-year supply in 1969.

Critics charge that the gas producers are perpetuating a hoax on the Federal Power Commission in an attempt to get it to raise rates.[18] They claim that the producers are deliberately underestimating the amount of their reserves in order to bring down the reserves-to-production ratio. While low estimates of reserves will encourage the FPC to raise prices, high estimates have no reward. The gas will be available in five or ten years when the producer needs it whether or not he goes through the additional effort to "prove" it by further exploratory drilling. Unproven reserves are as valuable as proven reserves. Some critics have gone so far as to accuse the American Gas Association of conspiracy. The FPC depends completely on statistics furnished by the A.G.A. It has no capability to investigate by means of independent tests. The U.S. Geological Survey conducts some on-site tests but lacks the resources to perform more than a superficial check on the producers. They cannot doublecheck specific wells because the FPC has allowed the A.G.A. to keep the specific information secret. Since the A.G.A. can manipulate the reserve figures, the FPC becomes its statistical prisoner. On the other hand the A.G.A. does not necessarily have to conspire. Reserve figures are always debatable. One geologist may estimate a much higher amount of gas in a field than another. No one can be sure until the well has been emptied. The geologists tend to err on the conservative side. The A.G.A. does not have to coordinate the producers to present a deceptively low reserve figure, for it is in the individual interest of each company to submit a low estimate.

The rationale for underestimating proven reserves is to encourage the FPC to raise the rates. Higher prices will attract more exploration, which will produce more gas. The American Public Gas Association charges that this is exactly the motive for the current gas "shortage." The A.P.G.A. is a consumer-oriented group in constant opposition to the producers' A.G.A. The A.P.G.A. represents city-owned utilities, the largest of which is the one in Memphis. The A.P.G.A. believes that the A.G.A. producers could easily supply the market with the gas that they are currently holding off the market for the purpose of creating an artificial "shortage" to stimulate higher prices. The producer has an incentive to delay as long as he believes that the price will be higher in the future. A series of FPC actions since 1969 has encouraged the producers to believe that the commission soon will raise prices. In 1969 it reopened the southern Louisiana case to increase the prices allowed. In 1972 it established an "Optional Certificate Procedure" under which the producer could ask for a rate increase without showing that his costs had increased. In 1973 it announced its intention of completely abandoning its regional rate structure in favor of a nationwide rate. This lack of firmness naturally encouraged the producer to believe that he could persuade the FPC to grant him more favorable rates in the future.

The producers' hopes for a rate increase climbed after President

Nixon sent his April 1973 energy message to Congress. Nixon asked for an end to controls on the prices of both old and new wells when the current contracts on them expire. The President blamed FPC regulations for the gas shortage. The "artificially low" prices had "artificially stimulated" demand. The administration was concerned that the low rates resulted in a maldistribution of resources. Cheap gas drew many buyers away from coal. Many more wanted to switch, but there was not enough gas available. City utilities had to deny service to new customers. The industry could supply only a small quantity at the cheap price. If the price could rise the shortage would end; those who wanted gas enough would pay the higher price, and those who didn't want it that much could choose an alternative fuel. The administration proposed to clear the market by means of the price system. The argument against this classical economic technique was the same that led to the Natural Gas Act of 1938. The market was not competitive; it was monopolistic. Hence the price needed to be regulated. The partisans of regulation feared that the Nixon policy was to end regulation by administrative means at the same time it sought the same thing by legislation. The Nixon appointees to the FPC all agreed with the President that the price should be determined by market forces.

Then in September 1973 the Federal Power Commission did the unthinkable. It voted to deregulate the price of natural gas. True, it was only a "temporary" action designed to avert shortages during the "energy crisis," but the decision was so contrary to the foundations established by the 1938 Natural Gas Act that it seemed inexorable. In keeping with the legalistic tradition of FPC regulation both parties appealed to the Supreme Court, which in December agreed to consider the case. The following month the high court accepted a companion case begun in 1971 challenging the southern Louisiana rate structure. Taken together the two cases vindicated the producers' assessment that the FPC's regulatory scheme was crumbling.

Consumer groups despaired at this course of events. Lee C. White, director of the Consumer Federation of America and a former (Democratic) FPC chairman, countered the Republicans' move toward deregulation by arguing that the solution was more regulation, not less. Congress should extend the FPC's jurisdiction to include intrastate as well as interstate sales. The two sides of the argument split along partisan lines. Democrats advocated allocation by regulation in the New Deal tradition, while Republicans advocated allocation by market forces.

The deregulation issue brought the Nixon commissioners, all appointed from industry, into bitter conflict with the FPC's Office of Economics. The commissioners justified their approach as a way to bring more gas into the market. The economists countered that deregulation gave assurance only that the producers would charge more, not that they would actually supply more. Letting prices soar would only hurt the consumer. For the Nixon Administration this was one more example of bureaucratic resistance to presidential policy. Throughout the federal government the bureaucrats tended to be more Democratic and more liberal than the political appointees, Nixon believed. Roosevelt had made the same complaint when he took office in 1933, but in reverse. Twelve years of Republican administration left him with a bureaucracy tending to be Republican and conservative and resistant to his policy innovations. Twenty years of Democratic administrations reversed the situation. The Nixon Administration's complaint was at least partly justified. Washington bureaucrats received many Nixon policies with slight enthusiasm. It was, however, not so much a bureaucratic plot as a natural reaction of anyone in their position. The federal bureaucracy has a vested interest in big government. Since many of the administration's programs were designed to cut down the government's responsibility, it was a natural reflex for the bureaucracy to resist. If the President's new regulatory scheme for natural gas went into effect the FPC would lose its traditional function. Its *raison d'être* would vanish. It should be no wonder that the staff resisted the elimination of its purpose. What would it do if there were no more rates to set?

In moving toward allocation by the market mechanism Nixon pleased the industry's owners. The National Petroleum Council's *U.S. Energy Outlook* recommendations, which represented the business point of view, called for freeing gas prices to climb to market-clearing levels.[19] In this it is on better ground in terms of optimal allocation of scarce resources than in its recommendations on oil, which urge continuation of special privileges. Gas, however, shares many of those privileges. As oil's twin, it is entitled to the 22 percent depletion allowance and special tax writeoffs for drilling expenses.

As this chapter shows, the physical properties of the fuel did much to shape its politics. First, gas's bulk made conventional transportation impossible. Its exploitation had to await the invention of electrical arc welding, which delayed its development until the 1930's, a period of federal activism contrasting sharply with the laissez faire era in which coal and oil emerged. Second, the large sums of capital needed to build the pipelines led to giant holding companies, fit targets for government regulation. Third, since gas is ready to burn as it comes out of the ground, it needs no workers to process it. Hence the labor movement that shook American society during the first half of the twentieth century by-passed the gas industry. In geographical terms natural gas paralleled the westward shift of coal and oil. The recent technology for liquification presages an international aspect that has hitherto not existed.

Market forces, which helped to explain the politics of coal and oil, yield less explanation in this arena. On one hand, demand has always been high, so gas never suffered the "sick industry" problems of coal or the booms and busts of oil. On the other, supply was generally predictable because of the long lead time to build transmission facilities. This, combined with gas's comparatively small share of the market, meant that there were no dramatic natural gas crises. In the natural gas arena market forces can be viewed three ways. First is in terms of the mammoth holding companies that flourished briefly in the 1930's between the time when the need for capital generation brought them forth and the time when the SEC implemented the 1935 Holding Company Act. Second is in terms of natural gas as the twin of oil. As such gas shares many of the features of oil such as common ownership of wells and identical tax benefits. But since oil is so much more profitable, gas is the weak sister tagging along. Gas's share of the total petroleum market is too small to significantly influence decisions about oil. The third perspective on the market structure is to view it as the result of politics rather than the cause. The natural gas market is really the dependent variable rather than the independent variable. The political process determines the issues of ownership, prices, and quantity consumed, which in coal and oil are decided privately. This may be considered the essence of government regulation. The free play of market forces gives way to political institutions' manipulation. To the extent to which the Federal Power Commission's trend toward deregulation succeeds, free market forces will be restored. Yet unless Congress goes so far as to completely repeal the 1935 and 1938 laws, natural gas will remain under close federal supervision.

Natural gas illustrates vividly the impact of transcending political issues. It is very much a product of the general political environment of the era of its birth. Since its physical properties ordained its sudden emergence in the 1930's it bears an indelible stamp of the New Deal. This was a time when federal activism promised to solve all problems; hence federal regulation was inevitable. The SEC and the FPC got the mandate and there it has remained. Since conflicts must be resolved within these institutions the process has tended to be more legalistic than in the cases of the other fuels considered. The Nixon Administration's desire to move away from regulation represents a straying from the New Deal direction, but it has taken nearly four decades for even this modest pullback from the New Deal mandate.

Strong as the New Deal legacy has proved, other transcending political issues have penetrated the politics of natural gas. In 1949 anti-Communism furnished Congress an excuse to rid the FPC of an unpopular commissioner. In recent years environmental concern has made pollution-free natural gas seem a panacea. Heightened demand puts greater pressure on the FPC. In comparison to oil, natural gas is more regulated. Furthermore this regulation is concentrated more narrowly (primarily in the FPC), whereas oil's lesser regulation is spread over a series of laws and government agencies at the state as well as federal levels. Since its profits are more dependent on the whims of a single commission, the natural gas producers have a greater incentive to manipulate that institution. Thus producers have a greater incentive to underreport the amount of their reserves, and pipeline companies have a greater incentive to contest an unfavorable decision in court.

Notes

1. Ralph S. Spritzer, "Changing Elements in the Natural Gas Picture," in Keith C. Brown, ed., *Regulation of the Natural Gas Producing Industry* (Baltimore: Johns Hopkins, Resources for the Future, 1972), pp. 114—16; Charles R. Ross, "Producer Regulation: A Commissioner's Viewpoint," in Brown, *op. cit.*, pp. 90—95; Harold F. Williamson *et al.*, *The American Petroleum Industry* (Evanston, Ill.: Northwestern, 1963), pp. 328—29.

2. Herbert K. Northrup and Gordon F. Bloom, *Government and Labor* (Homewood, Ill.: Irwin, 1963).

3. U.S. Senate, Temporary National Economic Committee, *Natural Gas and Natural Gas Pipelines in the U.S.A.* (Reports of the Federal Trade Commission, Monograph No. 36), 76th Congress, 3rd Session, 1940.

4. Ralph K. Huitt, "National Regulation of the Natural Gas Industry," in Emmette S. Redford, ed., *Public Administration and Policy Formation* (Austin: University of Texas, 1956).

5. Ralph K. Huitt, "Natural Gas Regulation Under the Holding Company Act," *Law and Contemporary Problems*, 19 (1954), p. 456.

6. *Ibid.*, p. 472.

7. Huitt, *op. cit.*, p. 64.

8. *Ibid.*, p. 93; Robert Engler, *The Politics of Oil* (New York: Macmillan, 1961), p. 321.

9. Spritzer, *op. cit.*, p. 116.

10. Engler, *op. cit.*, p. 413.

11. Spritzer, *op. cit.*, pp. 116—21; Ross, *op. cit.*, pp. 96—97.

12. "El Paso Pipeline," *CQ Weekly Report*, March 6, 1973.

13. *Ibid.*

14. Spritzer, *op. cit.*, p. 130.

15. Homer Bigart, "Gas Shortage," *The New York Times*, November 21, 1971.

16. David B. Ottaway, "Gas Project," *Washington Post*, June 9, 1973.

17. James P. Sterba, "H-Bombs Blast to Free Gas," *The New York Times*, May 20, 1973.

18. See U.S. Senate, Committee on Interior and Insular Affairs, *Hearings*, 92nd Congress, 1st Session, April 13, 1973; Paul W. MacAvoy, "The Regulation Induced Shortage of Natural Gas," in Brown, *op. cit.*, pp. 169—72. See also U.S. Senate, Committee on Commerce, *Natural Gas Regulation*, 92nd Congress, 2nd Session, March 22 and 23, 1972.

19. National Petroleum Council, *U.S. Energy Outlook* (Washington, D.C., 1972), p. 77.

5

Electricity

In its relationship to government, electricity shares many of the characteristics of natural gas. Locally, electricity, like gas, may be distributed by either a private or a municipally owned utility company. Indeed the same company generally furnishes both. Nationally, electricity, like gas, may be transmitted interstate by private companies. Both forms of energy come under the jurisdiction of the Federal Power Commission. Yet while electricity often shares with gas the status of a private utility under FPC regulation, at the national level electricity is in many other cases an entirely government owned enterprise. In the natural gas arena production and transmission are exclusively private, albeit strictly regulated, even when the wells are on federal lands. The Department of the Interior leases its rights to the private companies. Once produced, private pipeline companies pump the gas to the consuming cities. Even in the case of the pipelines it built during World War II the federal government turned them over to private companies once the war emergency ended. In contrast the government produces and transmits a major share of the electricity consumed. In addition to its own contribution it regulates the private companies' output much as in the case of natural gas. Thus in respect to electricity, government policies stand part way between the regulation without ownership that characterizes natural gas and the monopoly ownership that characterizes nuclear energy.

In terms of its physical properties, electricity is entirely unlike the other four types of energy treated in this book. They are primary forms. Electricity is a secondary form. The other four types produce energy directly. Burning the fossil fuels—coal, oil, and gas—or splitting the uranium atom produces power. Electricity, on the other hand, must be generated from one of the other fuels or from waterpower.

This leads to two political consequences. One is that geography plays a less important role in this arena than it did in those of coal, oil, and natural gas. As a secondary form of energy, electricity is produced everywhere in the nation. There are no "electricity states" comparable to the "coal states" of Pennsylvania and Kentucky or the "petroleum states" of Texas and Louisiana. On the other hand, electricity is more cheaply generated in some places than others. Waterpower makes electricity more efficient in Tennessee, New York State, and the Pacific Northwest. Hence electricity early became a political issue in those states. Cheap coal has recently done the same for electricity in New Mexico. Yet in spite of some regional variation geographic distribution is not the chief way in which physical characteristics influence the politics of the arena.

The second political consequence deriving from electricity's physical properties relates to its economies of scale. Large turbines can generate electricity much more cheaply than small ones, even including the costs of transmission over many miles and distribution to many users. While the individual household or business could run its own generator, it can far more efficiently buy power from the central plant. In economic terms this means that electricity is a natural monopoly.

Like natural gas, it is a natural monopoly because transmission and distribution are so costly and inflexible that competition would be inefficient. The duplication of facilities would cost more than the benefits of competition would be worth. To substitute for the hidden hand of competition, government feels it must regulate the utility to be sure that the consumers enjoy the savings and that the greater efficiency does not merely enrich the company.

Governments did not always view electricity this way. Prior to World War I most cities believed regulation was superfluous. Competition could keep the prices down. Cities would grant multiple franchises to electricity companies. Between 1882 and 1905 Chicago granted 29. The result was not healthy competition keeping down the consumer's bill, but many weak companies that were soon bought out by a strong one, thus leading to a monopoly. In the face of this trend local governments began to view utilities as natural monopolies and hence inevitable. This being the case the best solution seemed to be regulation by public commission.[1]

The private utilities were amenable to such regulation because the alternative appeared to be public takeover. It seemed better to be merely regulated by the government than to be owned by it. It was an era of reform, and for the reformers a commission was a panacea. Widespread corruption in urban government produced disgust with traditional city politics. The new middle class reformers abhorred the activities of the lower class party machines. They saw the bribery, vote stealing, and chicanery of the machine without seeing the redeeming services it performed of employment, welfare, and socialization into the political system. Since in the eyes of the reformers so many of the functions city government performed were not political, the solution was to depoliticize city government. Mayors and aldermen could be replaced by commissioners who could concentrate on the necessary technical aspects without wasting effort on the unnecessary political aspects. Likewise commissions could regulate the utilities, freeing them from the fickleness of city councils that would issue duplicative franchises in return for bribes. While these commissions could be at either the city or the state level both the reformers and the utilites tended to favor state oversight. In view of the notorious corruption of the city machines, the state alternative seemed more honest. Furthermore a state commission was likely to represent a different political coalition. In some cases that meant a different party. New York City was under the control of the Democratic Tammany Hall, while upstate was traditionally Republican. Even when the same party controlled both the city hall and state house, the broader and more rural orientation of the state usually promised to be more congenial.

State regulation began in 1907 in New York and Wisconsin and by 1922 had spread to 47 states and the District of Columbia. It was far from an unqualified success. While some states had strong commissions able to control the utilities, many did not. There the utilities effectively controlled the commissions, thus reversing the intent of the scheme. These lenient regulators failed to protect the consumers from high prices and poor services.[2]

An alternative to control by commission regulation was municipal ownership. The public benefited in two ways. Those served by the city electrical system enjoyed the low price directly. Those not served enjoyed the benefits of having a yardstick against which to measure their own prices. If a municipal plant could generate power at 4 cents per kilowatt, so could a private company. Sometimes the competition between public and private was direct. In Cleveland, Columbus, Los Angeles, and other cities, residents had a choice of hooking up with either municipal or private electricity. As a result these cities had some of the cheapest power in the country.

Even at its best commission regulation was conservative. Lack of innovation became a political issue in New York. Niagara Falls and the rapids of the Saint Lawrence River presented two obvious sites for hydroelectric power, but the private utilities were reluctant to develop them. When Franklin D. Roosevelt ran for governor in 1928 he made harnessing this power a major plank in his platform. In 1931 Roosevelt was able to push through the state legislature a law establishing the New York State Power Authority. The Power Authority was to develop the hydroelectric potential of the Niagara and Saint Lawrence sites. More significantly, the law specifically directed the authority to give domestic and rural users priority over industrial users. Furthermore, municipally owned distributors had priority over privately owned distributors. Roosevelt feared that his victory in the legislature could be undone by the private utilities through their control of the state regulation commission, so the law provided that the Power Authority be exempt from commission regulation. The authority had three means of benefiting the public: (1) When it sold power to private distributors, its contract would specify the prices the company was to charge consumers. (2) It would publish its "true costs" so that the public could compare the Power Authority's costs to those of its own utility. (3) The Power Authority would sometimes compete directly; if necessary it could build its own transmission lines to industries in the region. Roosevelt called the alternatives the Power Authority's "whip hand" and "trump card."[3]

The New York State Power Authority was not to crack that whip or play that trump card for over two decades, for the Saint

Lawrence project had many enemies. Within New York these were the private power companies. They managed to handicap the project by successfully opposing the Power Authority's plans to sell electricity directly to the public. But greater opposition came from outside the state. Along with its hydroelectric plants the project planned to improve navigation. The Saint Lawrence rapids and Niagara Falls prevented ocean-going ships from entering the Great Lakes. The project envisioned the creation of a Saint Lawrence Seaway with a 27-foot deep channel which would allow 70 percent of the world's ships to sail the Great Lakes. This won the support of most of the Midwest. They could easily see the benefits of cheap ship rates from as far west as Duluth. But the Saint Lawrence Seaway stirred the opposition of those with vested interests in alternative forms of transportation. The Atlantic seaboard ports realized that they would lose much business if ships could sail directly to Cleveland, Detroit, or Chicago. Mississippi Valley states feared both that the seaway would take away business and that it might decrease the amount of water available from the Great Lakes, thereby lowering the level in the nine-foot-deep Lakes-to-the-Gulf waterway. Railroad owners and unions feared the competition, as did Great Lakes and New York State canal shippers. The combined opposition to both the hydroelectric and navigation elements blocked the development scheme until 1953.[4]

Thus the national impact of the New York State Power Authority did not come from its engineering achievements; the Saint Lawrence turbines did not generate their first power until 1957, and the Niagara Falls turbines, until 1961. Rather the impact came from the political philosophy behind the Power Authority: that government should actively promote cheap electricity for the benefit of its citizens. The New York power policy became the national power policy. Roosevelt made public power a campaign issue in his 1932 race for President just as he had in his 1928 race for governor. Roosevelt brought both the development plan and many of the men to implement it to Washington from New York State.

Upon assuming the Presidency in 1933 Roosevelt faced the issue of how to proceed on a number of hydroelectric projects that had been suspended for many years. The chief among these was a dam at Muscle Shoals in northern Alabama. During World War I President Wilson had begun this dam on the Tennessee River in order to manufacture synthetic nitrates for explosives. When the construction of the dam and nitrate plant ended in 1925 the logic of government ownership for war production had disappeared. Washington could not decide what course to follow. Private manufacturers sought to buy the property. Others urged that the federal government retain ownership. As an interim measure the government sold the power to the Alabama Power Company at a bargain rate. Senator George Norris, a Republican liberal from Nebraska, proposed that the Muscle Shoals dam, now named in honor of President Wilson, become the first in a series of dams on the Tennessee River system to supply electricity to the entire region. The prices this publicly owned utility charged would serve as a yardstick against which to measure the efficiency of privately owned utilities. When Congress voted such bills in 1928 and 1930 they were vetoed by Presidents Coolidge and Hoover. Roosevelt had a different attitude. For him, Wilson Dam was exactly the starting point he needed to apply the New York State power policy on a national scale. The new President moved immediately to keep his campaign promises.

Roosevelt signed the Tennessee Valley Authority Act on May 18, 1933. The act provided for the total development of the valley. Wilson Dam was to be joined by a series of other dams to generate cheap power. TVA was to make the same sort of contract with the utility companies, fixing the fees to be charged the consumers, as was provided for in the New York State Power Authority enabling legislation. This would assure that the benefits were passed on to the public rather than merely enriching the private utilities. The river would be made navigable with a nine-foot deep channel. The reservoirs would control the notorious flooding in the watershed. The Muscle Shoals nitrate plant would convert to fertilizer production. TVA would foster the growth of industry so that the cheap electricity could be translated into high employment. Finally, a major concern of the Tennessee Valley Authority was to involve the people of the region in the decision-making process, bringing them out of their apathy. The federal government would socialize them into the political system much as the political machines had socialized the immigrants in the northern cities.

By nearly all standards TVA must be judged a success. Today Wilson Dam is one of 32 major dams owned or controlled by the authority. The neighboring Cumberland Valley has eight other dams—one owned by the TVA and the other seven by the U.S. Corps of Engineers—which feed power into the TVA system. In 1933 the region was one of the least electrified; today it is one of the most. Consumers pay rates well below the national average. Furthermore the threat of TVA power has reduced the rates in nearby regions. Once TVA began generating, Cincinnati applied to buy electricity even though it was 200 miles distant. To forestall this threat the city's private utility sharply reduced its charges to match the competition. Farther afield, where TVA power was not a direct menace, it served as a measure of the efficiency of the local companies.[5]

The Tennessee River is now navigable for over 600 miles from its mouth. Since the locks opened in 1945 the cargo transported has risen from 2 million to 24 million tons. Floods have been contained. The authority estimates that the system has averted over a half-billion dollars of flood damage since 1936. Fertilizer produced has revolutionized the backward farming practices that previously characterized the region. Industry has moved in to take advantage of the cheap power. Thousands of local residents have become politically active as a result of TVA's programs to involve them in the decision-making process.

Yet the TVA program has had impacts beyond those Roosevelt anticipated when he signed the act in 1933. When TVA sold its first half-million kilowatt hours in 1934, virtually all were generated by water. But as the years went on the authority found that hydroelectrical power was not sufficient to meet the demands of the public so it began to build steam-driven generating plants fired by the cheap coal abundant in the region. Of the 93 billion kilowatt hours sold in 1970, 82 percent were generated by steam and only 18 percent by water. TVA's chief customer today is one undreamed of in 1933: the Atomic Energy Commission. Its two major installations at Oak Ridge, Tennessee, and Paducah, Kentucky, have voracious appetites for electricity. At the 1957 high point the AEC consumed 3.7 million kilowatt hours.

In its social mission the TVA has failed to achieve the goal of democratizing the region, which many of its early supporters believed outshone any practical goals of more electricity or more fertilizer. In order to survive and grow in a moderately hostile political environment the authority had to adapt to the existing conditions. To the extent to which TVA had to rely on existing institutions it ended up supporting the status quo. In its agricultural program it allied with the land-grant agricultural colleges, strengthening them at the expense of the independent colleges. It chose county agents to demonstrate the benefits of fertilizer, thereby strengthening the Extension Service. In labor relations it favored the A.F.L. craft-based unions in constituting the Tennessee Valley Trades and Labor Council, thereby disadvantaging C.I.O. industrial-based unions. One aspect of the status quo TVA ended up supporting, intentionally or not, was racial discrimination. By acting through local institutions TVA perpetuated local prejudices.[6]

Because of its broad scope and political goals TVA was the most important federal power project developed during the 1930's, but it was not the only one. Washington's other involvement in hydroelectric power came indirectly. Its entanglement was a by-product of two other duties, in addition to the wartime need for explosives that led to the Muscle Shoals dam and nitrate plant. First, Congress had given the Interior Department authority to store and distribute water for irrigation in the arid lands of the West. These irrigation reservoirs generated their own electricity to run the pumps for distributing the water. In 1906 Congress authorized the Secretary of the Interior to sell any excess electricity generated. As the size of these projects increased during the 1920's the Republican administrations faced the dilemma that they might be competing with private enterprise. President Hoover was particularly concerned in 1928 as Congress debated the Boulder Canyon Project Act. California and Arizona actively sought this multipurpose dam, which was to supply water for irrigation, drinking, electricity, and flood control. Only when a compromise provided for greater participation by a private utility company did Hoover sign the law authorizing the dam later to bear his name.

The second duty of the federal government that eventually drew it indirectly into hydroelectrical generation was its jurisdiction over navigable water. The responsibility for rivers and harbors traditionally belongs to the Army Corps of Engineers. When Congress first appropriated funds to dredge the Mississippi River in 1822 the Army was the logical choice. West Point was the biggest engineering school in the country. As time went by the Corps of Engineers grew more firmly entrenched in its public works role and grew increasingly civilianized. It became an autonomous agency with strong ties to the public works committees of the House and Senate. Only a few of its staff were actually Army officers, and the military abandoned all but titular control. Until 1909 the Corps of Engineers discouraged building dams as a means of deepening a river channel. It preferred dredging. Indeed the government's policy at the time was often to refuse private utilities permission to build hydroelectrical dams because they would interfere with navigation. In 1903 Theodore Roosevelt had refused the Alabama Power Company's request to build at Muscle Shoals for that reason. In 1909 Congress required the Engineers to consider hydroelectrical power in their river studies. In 1925 it more forcefully required the Engineers to recommend locations that might be developed for hydroelectrical power.

The Columbia River at Bonneville was among the first the Corps of Engineers recommended. Nothing happened for ten years, however. The Republican administrations had not accepted the rectitude of the government's competing with private utilities. Furthermore, demand was low. Compared with other areas, Oregon and Washington have less need of water for irrigation and drinking. There was no Los Angeles thirsty for water and hungry for power. There was no Imperial Valley dependent on an irrigation canal from Mexico. On the other hand, there was a tradition of public ownership emanating from the municipally owned utilities in Seattle and Tacoma. Once the TVA Act of 1933 announced the power policy of the New Deal, the Bonneville project followed naturally. Three federal agencies shared the endeavor. The Corps of Engineers supervised the construction. Funds came from the Work Projects Administration. The WPA was one of the series of New Deal "alphabet agencies" Roosevelt created to bring the country out of the Great Depression. Like TVA it was established in a flurry of legislation that marked the Hundred Days at the beginning of Roosevelt's Administration. The WPA loaned and granted funds to local and state governments for bridges, hospitals, water systems, and the like. Roosevelt used the WPA money to advance his national power policy. The third agency sharing the Columbia River project was the Bonneville Power Administration. Created as an independent agency to administer the Bonneville Dam along with the Grand Coulee Dam later built upstream, the BPA later came under Interior Department jurisdiction.[7]

The BPA shared many of the same objectives as TVA. It was to encourage development of the region through cheap power. It was to give preference to publicly owned utilities. It was to encourage the distributors to pass on the savings to the consumers. But the BPA was less influential than TVA. Its retail rates schedules were not binding, as were those of TVA. It had no comprehensive program for the total development of the region as did TVA. It lacked TVA's fervid ideological commitment to restructuring the politics of the region. A partial explanation for the BPA's more relaxed approach comes from a comparison of the two regions. The Pacific Northwest was never as economically backward as the Tennessee Valley. Even in the midst of the Depression it was a comparatively prosperous area. It already had a number of publically owned distributors. Politically it was more liberal. Indeed, Washington State had a tradition of radicalism, earning it the sobriquet of the Soviet of Washington. A second partial explanation for the BPA's less vigilant adherence to the New Deal power policy comes from the role of the Department of the Interior. The Tennessee Valley had its own agency, TVA, newborn with a mission and a staff dedicated to that mission. This spirit was exemplified by Commissioner David Lilienthal, who combined administrative skill with a missionary devotion to the New Deal ideology. TVA's compromises came as it butted up against external problems. Internally it was pure. In contrast the Interior Department brought its bureaucratic heritage with it. One of the most important parts of that heritage was its traditional job of supplying water for irrigation. Hydroelectric power was secondary. Hence concern with industrial development, public utilities, and consumer savings was secondary, too.[8]

One of F.D.R.'s special concerns when he brought the New

York State power policy with him to the White House in 1933 was electricity for the farmer. It dated from 1924, when he had traveled to Warm Springs, Georgia, seeking therapeutics for his paralysis. Upon settling into his bungalow at the health spa he was shocked to find the electric bill four times what he paid in Hyde Park, New York. He also learned that many farmers could get no electricity at all. The utilities confined their service to the cities and towns where they could connect many customers per mile of line, ignoring the sparsely settled countryside. Only if a farmer lived near a town or along a transmission line between towns would the utility string a short line to him. When elected governor, Roosevelt incorporated preference for rural consumers into the New York Power Authority Act of 1931. Roosevelt's concern for supplying cheap electricity to rural areas had further impetus from some practical experiments. Intensive electrification of 20 farms near Red Wing, Minnesota, showed that cheap power could increase agricultural productivity through use of incubators, milking machines, and power tools. Meanwhile in Pennsylvania a reformer from a patrician Philadelphia family, Morris Cooke, challenged the utilities' assertion that they could not afford to connect rural areas. Cooke showed that the companies' cost estimates for stringing wire were based on outdated figures. Though the figures were formerly true, current costs had dropped considerably, so many more areas could be served economically. Finally, TVA had promoted electricity for rural consumers. Farmers in Alcorn County, Mississippi, formed a cooperative to buy power generated at Wilson Dam. The Alcorn Associates strung 100 miles of wire, charged rates no higher than in the towns, and made enough profit in one year to repay half of the funds TVA had loaned it the previous year to establish the service. This cooperative furnished the model for the typical R.E.C.— Rural Electrification Cooperative.[9]

In 1935 Congress was in a mood not often seen since. It was looking for more ways to spend money faster. The Roosevelt Administration was won over to a Keynesian economic policy. Lord Keynes advocated that in a depression the national government should spend more money than it took in in revenues in order to stimulate the economy. Since this was a great depression it called for great spending. Rural electrification seemed to meet the requisite conditions. It was expensive. It would generate jobs for the unemployed. It was an investment leading to increased productivity. So on May 11, 1935, the President signed Executive Order 7037 creating the Rural Electrification Administration. Congress incorporated the program into the Emergency Relief Act of 1935. F.D.R. named Morris Cooke to head the agency.

Cooke soon found REA could not be administered as a relief agency. The process was too technical. There were few jobs suitable for the unskilled unemployed. The careful planning precluded spending large amounts of money. Learning this Roosevelt restructured the REA from a relief agency into a loan agency. Cooke first tried to accomplish his mission through the private companies. They were established in the field with the technical knowledge and equipment to do the job. But the utilities' attitudes precluded success. They clung to the idea that rural customers could not be served cheaply. They refused to lower their rates unless the REA extended long-term, low-interest loans as a subsidy. If the privately owned utilities would not collaborate, the next best option seemed to be the municipally owned utilities. These public power companies could expand into the countryside to serve the farmers. But the municipal companies proved unsatisfactory too. First, like the private utilities they had little enthusiasm for rural extensions that would neither serve their own residents nor return much profit. Second, a series of adverse court decisions cast doubt on their legal right to provide electricity beyond their city boundaries. Cooke then turned to the Alcorn cooperative as a solution. The farmers had a clear incentive for speedy electrification. There would be no foot dragging as was the case with the private and municipal companies. Their legal right seemed clear. Thus the cooperative—the R.E.C.—became the chief vehicle of rural electrification. Of the first ten loans made in 1935, seven were to cooperatives, two to public utilities, and one to a private company. The individual R.E.C. was based on the TVA model. This meant all farms were to be covered on an area basis, not just the most profitable ones. If electricity was instrumental to the economic development of the area, rates should be low to promote maximum usage. The private companies countered by "skimming the cream," connecting the most profitable customers, while ignoring the others. They built "spite lines" to compete with R.E.C. lines. They attacked the cooperatives as socialistic and communistic or at least unfair government ownership. In fact the cooperatives were not government owned but privately owned by their members. They were, however, financed by the federal government.

Following the Alcorn Associates' example, the R.E.C.'s bought their power from the established utilities. Their purpose was distributing electricity, not generating it. For those cooperatives with access to TVA or other federal hydroelectric power this presented no problem, for following the New York State Power Authority example federal projects gave preference to the cooperatives. Obtaining power from private producers was often more difficult. Federal or state intervention was often required to force the private companies to sell. Difficulties in getting dependable and cheap power led the R.E.C.'s to join to construct generating and transmission cooperatives. These supercooperatives, funded by REA loans, posed a greater threat to the private companies than the small R.E.C. distributors. The private utilities fought their producing rivals, known as G and T's, by offering the R.E.C.'s reduced wholesale rates and blocking their expansion into their territorial franchises.

The private utilities came under a two-pronged attack in 1935. The REA threatened their physical structure by creating a rival network of power generation, transmission, and distribution through the G and T's and R.E.C.'s. Congress threatened their financial structure through what became the Public Utility Holding Company Act of 1935. The legislation brought to the fore some of the personalities who were to dominate national politics in the years to come. The bill's sponsor in the House of Representatives was Sam Rayburn, later to become Speaker for 17 years. The bill's chief opponent was Wendell Willkie, then president of the Commonwealth and Southern Company and later the Republican nominee for President against Roosevelt in 1940. Willkie began his career as a Democrat. As such and as a liberal he stood out from his generally Republican and conservative business associates. His aggressiveness and business acumen carried him from crusading reformer of the Ohio Edison Company to the presidency of the

New York-based Commonwealth and Southern, one of the country's biggest holding companies. The goal of the 1935 Holding Company Act, as discussed in Chapter Four, was to reorganize the complex financial arrangements in order to end the abuses to which the public utilities and their investors were subjected. Pyramiding resulted in undue concentration of power and made possible a legion of frauds. The fiery and articulate Willkie made a good spokesman for the private companies. He energetically took his side of the story before congressional committees and public audiences. While he lost in terms of blocking the law's passage, he won in terms of catapulting himself into national attention. Through his dazzling rhetoric on behalf of business, Willkie converted himself into a Republican. In 1940 he stormed into the party's convention in quest of the presidential nomination. He was the first candidate in either party to go to a convention to promote his own selection. Previously the hopefuls had discreetly (though nervously) waited at home while their managers negotiated the deals to build a winning coalition. Even going to the convention to give an acceptance speech once nominated was Roosevelt's 1932 innovation. But Willkie went to the G.O.P.'s 1940 Philadelphia conclave to force himself upon the party. He did so through charisma and thousands of demonstrators whom he packed into the galleries of the convention hall to scream "We want Willkie." On the floor the delegates cast their votes in the paradoxical pattern they were to repeat in every national convention until 1964. The party that was basically midwestern and conservative nominated a presidential candidate supported by its eastern and liberal wing. After Willkie this group was to nominate Dewey twice, Eisenhower twice, and a liberal Nixon once. Not until Goldwater broke the pattern and the new conservative-based Nixon repeated it was the Willkie legacy abandoned.

The 1935 Holding Company Act that brought Willkie into the national political limelight affected the electric utilities in the same ways as it affected the national gas utilities. The Securities and Exchange Commission supervised the financial structure of the holding companies. It forced a separation between the major electric and natural gas components (although this was not required at the local level). As with gas, it required the electric companies to simplify and organize regionally. The SEC had to approve new stock issues. In doing so the commission exercised detailed supervision of companies' finances. It told the utilities which percentage of their capital should be in common stock, preferred stock, or bonds. While the goal of this close regulation was to make the investments safe for the public, critics charged that it retarded the flow of capital and hence the growth of the industry. The SEC protected the investor, but the price was less electricity available for the consumer.

When Congress passed the Holding Company Act of 1935 it amended the Federal Power Act to give the Federal Power Commission jurisdiction in regulating the public utilities that are actual operators. The SEC is responsible for the holding companies; the FPC is responsible for the operating companies. While it might have been more logical to give the FPC jurisdiction over both levels, in 1935 Congress did not believe the FPC had the financial expertise to tangle with the holding companies. The law exempts the local utilities from regulation if they are already subject to the jurisdiction of a state commission with power to regulate securities issues. Thus the FPC devotes little of its time to capitalization and most of its time to more practical aspects of hydroelectrical power transmission and sale.

Thus by 1935 Franklin Roosevelt had charted an electrical power course the nation was to follow without serious challenge for 19 years. The Tennessee Valley Authority Act of 1933, combined with the Holding Company and Federal Power Acts of 1935 and the rural electrification program, presaged an expanding role for the federal government. Hydroelectric projects promised to be a panacea for the nation. Building the dams offered employment. Their cheap power offered economic development. Their reservoirs offered irrigation, navigation, and recreation. Critics referred to this as the "dam mentality."

During this period the responsibility for developing hydroelectric projects fell to a number of federal agencies. The independent Tennessee Valley Authority had jurisdiction in the watershed from which it took its name. Department of the Interior agencies covered three-quarters of the rest of the country. The Bonneville Power Administration, established in 1937, covered the Pacific

Northwest. The Bureau of Reclamation, established in 1902, covered 17 western states. In 1943 and 1950 the Secretary of the Interior created two other bureaus: the Southwestern and Southeastern Power Administrations. Unlike other agencies these two do not operate any dams but supervise the distribution of power from dams belonging to other federal agencies, primarily the Army Corps of Engineers. These two bureaus buy power for redistribution from private sources as well. The lack of unity in the field began to cause problems in the late 1930's as the New Deal's dam mentality brought the various agencies into conflict over who was to dam which rivers. After victory in World War II allowed resumption of dam building, President Truman proposed that the Interior Department's Bureau of Reclamation develop the Missouri River. The Corps of Engineers protested that it should be the one to do the building. The Fort Peck Dam in Montana, which it built prior to the war, gave it a claim to the Missouri. The Corps took this position in defiance of presidential instructions. Presidents have seldom been able effectively to control the Corps. The Corps has its own direct lines to the Public Works Committees of the Senate and House. Each year Congress passes a "pork barrel" law authorizing the Corps to construct a series of public works projects. This "pork" rewards the committee members and their friends. Since a senator or congressman is always eager to have a federal public works project in his state or district the pork barrel includes something for everyone, even though the aggregate result is to inflate federal spending with needless projects. This cozy relationship between the Corps and Congress gives the Corps great autonomy. It pays little attention to the President's calls for budgetary restraint since it knows Congress will give it all the money it wants. The conflict between the Corps and the Bureau of Reclamation for jurisdiction over the Missouri River became so intense that Truman finally called the two antagonists to the White House to negotiate a peace treaty. The two sides finally compromised by dividing the job.

The bureaucratic squabbling between the Corps of Engineers and the Bureau of Reclamation did not challenge the Democratic administration's commitment to federal development of cheap electricity. This changed, however, once the Republicans took office in 1953. Eisenhower won the Presidency pledged to roll back "creeping socialism." He soon had an opportunity. TVA requested the President's Bureau of the Budget to include funds to build a new plant to generate electricity for Memphis, Tennessee. It was to be a steam plant. Most of the good dam sites were already used up. TVA was then generating two-thirds of its power by steam. For the private utilities this seemed to be the logical point at which to stop TVA's creeping. While there might be a logic and tradition to the federal government's building hydroelectric plants, there was none such for steam plants. Two private utilities just across the river from Memphis proposed as an alternative to build jointly a steam plant to supply Memphis. The alternative proposal took its name from the two utilities' presidents: Edgar Dixon and Eugene Yates. The Dixon-Yates proposal drew enthusiastic support from the business-oriented administration. The scheme was to use the Atomic Energy Commission as an agent for supplying private power to Memphis. Memphis would not accept the power directly, nor would TVA, and the administration was afraid to meet the issue directly. Therefore it directed the AEC to buy the power from the Dixon-Yates plant—not actually for the AEC to use but to replace the electricity the TVA supplied to the AEC's Paducah, Kentucky, installation. "Laundering" the private power by supposedly passing it through AEC hands was intended to satisfy partisans of public power. The AEC resisted the plan since it was to pay $4.1 million more per year and receive nothing in return.[10]

The Republican assault on TVA aroused Senator Estes Kefauver. The Tennessee Democrat was a staunch backer of public power, particularly in his own state. Kefauver held to the southern tradition of populism. To enhance his image as a man of the people he adopted the pioneers' coonskin cap as his symbol and avoided mentioning his LL.B. from Yale Law School. Kefauver had recently demonstrated the popularity of his populism by defeating President Truman in the 1952 presidential primary in New Hampshire. The 20,000 to 16,000 loss caused Truman to announce that he had not really intended to seek another term anyway; he was retiring. To launch his attack on the Dixon-Yates proposal in 1955 Kefauver secured his own appointment as chairman of a subcommittee to investigate the deal. Two others named to the five man committee shared Kefauver's support for public power. The Kefauver committee hearings quickly exposed compromising behavior within the administration. The Bureau of the Budget had based its decision on a report of a consultant guilty of a conflict of interest between his government assignments and his private business. In related developments Sherman Adams, Eisenhower's "assistant president," had intervened in the adjudication of the case before the Securities and Exchange Commission.[11]

In the midst of the hearings the city of Memphis announced that it would withdraw from the TVA system and build its own municipal plant. With no one to use the private power, Eisenhower was stymied. The Dixon-Yates contract had to be canceled. Kefauver was jubilant at the victory for public power. It soon became his leading issue as he renewed his quest for the Presidency in 1956. While his popularity was not enough to secure the first spot on the Democratic ticket, he did win nomination for the Vice Presidency, narrowly defeating John F. Kennedy for the honor.

Analysis of the Dixon-Yates affair indicates an institutionalization of the sharp split between public and private power. The participants divide into two camps bitterly opposed to each other. Very few remain neutral. The participants have a vested interest in feeding the controversy, since their careers as public or private officials depend on the vigor with which they attack their opponents. Their career and emotional commitments to their side overcome their ability to compromise or even to see where the profits lie. Their cause becomes an ideological crusade.

On the private power side the institutionalization of the conflict brought to the front such men as Dixon and Yates and their allies in the Eisenhower Administration. On the public power side it brought forward such men as Estes Kefauver. Politicians tend to affiliate with one of the two sides on the basis of party and geography. Democrats generally favor public development, while Republicans generally favor private. Westerners generally favor public, while others do not. The partisan dichotomy reflects the two parties' orientation toward the degree to which the federal government should participate in business. To the Republicans public power is "creeping socialism." The geographic dichotomy reflects rainfall. The western states favor public hydroelectric projects because the power is a by-product of the water for irrigation. Besides westerners, those politicians in states with public power tend to be strong supporters. Virtually every senator from the TVA region supported Kefauver's probe of the Dixon-Yates contract.

Public power has recently come under attack from economists who challenge the value of the projects. Their basis of judgment is opportunity cost. What alternative opportunities were sacrificed so that this project could be built? When TVA (or any other public or private power producer) builds a dam or a steam plant to generate electricity it calculates the costs of the facility in terms of the price it can charge for the power it will produce in the future. If the project is economical it proceeds to borrow the money to build the facility. The problem is the rate of interest to be paid. For a private company the interest rate is clear. It is whatever it must pay on its bonds in order to attract buyers. But for a public producer it is not necessarily clear. If it issues the bonds (as for example TVA and the New York State Power Authority do) then it is much like a private company. But the federal government does not generally issue bonds for specific projects. This has fostered the attitude among some congressmen that the interest rate is zero. Why not build a dam since the money is free? The logical conclusion of this fiscal naiveté would be for the government to do all the nation's investing since it can do so for zero percent while private business must pay 8, 10, or 12 percent. The actual procedure adopted by the government was only slightly less naive. In 1962 the President's Water Resources Council, composed of the Secretaries of the Army, Interior, Agriculture, and Health, Education, and Welfare, decided on an unrealistically low 3⅛ percent. The Treasury objected that at best it had to borrow the money from the public at 4¼ percent, thereby losing 1⅛ percent, or approximately a quarter of its value, every year. The effect of using low interest in calculating the value of a project is to make the project look more advantageous than it should. Thus the government may decide to build a dam that a private company would decide not to build because it has to pay competitive interest rates. This is economically wasteful because it moves money out of the private sector, where it would respond to true efficiencies, into the public sector, where it does not really produce as much benefit. The solution is to have the government calculate the value of a dam based on an interest rate comparable to private business. Then if the project is still efficient it should be built.[12]

The controversy between public and private power was not solved by the economic logic of comparing interest rates. Rather it died down of exhaustion after the Dixon-Yates episode. The aftermath of the dispute was a truce between TVA and its privately owned neighbors. The private companies ceased trying to roll back TVA, and TVA agreed to limit its territory to the region it already served.

Like the three forms of energy already considered in this book electricity faded into a period of political quiescence in the 1950's. Its existence secured but its expansion blocked, TVA ebbed from the vortex. The Department of the Interior family of power agencies, less controversial from the beginning, maintained an even lower profile. The New York State Power Authority, established by Governor Roosevelt in 1931, finally built its two big generating plants at Niagara Falls and the Saint Lawrence rapids but did not move on to further projects. In general those cities with municipal systems kept them, and those with private systems kept them. Again like the three forms of energy considered thus far, electricity re-emerged into political controversy as a result of the environmental movement.

TVA typified the pollution of electric power. As the authority came increasingly to rely on steam plants to generate its power it moved from environmentally pure water to environmentally destructive coal. In its massive purchases of coal TVA acted counter to many of the original goals of the agency. The authority's purpose was to develop the South. Its effect sometimes has been to ravage it. Its purchasing policy has encouraged strip mining of the most destructive sort. Its economic giantism has driven prices to rock bottom. In 1970 the National Coal Association charged that TVA used its position as a monopsonist to force prices down. The authority has indulged in such tricks as seeking competitive bids for a large quantity, then accepting the lowest bid, but only for a fraction of the original quantity. It then turned around and used this low bid to force down other coal companies' offers. Because of its size TVA could buy coal at nearly half the going price. Faced with such a low price the coal operators could stay in business only by adopting irresponsible mining techniques. They would "cream the contours" and fail to restore the land they gouged. Most of the coal comes from areas of Kentucky outside the authority's boundaries. TVA has a mission of benefiting the Tennessee Valley, not Kentucky. The Paradise steam plant, currently the world's largest, was TVA's first "mine mouth" plant. Each day it burns 21,000 tons dug from the coal bed on which it stands. Environmental groups sued TVA after the passage of the National Environmental Policy Act of 1969, charging that the authority failed to file environmental impact statements. TVA responded with a general statement in December 1972 but refused to file specific statements for each of its 30 to 40 purchasing contracts.[13]

TVA's promotion of electricity has been wasteful. When the agency began in the 1930's it had to convince its consumers that electricity was worthwhile. Since then it has been all too successful. It encouraged homeowners to install electric heating. It takes 7½ tons of coal to generate the electricity to heat the average home for a winter, but four tons would be sufficent if the coal were burned directly. Roughly 60 percent of the fuel's energy value is wasted when the coal is converted into electricity, as compared to about 20 percent when the coal is burned directly. A 40 percent loss of efficiency seems a high price to pay for concentrating the air pollution from the coal fire at one generating plant rather than spreading it from each house's chimney.

The siting of generating plants traditionally falls to the states. With the emergence of the environmental movement the construction of a new plant has become the occasion for the environmentalists to wage a holy war against the power companies, whether public or private. To the champions of nature any proposal is wrong *ipso facto*. Their duty is to block construction, and they have frequently succeeded in doing so. The utilities are vulnerable. Construction plans must be determined years before any electricity is generated. The public does not tolerate shortages or interruptions of power. Since electricity cannot be stored and the demand varies greatly, the plants must have a wide margin of excess capacity. With electricity consumption doubling every decade the utilities are desperately trying to start construction on enough plants to meet the anticipated demand.

The clash of these forces has locked the two sides into a conflict that paralyzes the industry. Environmentalists are able to delay construction for years by intervening each time the utility needs permission from the state or local government to move to the next step in building the plant. The obstacles are numerous. A typical fossil fuel installation requires 20 to 30 separate hearings to gain permission to move forward to its completion. A nuclear plant requires more. One consequence is for the utilities to follow the course of least resistance by resorting to temporary generating equipment, which does not require extensive government approval. They install jet turbines that run on kerosene rather than build a permanent steam plant. The cost is much higher, but they must do so since they cannot obtain the clearances required for the more efficient method.

Several states have radically reordered their public utility approval process to solve this problem. Minnesota created a single commission composed of utility officials, government officials, and citizens to handle the entire process. If none of the company sites meets the commission's approval, the commission must provide a site of its own for the plant. Maryland enacted a Power Plant Siting Law designed to serve the same purpose. The law requires a company to disclose its plans ten years in advance to allow adequate time for careful evaluation. The state government then has two years in which to evaluate environmental impact on the sites. In addition the state must develop a "land bank" of four to eight sites, each of which is environmentally approved. The state buys these sites and then sells or leases them to the power companies if requested. To bear the cost the consumer pays a tax of 10 to 20 cents a month on his electric bill. For the citizen the law offers careful and unhurried evaluation of a plant's impact on the environment. The utility company can no longer confront him with a last minute crisis in which the state must approve its plans or face an immediate power shortage. For the company the law offers a guarantee of timely approval of a satisfactory site. Citizen intervenors can no longer block costly construction at the last minute. The company faces only two hearings rather than the 20 or 30 it previously faced.[14]

Sound as the law appears, compliance is still based on cooperation. In its first test the result was a compromise in which the Baltimore Gas and Electric Company agreed to modify some of its facilities to reduce pollution but not to the degree that the state originally required. The negotiation was still politically based on the relative bargaining strength of the two parties rather than on firm technical standards. On the other hand the law did provide some standards, even though they were not firm. Without them B.G.&E. would have been less likely to limit its pollution. The company's argument was that the new plant would actually reduce air pollution by allowing the utility to close older and dirtier plants within the city limits. The Maryland foray into power plant ecology is a delicate undertaking. It is potentially expensive. A two-year intensive study required for a site costs $1 million. Routine statewide monitoring costs $1 million each year. Citizen input is small, while utility input is great. If it works in spite of these problems it promises to be a model for other states to imitate in reconciling their energy needs with their environment.

The Nixon Administration's concern that environmental protection was blocking power plant siting led it to propose federal legislation that would require each state to establish a plan similar to Maryland's. First introduced in Congress in 1970, the bill languished in committee despite administration appeals that the site selection process had to be streamlined to meet Nixon's goal of energy self-sufficiency by 1980.

The balance between energy and environment shifted slightly in favor of nature as a result of a 1965 decision by the U.S. Court of Appeals for the Second Circuit. The Consolidated Edison Company of New York proposed to build a $162 million pumped storage facility at Storm King Mountain on the Hudson River. The installation was to serve as a primative battery. Unlike other forms of energy, electricity cannot be stored (except in tiny amounts). Since demand fluctuates greatly hourly and consumers will not tolerate shortages, the utilities must have enough generators to supply the peak demands even though much of this equipment sits idle during slack periods of the day. A pumped storage plant seemed a partial answer to Con Ed. If its physical properties are such that electricity cannot be generated during slack periods and stored, at least water can be used as a surrogate. During the day when the consumer requirements were low the surplus power from steam plants in New York City would pump water up to a 12 billion gallon reservoir atop the mountain. Then in the evening 8 billion gallons of water would rush back down, generating power for the city. Hudson Valley residents objected to the construction for it would destroy Storm King. The reservoir would gouge out the mountain, and the plant transmission lines would deface its wild beauty. Forming the Scenic Hudson Preservation Conference, they intervened against Con Ed in hearings before the Federal Power Commission. When the FPC dismissed the complaint the conference appealed. The Court of Appeals reversed the power commission in language that redefined the commission's role. The court held that since the FPC was a public body it must vigorously advance the public's interest. It must move from a passive to an active role. The court wrote:

> In this case as in many others the commission has claimed to be the representative of the public interest. This role does not permit it to act as an umpire blandly calling balls and strikes for adversaries appearing before it; the right of the public must receive active and affirmative protection at the hands of the commission.[15]

This pointed the FPC in a new direction, away from merely smoothing the industry's way by following the path of least resistance toward one of questioning the industry's growth when that growth might conflict with the environment or some other public interest. Though hailed by environmentalists at the time as a legal breakthrough, the *Scenic Hudson Preservation Conference* v. *FPC* has since proved a disappointment. The commission has moved slowly in actively putting forward the public side.

The FPC was more influenced by another event that occurred in 1965: the massive power failure blacking out the northeastern United States and much of Canada. At 5:16 p.m. on November 9, as a single relay switch malfunctioned, first one, then all five of the high voltage lines carrying power from Ontario Hydro's Sir Adam Beck Plant Number Two at Niagara Falls north to Toronto went dead. Cutting transmission to Toronto sent 1.5 million kilowatts surging across the border into the United States. As the automatic switches cut off power to counter this massive overload, they created imbalances farther east and south in regions that only a few minutes before were drawing power from the Niagara plants. Within 12 minutes 30 million people from Toronto to New York and from Buffalo to Boston were plunged into darkness for up to 13 hours. In New York City the cutoff trapped people in subways and elevators. Consolidated Edison could not restart its generators. Unlike the upstate system, it has no hydroelectric facilities. Those can start themselves with water power but Con Ed's steam plants required electricity. The company had never contemplated all its generators failing at once. It had to restart one plant at a time using power from the Pennsylvania-Jersey-Maryland (PJM) system.

The 1965 blackout brought to national attention the interconnections of the regional systems into grids covering nearly the entire country and extending into Canada and northern Mexico. The national grid was the result of FPC leadership. Since 1935 the commission had urged local and regional interconnections as a means of increasing efficiency and reliability. Pooling generating capacity spread the burden of meeting peak loads and gave smaller systems access to major hydroelectric facilities. When it ordered the National Power Survey in 1962 the FPC proposed the goal of the complete integration of all electrical power systems. But experience soon showed that the FPC policy was outrunning technology. Two years later, when another massive blackout hit the Pennsylvania-Jersey-Maryland pool, the FPC admitted that while it learned how the malfunction occurred, it did not know why.[16]

The blackouts caused the commission to turn more cautious. Unlike most regulatory bodies, the FPC was on the forefront of technological development. Successful interconnections are a boon to the consumer, saving him money and improving service, but the smallest errors could suddenly explode into major disruptions for the public. Current FPC policy with respect to the regional pools has shifted from haphazard expansion to concern with access. The commission has generally supported applications by municipally and cooperatively owned utilities for admission into the regional systems. The private companies have opposed sharing their power, proposing instead to consolidate all utilities into about a dozen (privately owned) giants to obtain economies of scale. The public utilities counter by arguing that their admission into the regional pools would do the same.[17]

As America moved into the 1970's it increasingly became concerned with shortages of electricity. The 1965 blackout of the Northeast planted the seed of worry that there would not be enough. Within five years brownouts had become a summertime routine. As a heat wave brought excessive demands to power the ever more popular air conditioners, the companies reduced power 2 to 5 percent as an interim measure to conserve electricity. In 1974 the nation went onto year-round daylight savings time for the first time since World War I. The utilities urged consumers to turn their lights off whenever possible and to turn their thermostats down in winter. They launched propaganda campaigns to convince the public to save electricity and support their efforts to build new generating plants in the face of environmentalists' opposition. One company pamphlet stated its position boldly: "We are not in battle over environmental objectives. We are dealing, rather, with a question of survival."[18]

Such desperate cries of alarm foreshadowed shifting the balance away from the environment. The chief victim was air quality. Clean air standards established under the 1970 Clean Air Act were sacrificed so that electric power plants could continue to burn high sulfur coal, and in some cases even convert to coal from less polluting oil or natural gas. Concurrently power systems in the Northeast, which depended largely on oil, arranged to buy electricity from coal fueled midwestern plants. A consortium of utilities from as far west as Wisconsin agreed to sell 500,000 kilowatts of off-peak energy to New England, transmitting it via the FPC sponsored regional grid systems.

Assessment of the impact of physical characteristics of electricity on the politics of the arena focuses on the properties of the fuel. The impossibility of storing electricity has several consequences. A crisis will be dramatic. A power blackout conveys the power shortage to the average citizen at the speed of light. Electrical companies don't have to persuade the public that a crisis exists with arcane statistical summaries of distant reserves lying far underground. This same impossibility of storage has led the FPC to foster the development of grids allowing power transfers during peak hours. As a fuel, electricity appears environmentally clean. It does not pollute the air or water when it is used. But this purity is superficial, for, while it is clean in its use, it is polluting in its generation. In the balance, however, electricity may still be preferred on environmental grounds since emissions from coal or oil burned at a single large plant may be cleaned efficiently, which cannot be done at a multitude of individual houses and businesses. The federal role in electricity derives from physical properties of hydroelectric power. An efficient plant requires a sufficient "head" (force with which the water falls). This usually means a massive dam involving a large capital investment and the legal right to condemn land.

The market forces that undergird the industry have had less of a political impact because they have generally been benign. Consumer demand has grown rapidly but smoothly. Electricity has been far from being a sick industry like coal. Nor has it been an unstable one like oil. Rather it has been exceptionally healthy. Demand has been strong and predictable like natural gas. High capital needs deriving from the physical characteristics of the fuel make electricity a natural monopoly like gas, hence in need of regulation; but obvious and measurable inputs of equipment and primary fuel have made calculating appropriate rates less of a mystery than was true for natural gas production.

The politics of electricity bears the strong imprint of the general political environment of the 1930's. The public versus private dichotomy was a leading issue of the era and ultimately came to rest along the lines established by the New Deal. Still, the electrical industry developed over a long period, and a variety of other political environments left their marks. Public ownership traces back to the beginning of the century, when many cities established municipal plants. Multipurpose federal dams, which generated electricity as a by-product, are another pre-Roosevelt legacy. The Republican return to office in 1953 renewed the public versus private struggle. In keeping with the tenor of the times its opponents criticized TVA as a "socialist plot" not far removed from communism. The effect of these various forces has been a regulated industry with highly polarized political roles. The conflict between public and private partisans, now half a century old, has become institutionalized along positions nearly identical to those delineated by Franklin D. Roosevelt when he was governor of New York. The now sterile conflict continues along ritual lines.

Building a dam became the Democrats' standard response. Harry Truman proposed a TVA equivalent on the Missouri River. In 1965 Lyndon Johnson proposed developing the Mekong River Valley as a solution to the Vietnam War. If American-built hydroelectric stations and nitrate plants could bring cheap power and fertilizer to the four nations of Southeast Asia the fighting would end. While Johnson's proposal may have been naive in terms of the harsh realities of international politics, its genesis lay deeply rooted in the traditions of the Democratic party.

Notes

1. Richard Hellman, *Government Competition in the Electric Utility Industry* (New York: Praeger, 1972), p. 9.

2. Twentieth Century Fund, *The Power Industry and Public Interest* (New York, 1944), p. 20.

3. Twentieth Century Fund, *Electric Power and Government Policy* (New York, 1948), p. 570.

4. *Ibid.*

5. Hellman, *op. cit.*, pp. 123–32.

6. See Philip Selznick, *TVA and the Grass Roots* (New York: Harper Torchbooks, 1966).

7. Twentieth Century Fund, *Electric Power*, p. 512; Hellman, *op. cit.*, pp. 34–35.

8. Hellman, *op. cit.*, p.36.

9. Marquis Childs, *The Farmer Takes a Hand* (Garden City, N.Y.: Doubleday, 1952), *passim.*

10. Aaron Wildavsky, *Dixon-Yates: A Study in Power Politics* (New Haven, Conn: Yale, 1962), *passim.*

11. *Ibid.*

12. See Robert L. Banks and Arnold Kotz, "The Program Budget and the Interest Rate for Public Investment," *Public Administration Review*, 26 (1966), 283–91.

13. Osborn Segerberg, Jr., "Power Corrupts," *Esquire*, March 1972, pp. 138ff.

14. John Noble Wilford, "Nation's Energy Crisis: It Won't Go Away Soon," *The New York Times*, July 6, 1971; Peter E. Wagner, "Power Plants and the Law," *The Johns Hopkins Magazine*, March 1973, pp. 20–25.

15. *Scenic Hudson Preservation Conference* v. *FPC*, 354 F. 2d 608; see also Alan R. Talbot, *Power Along the Hudson* (New York: Dutton, 1972).

16. Louis M. Kohlmeier, Jr., *The Regulators* (New York: Harper and Row, 1969), p. 190; Federal Power Commission, *The 1970 National Power Survey*, Vol. I, Ch. 13, pp. 1–18.

17. Hellman, *op. cit.*, p. 44.

18. Pamphlet of Public Service Electric and Gas Company, Newark, N.J., 1973.

6

Nuclear Energy

The political importance of the atom derives from its potential rather than its present production of energy. While its potential power is awesome, its current contribution is paltry. Measured in terms of B.T.U.'s, nuclear energy contributed only 0.6 percent of the United States' 1971 output. Measured in terms of its contribution to electrical power generation (which accounts for nearly half of the nation's primary consumption of energy) nuclear plants generated 1½ percent in 1971. By the end of 1973 the contribution was up to 5 percent. By 1985 it will expand to 42 percent, and to 60 percent by the end of the century.[1] As the electrical sector grows, the proportionate nuclear contribution will grow as well. Impressive as the long range potential for nuclear power is, it was another sort of potential nuclear power that set the politics of the atom on its original course.

It was and is a political course dominated by the physical properties of the fuel. To an extent greater than for any of the other four forms of energy considered, a single variable—the fuel itself—offers the key to understanding the politics of the arena. The other physical variable, geography, explains little. Likewise market forces and the general political environment are less useful explicands than in the previous four cases.

That other sort of potential power which gave nuclear energy its original political course is, of course, its cataclysmic release in the form of a bomb. The United States first developed atomic power as a weapon, and its military role long overshadowed its civilian one. Besides killing 150,000 people and ending World War II, the bombs dropped on Hiroshima and Nagasaki brought the President and Congress to the realization that they had to establish a suitable institution to manage the accouterments of the atomic age. The novelty and power of the bomb awed Congress. It seemed to call for a unique administrative structure to match its unique physical power. The Atomic Energy Act of 1946 created the Atomic Energy Commission. Five commissioners headed the agency. All were civilians, reflecting a concern over military dominance. In a period when the military stood at the height of prestige after its global victory, the civilian makeup of the commission indicated a vague distrust and a wish to return firmly to the prewar tradition of civilian dominance. The AEC was not to be part of the military establishment or any other existing department. It was to have a direct line of authority to the President. Congress, feeling that it should have special arrangements for overseeing the atom, included several unique provisions in the 1946 law. A single joint committee composed of nine members from each house would be responsible, instead of the usual two committees, one for each house. The authority for the joint committee derived from the act rather than from the rules of procedure as was the case for all other committees. The joint committee was staffed by personnel from the AEC and had special rights to delve into the commission's administrative affairs. This exceptionally endowed committee has been able to wield more control over its executive branch charge than is often seen in Washington.

For the first three years, however, the Joint Committee on Atomic Energy was restrained in the exercise of its pervasive power to supervise the AEC. In part this came from a tension between the Republican-controlled 80th Congress and the Truman-appointed commissioners. The President named David Lilienthal to head the agency. A staunch New Dealer and former head of TVA, the controversial Lilienthal believed the best strategy was to keep relations with the JCAE to a minimum. In part the joint committee's restraint in the 1947—48 period came from its lack of expertise. If the 18 senators and representatives stood in awe of the atom, they also stood in ignorance of it. They had little to contribute to the AEC, not even intelligent questions. The commissioners themselves knew little more of the physics involved in the fission process than did the congressmen. For advice they turned to the one group that did have the expertise: the scientists who built the bomb. The commissioners appointed the most prominent of these scientists to a General Advisory Council. For the first period in the commission's history the GAC scientists set the policy.[2]

The scientific advisory council's influence declined and the congressional joint committee's influence grew in 1949 as a consequence of a confluence of events, some foreign and some domestic. The Soviet Union's successful testing of an atomic bomb caused the JCAE to question the scientists' advice. The General Advisory Council had been lackadasical in realizing the threat the test presented to foreign and military policy. The American monopoly was broken. The United States could no longer depend on the bomb to enforce its will anywhere in the world. The scientists had predicted no Russian bomb until 1952. Internationally the United States had suffered setbacks from the Communists. The Communists blockaded Berlin, seized the government in Czechoslovakia, and conquered China from Chiang Kai'shek. At home the AEC lost four grams of U-235 to thieves, sent isotopes to Norway contrary to the provisions of the law prohibiting export of radioactive material, awarded a graduate fellowship to an avowed Communist at the University of North Carolina, and had been found lax in its security procedures. These AEC mistakes came out as a result of investigation by Senator Bourke Hickenlooper of the joint committee. The effect of the Hickenlooper probe was to discredit the scientists. Along with Lilienthal's departure as commission chairman, the AEC's guidance was shifted from the General Advisory Committee to Congress. This, in turn, aimed it away from a solely military orientation to one more civilian. The scientists, though civilian themselves, focused their attention on building bombs. The members of the JCAE, however, included some interested in the atom's potential for generating electrical power.

The development of this potential was slow and uneven. The AEC began building an experimental reactor at its Knolls laboratory in 1947. With no success as of 1950 it abandoned the project. The following year another experimental reactor at Argonne laboratory's Idaho test station did succeed in producing 100 kilowatts of electricity. This reactor, however, was not for civilian power but to propel the submarine *U.S.S. Nautilus*. The reactors designed to produce power derive from a project initiated by private industry. In 1951 two groups—Monsanto Chemical and a Dow Chemical-Detroit Edison consortium—applied to develop reactors that would generate electricity for commercial use. At the urging of the joint committee the AEC developed an Industrial Participation Program to allow them to do so.[3]

This program marked a sharp departure from the previous Atomic Energy Commission policy. It was the first step away from the absolute monopoly it had maintained since its inception. During the war the Manhattan Project, which developed the bomb, kept an absolute monopoly in order to assure military security. Knowledge of the bomb's design or even of its existence could have put the Allied victory in jeopardy. Appropriations were hidden in the budgets of other departments and approved secretly by the chairmen of the military affairs and appropriations committees of the House and Senate. Even President Truman did not know of the bomb until he had been in office three days after Roosevelt's death.

At the time Congress debated and passed the Atomic Energy Act of 1946 it did not consider any alternative to a strict government monopoly. The rationale for the monopoly was national security. Until Monsanto and Dow-Detroit Edison applied to develop reactors for large-scale power generation, the AEC reactor research was oriented toward military requirements. The chief achievement was the new class of nuclear submarine capable of remaining undetectable underwater for patrols lasting six months. Just as in the case of weaponry, the transcending issue of national security dictated a strict government monopoly. The legacy of this military-inspired monopoly remained with the AEC as it moved into the development of civilian reactors. Thus the AEC's strict regulation of the nuclear industry derives in part from a different source than the regulation of nonnuclear electricity or of natural gas. Regulation of conventional electricity and gas is based on its characteristics as a natural monopoly. Since competition would be uneconomical, the government steps in to assure that the consumer gets a fair price. Virtually all power produced by nuclear reactors is distributed in the form of electricity, so it is logical to subject it to the same type of regulation after it leaves the generator. But because of the military legacy of atomic power, Congress saw fit to keep the government monopoly on it at the earlier stages as well. The uranium fuel to power the reactor was subject to tight AEC control; only the commission could own it (and at first only the commission could own the reactor as well). This was not because it was a natural monopoly. The ore could be mined by small operators and easily transported like coal. Control was, rather, a by-product of the national security ethos that the agency followed.

The breakthrough in AEC's movement into the civilian reactor field came at the urging of the joint committee. Congress appropriated extra funds in the spring of 1953 to construct a pilot power plant. Westinghouse received the contract to build the reactor, and the Duquesne Light Company received the contract to build and operate the generating plant at a site on the Ohio River near Shippingport, 35 miles northwest of Pittsburgh.

The joint committee's hearings and discussions leading up to its decision to direct the AEC to build the Shippingport reactor revealed dissatisfaction with the 1946 Atomic Energy Act. Among the foremost faults of the act was its neglect of civilian power development. Contemporaneously President Eisenhower became dissatisfied with the act as well. Addressing the United Nations General Assembly in December 1953, Eisenhower proposed an Atoms for Peace plan. The United Nations would establish an agency to oversee worldwide applications of nuclear energy in agriculture, medicine, and electric power generation. Behind the Eisenhower proposal lay two goals. One was the propaganda advantage to be gained. The nonnuclear nations had heard of nothing but the destructiveness of the weaponry and were growing nervous and resentful. Peaceful applications would soothe them. The other was a military advantage. An AEC test explosion the previous March demonstrated the practicality of a cheap "uranium" bomb. Up to this point the United States had relied on the difficulty in producing large quantities of plutonium to limit the explosive capability of potential nuclear nations. But this experiment showed that a small amount of the hard-to-produce plutonium could be combined with a large amount of the easy-to-produce natural uranium to create a bomb of unlimited size. The United States had to gain firmer control over nuclear research and development around the world in order to keep down the amount of weaponry that could be built. The Atoms for Peace proposal seemed the ideal way. A United Nations atomic energy agency would give the United States a window on the progress of foreign countries' research. This fit in with a related policy created by the President's National Security Council to deny nuclear weapons to the United States' NATO allies. Since the "uranium" bomb test showed that nuclear capability could increase so enormously, it seemed best to keep as many countries as possible completely out of the weapons technology. Atoms for Peace would mollify them. The new policy called for sharing nuclear material, something forbidden by the 1946 law.

This double pressure for civilian power development and international cooperation combined to bring a revision of the Atomic Energy Act of 1946. In his January 1954 budget message Eisenhower called for amendments to effect these changes. The AEC sent the joint committee two draft amendments embodying the President's proposals—one to allow private industry to build power plants and the other to allow international exchanges. But before the JCAE or Congress could consider the two drafts the committee chairman, Representative Sterling Cole, and the vice chairman, Senator Bourke Hickenlooper, rewrote them into a single bill that completely reworked the 1946 act. On one hand, Cole and Hickenlooper were dissatisfied with the AEC drafts because they took authority away from the joint committee. On the other, they feared that if presented individually each proposed amendment might be defeated, whereas if combined they would pass. Democratic liberals would be likely to oppose giving away free to private industry the benefits of years of government research. Republican isolationists would be likely to oppose giving away the same to foreign countries.[4]

Cole and Hickenlooper underestimated the ease with which this combined bill would pass. The issue was joined immediately along partisan lines, first in the JCAE and then on the floors of the House and Senate. The question was the traditional one of public versus private power. The Democrats supported the former and the Republicans the latter. The argument for public power stressed that nuclear reactors were a means of bringing cheap electricity to the entire nation the same way TVA brought cheap power to the Tennessee Valley. To accomplish this the government should invest massive funds in research, development, and construction. The policy should stress aggressive promotion in the New Deal tradition. To turn the program over to private industry would mean stagnation, costly rates, and a windfall for the utilities. The private companies were not entitled to the free use of the government-invented technology. The argument for private power countered that when nuclear power became commercially economical it should be distributed in the traditional American manner: through private business. In this the Eisenhower Administration and the Republicans in Congress concurred.[5]

The issue provoked a series of hotly contested congressional votes. Although generally once a congressional committee agrees on the provisions of a bill, the parent chamber will accept it, the Cole-Hickenlooper bill was too controversial. Committee members even lost their usual roles in guiding the bill through floor debate. The overall party leaders usurped their functions. Amendments to allow the AEC to undertake commercial production lost in the face of Republican opposition. On the other hand, the public power advocates gained amendments requiring private firms to share with the government patents on discoveries and inventions made while working on AEC contracts. They also gained provisions bringing nuclear-generated electricity under the regulation of the Federal Power Commission and giving preference to publicly owned utilities.[6]

In the balance the Eisenhower Administration and the Republican-controlled 82nd Congress had their way. Private power won. But the exact terms of the settlement merely divided up the new industry according to a pattern virtually identical to the one already existing in the electric power industry. As far as generation and distribution, the 1954 law projected the status quo onto a new field. Private power would be the chief form, but public power would continue to have preference in licensing and in access to AEC experimental plants (just as to federal hydroelectric facilities) and the FPC would regulate rates.

It was in the provisions for supplying the fuel to the reactors that the 1954 Atomic Energy Act established procedures that were new. Here the AEC kept its military-based monopoly. All nuclear fuel produced in the United States would continue to be the property of the government, but the AEC would lease the utilities the quantities they needed to run their reactors. Furthermore the utilities could build and operate reactors only under license of the AEC. The commission would issue two types of license: experimental and commercial. The experimental licenses were for research or prototype plants, which normally would receive an AEC subsidy as well. Commercial licenses were for power generation at competitive rates. In fact none was issued for ten years.

Within two years the public power Democrats on the joint committee rallied to attack the AEC's lack of progress in developing civilian reactors. Senator Albert Gore of Tennessee and Representative Chet Holifield of California led the assault. Private industry had failed to take the initiative in developing nuclear power that the 1954 act envisioned. As a consequence the United States was losing the electricity race with the Russians. To prod the AEC into action Gore and Holifield introduced legislation to "direct" the commission to construct six large-scale reactors around the country. The AEC opposed this, claiming that it was already doing enough. The real problems holding back private development were inability to get insurance and possible violations of the Public Utility Holding Company Act of 1935 if private companies tried to build joint facilities. In order to get the JCAE to report the bill favorably to the floor, the committee Democrats compromised, sacrificing much of the thrust of the Gore-Holifield bill. Even this watered-down bill met defeat. The next year the Democrats tried a new strategy. They secured the cooperation of Chairman Clarence Cannon of the House Appropriations Committee. Cannon threatened to block AEC funds until the committee agreed to greater JCAE supervision of the civilian reactor program. Once the initial coercion impressed the AEC with Congress' power, the commission decided the best policy would be to acquiesce to the JCAE's wishes. Accordingly the AEC and the JCAE members and staff held a series of meetings in 1958 and 1959 to evolve a mutually agreeable policy. The result was to set a goal of competitive nuclear power within ten years.[7] Where private companies failed to develop facilities, the AEC would step in.

In fact this amounted to subsidizing uneconomical plants for their symbolic value. Democrats in the 1950's chose to subsidize nuclear reactors surreptitiously for the same reasons they chose in the 1930's to subsidize TVA—among other things, to provide visible signs of an invisible dedication to the welfare of the common man. Where once a senator sought a dam in his state as a symbol that he had served his constituency, now he sought a nuclear plant to point to when he ran for re-election. On the other side of the aisle Republicans in Congress backed President Eisenhower's proposal to build a nuclear powered merchant ship to demonstrate the use of Atoms for Peace. The same type of reactor as used in the *Nautilus*-class submarines was to propel the ship. No one argued seriously that nuclear energy was an economical fuel for the merchant marine. Merchant ships already use a comparatively cheap fuel and have no need to cruise underwater or be away from ports for months at a time. The ship was primarily for propaganda —to enhance American prestige. The joint committee eliminated construction funds when the administration first proposed the ship for the 1956 fiscal year budget, but the following year it slipped by unnoticed as attention focused on the Gore-Holifield bill controversy. Support came from the Republicans eager to sustain the President even though this meant supporting a public facility in an industry traditionally private. Construction began on the *S.S. Savannah* in 1958 with Mrs. Richard M. Nixon presiding at the keel-laying ceremony.

Less than a decade later the Johnson Administration was rudely to learn the symbolic importance of nuclear fuel when it built a new aircraft carrier to be named the *U.S.S. John F. Kennedy*. The Pentagon recommended the more efficient conventional engines in preference to a less efficient atomic reactor. Department of Defense cost effectiveness studies showed the nuclear system to be too costly to be practical. But Kennedy loyalists believed that choosing oil over atoms implied a slight to the memory of the martyred President. Symbolically, as Johnson discovered, nuclear energy outranks conventional energy.

The intense partisan controversy of the late 1950's reflected the division of control between the Presidency and Congress. Once the 83rd Congress convened in January 1955, a Republican President faced a Democratic majority in both houses for the remainder of his two terms. Eisenhower was not a strong President. He believed both personally and in keeping with Republican ideology that his role ought to be more passive than Roosevelt's or Truman's had been. Not only should the President defer to Congress, but the entire federal government should restrain its use of power. Political power should be returned to the states and to the people after Washington's power-grabbing under 20 years of Democratic rule. To the Democrats, the Eisenhower attitude meant a leadership vacuum at best and a sellout to private greed at worst. As their party's leaders in Congress, Senate majority leader Lyndon Johnson and House Speaker Sam Rayburn led the Democrats to offer a series of alternatives to Republican policy. Their aggresive promotion of their own programs stirred up controversies in other areas comparable to the one on nuclear reactors.

Not all AEC controversies came before Congress promptly. A chief commission advantage in maintaining its monopoly was its ability to suppress issues. One of these was the danger inherent in the physical properties of uranium. In 1949 the commission became concerned that it depended on uranium ore imported from the Belgian Congo for 85 percent of its supplies. To achieve autarky it fostered the development of an American mining industry; to keep down the price it neglected safety. European experience in radioactive mines going back a century showed the miners faced increased risks of lung cancer. The uranium in the mine slowly changes into radium, which in turn changes into radon—a radioactive gas. The radon then produces a set of "radon daughters" which the miners inhale into their lungs where they cause the cancer, usually 10 to 20 years later. The solution the Europeans learned in the 1930's was thorough ventilation of the mines. The AEC denied that the health problem existed in America. When evidence of the risks accumulated, it claimed that there was no conclusive proof that the radioactivity caused the lung "damage" (the AEC avoided calling it "cancer"). Meanwhile it denied responsibility for mine safety since its monopoly technically began only after the uranium left the mine. The AEC went so far as to use secrecy to prevent the health officials from investigating the dangers. A Colorado state health inspector was denied access to mills processing the ore for many months until he received the AEC's supersecret Q clearance. The Colorado health department was the only one that vigorously pursued the issue. This it had to do in the face of AEC hostility. Public opinion handicapped the health department as well. During the 1950's nuclear weapons were so identified with the popular anti-Communism that health officials critical of uranium mining were suspected of lack of patriotism.[8]

U.S. Public Health Service investigations supported the Colorado health department's concern, but it was not until 1959 that the Joint Committee on Atomic Energy even held a hearing on the subject. The JCAE did not welcome reports that uranium was killing people. It admitted in the 1959 hearing that a danger existed but did not pressure the AEC to remedy the situation. Eight years later, when the Secretary of Labor imposed on the industry safety regulations to control radioactivity, the chairman of the JCAE, Chet Holifield, castigated him for singling out the uranium mines.

Uranium miners were not the only ones to face the risks of radon. Careless management literally brought home the dangers to the ordinary citizens. Grand Junction lies in the midst of the Colorado uranium fields. Its Climax Uranium Company mills are among the biggest refining the ore for the AEC. Over the years Climax sold its tailings (the fine sand remaining after the ore was processed) to construction companies building houses in the area. The sand made an excellent fill on which to pour a concrete floor. The result was to make every new house in town as lethal as a uranium mine. The gaseous radon daughters seeped up through the floor to poison the air. The radium trapped below emitted gamma rays. Babies and toddlers who remained home all day and played on the floor received the heaviest doses. They, along with the unborn, were the most vulnerable to genetic damage from the gamma rays.

The danger came to public attention only after 1966, when a public health official serendipitously recognized that the fine white sand used in construction was the radioactive tailings. After mapping the areas affected, the Colorado health department sent official warnings to 5,000 home owners. For the 10 percent most in danger, the dosage equalled 500 chest X-rays a year per person.

Removing the tailings typically cost up to one-half the value of the house. Veterans Administration loan officials considered refusing to guarantee mortgages on houses in which the radon exceeded safe limits. The episode stirred resentment against the AEC. The people of Grand Junction noted that between 1952 and 1966 the AEC inspectors permitted the Climax Company to sell 200,000 tons of tailings to the builders. The AEC tried to suppress or minimize the dangers from radon after the Colorado health department began exposing the problem. The commission belittled the risks, blocked funds for research, and denied responsibility.

The AEC's handling of the problem prompted the charge that it resorted to deceit. When the commission came under fire for negligence, one of its defenses was a letter it claimed to have sent nine state health departments in 1961 warning of the danger. But none of the nine health departments could remember receiving the letter or could find it in their files. The implication was that the AEC fabricated the letter after the controversy arose so that it could shift the blame to the states.

While geography confines the dangers of radon poisoning to the Rocky Mountains where the uranium is mined, the building of nuclear power plants brings the danger home to the millions of Americans whom these plants serve. Nuclear power plants endanger their environment two ways: accidentally and routinely. Congress faced the risks of a reactor explosion in its 1957 passage of the Price-Anderson Act, which provided government indemnity to back up private companies insuring nuclear reactors. That same year in England just such an accident occurred. As its staff restarted the Windscale Pile Number One after a routine shutdown for maintenance, the reactor began heating up uncontrollably. A nuclear "fire" began raging violently. The fire destroyed the safety equipment needed to contain the pile's energy. Radioactive contamination escaped into the atmosphere. After battling the nuclear fire unsuccessfully for three days, the plant management took a desperate step. It decided to use water to cool the reactor. The risk was that the water striking the uranium might trigger an explosion of the entire reactor. Local police prepared to evacuate nearby residents, and plant workers took shelter. Fortunately the reactor did not explode, and after 24 hours of hosing the pile was cold.

Windscale Pile Number One was a total loss, and large amounts of radioactive iodine contaminated the region. Since milk from cows grazing in a 200 square mile area downwind was poisoned, the government bought and destroyed it. The fallout, with about one-tenth the radioactivity of the Hiroshima blast, spread over England, France, the Low Countries, Germany, and Denmark.[9]

In 1961 an experimental reactor exploded at the AEC's National Reactor Testing Station in Idaho Falls. A mismanaged control rod produced a power surge in the 3,000-kilowatt reactor. The explosion killed three workmen. The official report claimed they died from the blast. The union that represented the Idaho Falls workers charged that this was a "whitewash," that they had died of exposure to radioactivity. The union complaints grimly proposed that if the AEC could not prevent the deaths at least it could provide lead caskets for a dignified burial rather than the unceremonial disposition that the AEC gave to the irradiated bodies.[10]

The Idaho accident prompted the AEC to issue safety guidelines based on distance. Reactors were to be built only in sparsely populated areas far from cities. These 1961 guidelines stopped, for example, the Consolidated Edison Company's plan to build a nuclear plant in the heart of New York City. The reactor's East River site would have been perfect in terms of electric demand but disastrous in case of an accident. By 1967, however, the AEC began to relax its tough demands for safety through distance. The electric utilities argued that no sites within economical transmission distance of the cities they served were available to meet the AEC's standards of sparse population. The commission's response was to abandon safety through distance in favor of safety through engineering. The utilities could build reactors close to cities provided that they incorporated safety redundancies into the design. Thus the AEC recommended the licensing of New Jersey's Public Service Electric and Gas Company's plant on Newbold Island on the Delaware River, even though the site is only five miles south of Trenton and ten miles north of Philadelphia.

A 1966 accident at the Enrico Fermi Atomic Power Plant near Detroit points up the dangers faced even when radiation is not released into the atmosphere. The Detroit Edison Company was one of the pioneers in nuclear generation of electricity. Its 1953 proposal to develop the techniques for civilian use prompted Congress to restructure nuclear policy in the 1954 Atomic Energy Act. But Detroit-Edison had little technical success. Its Fermi reactor was plagued by difficulties and did not begin to generate electricity at full power until January 1966. The accident occurred in October. A bit of sheet metal chipped off, blocking the sodium pumped through the pile to keep it cool. The result was a nuclear "fire" similar to the Windscale accident in England. In this case the safety devices did work properly and extinguished the fire. Had the safety controls failed the result would have been what reactor experts call the "China syndrome." Within two minutes of a drastic coolant failure the reactor heats up to 3,360 degrees Fahrenheit and the core collapses. Within an hour the molten mass burns through the bottom of its container, accompanied by steam explosions. Within a day it burns through the concrete containment slab under the plant. The fiery fuel forms a glob in the earth 100 feet in diameter. Some predict that the molten mass of the reactor will burn its way down deeper through the earth directly toward China. More likely it will lie burning at the bottom of its self-dug pit for over ten years.[11]

To foster safety the AEC subjects proposals to build nuclear reactors to a series of reviews. The utility must file a Preliminary Safety Analysis Report. The AEC staff examines the preliminary report and confers with company officials. The AEC then submits the preliminary report to its Advisory Committee on Reactor Safeguards. This committee frequently demands design modifications. The third safety review is a public hearing before a three-member board selected from the 23-man Atomic Safety and Licensing Board Panel. Members of the public may intervene at this stage and have sometimes prevented the utilities from securing their construction permits. The final review precedes issuing an operating license after the plant is built. The public can again intervene. The problem with the review system is that it is all internal. At every stage it is within the AEC. No disinterested agency ever reviews the application. Public intervenors can challenge only what they know about, and the system keeps them in ignorance. Critics suggested that Congress transfer the responsibility for safety to the U.S. Environmental Protection Agency, where it would be unbiased by the AEC goal of promoting atomic energy. The commission's response was to reorganize the review procedure to make it more independent. But it remains within the AEC, so its new autonomy remains questionable.

A chilling variation of a nuclear accident is the purposeful criminal act. In 1970 a fourteen-year-old honors science student threatened to blow up Orlando, Florida, with a hydrogen bomb unless the city paid him $1 million.[12] He included a diagram of his homemade bomb that convinced an Air Force nuclear armament officer that the threat was credible. Fortunately for Orlando it was a hoax. The boy had no hydrogen fuel, only the expertise. But with the proliferation of civilian reactors, obtaining the material for a bomb will become easier. Building a bomb would not be necessary for a would-be extortionist. Plutonium is so highly toxic that a criminal could merely threaten to dump a bucketful out of a window whence it would poison the atmosphere. The civilian power era has freed nuclear fuels from the tight security with which the military used to guard the material. Now it is shipped about the country by commercial air freight, a form of transportation notoriously subject to pilfering.

While ordinary criminals or high school science students may be unlikely to build bombs successfully with fuel intended for reactors, a foreign power's doing so is not so unlikely, as India reminded the world in May 1974. Israel, Egypt, Iran, and South Africa are all countries with both scientists to build a bomb with plutonium from civilian reactors and the reason to do so. When President Nixon announced during his 1974 visit to Cairo that the United States would give Egypt a nuclear reactor, his critics charged that that was tantamount to giving the Egyptians a bomb. Nixon's defense was that if the United States had not supplied the reactor, France would have, and then the United States would have had no control or monitoring role. As if acting on cue, France promptly announced that it was giving a reactor to Iran, an oil rich country scarcely in need of energy (unlike Egypt).

Accidents and bomb builders are not the only risks nuclear power plants present. Many of the dangers are routine. The ordinary operation of a reactor pollutes its environment. The more benign form of pollution is thermal. The nuclear plant is only 30 percent efficient. While 30 percent of the energy it produces becomes electricity, 70 percent is wasted in the form of heat. This waste heat is removed by circulating cold water through the plant. The then heated water returns to the river, bay, or ocean whence it came. Cooling is not a new problem for electric generating plants. Fossil fuel plants require water for cooling as well. But they operate more efficiently (at 40 percent for coal), and they vent much of their heat into the atmosphere via tall smokestacks. The water coolant must absorb all of the nuclear plant's large heat wastage. Biologists fear the effects of this thermal pollution on aquatic life. Marine plants and animals respond to slight changes in water temperature. The warm discharge into Oyster Creek from the Jersey Central Power and Light Company nuclear plant tricked many fish into remaining in the creek for the winter when normally they would have migrated to their winter habitat. When the plant shut down for maintainance in the early spring the warm discharge ceased and thousands of fish died. In the Chesapeake Bay the bluefin crabs winter just off the Calvert Cliffs site of the Baltimore Gas and Electric Company's nuclear facility. The bay's commercial fishermen fear that the heat will upset their source of livelihood. Fishermen, both commercial and sport, express similar concern about Lake Michigan. Waste heat might upset the equilibrium between two layers of the lake's water. Limnologists do not understand the relationship well and fear that thermal pollution may upset the balance before they learn what is happening. A single plant might not be a danger, but the utilities plan to ring Lake Michigan with dozens in the next 25 years. Chesapeake Bay, too, faces thermal pollution from multiple sources, as do many other bodies of water. A remedy for discharging heated water is to use cooling towers. These hyperbolic structures reaching 500 feet in height cool by evaporation as the water splashes down their sides. Unfortunately they also generate fog, rain, and snow downwind. They are unsuitable for salt or brackish water since the salty spray destroys farm crops. For such water the plant must build dry, rather than wet, towers similar in principle to an automobile radiator. In either case many citizens consider the huge towers so ugly that they object more to the scenic pollution than to the thermal pollution.

The routine operation of a nuclear generating plant produces pollution more deadly than heat—radioactivity. The story of how the dangers of radiation emerged as a public controversy illuminates the flow of information and the decision-making process within the closed world of the nuclear arena. The AEC sought to preserve its bureaucratic dogma with the ruthlessness of the medieval Church suppressing heretics. In 1969 Dr. Ernest J. Sternglass of the University of Pittsburgh published predictions that radioactive fallout would cause the deaths of 400,000 babies. To counter this "prophet of doom" the AEC asked two of its own scientists to rebut Sternglass' article. The two, Arthur R. Tamplin and John Gofman, answered the challenge by showing that only 400 babies would die. This upset the AEC administrators, who did not want any number placed on the casualties from radioactivity. They pressured Tamplin and Gofman to revise their report, but the two scientists refused and published it uncensored. Furthermore the AEC's attempt to intimidate Tamplin and Gofman transformed them into vocal critics within the commission itself. The commission is unable to discipline them for three reasons. First is because they possess expertise. As scientists they speak with authority that the administrators cannot refute. Their technical skills give them autonomy, which they would not have if they had no claim to specialized knowledge not generally possessed. The second reason the AEC is unable to discipline them is the publicity. Once their situation is widely known the commission cannot apply sanctions against them or even appear to apply sanctions against them without sparking an outcry from their supporters or from neutral observers concerned with hearing both sides of the argument. Their audience and/or supporters come from within the scientific community. They share the values of free flow of information and are offended by attempts at censorship. This freemasonry of scientists will lend support to its own when they are attacked by "administrators." A third reason for Tamplin and Gofman's immunity from AEC pressure is that their jobs are tenured. They cannot be fired for advocating a particular position.

In the past the AEC was less willing to tolerate dissent. In 1954 it revoked Robert J. Oppenheimer's security clearance. Oppenheimer was the leader of the Los Alamos research team that built the first atomic bomb during the war and a professor of nuclear physics at Princeton University, but he offended the AEC headquarters for unnamed reasons. Because atomic science was so secretive, revoking his clearance cut Oppenheimer off from any significant research. He became a pariah to the AEC. Though in 1963, at the instigation of President Kennedy, the AEC rescued him from disgrace by presenting him with the Fermi Award at a White House dinner, Oppenheimer's ultimate vindication could not recompense him for the years of lost access to ongoing research.

When scientists disagree, who is right? This is the insoluble problem that the controversy over radiation safety presents. Sternglass claims radioactive pollution kills 400,000 babies. Tamplin and Gofman claim 400. Ralph Lapp, a Washington based "consulting physicist," claims only 4. Each expert attacks the others' statistics, asserting that only his are correct. For the nonscientist in the AEC, Congress, or the public, this presents a dilemma. If he must make a decision what is the basis? He can go with the weight of the evidence. He can choose the average or the conservative estimate. Nuclear reactors now under construction emit only 1 percent of the AEC allowed level of radiation. Is this a safe, conservative strategy or one aimed more at public relations? The utilities believe it is better to pour a few tons more concrete as a safety shield than to have their application for an operating license delayed. The nonexpert can accept the advice of an expert he knows personally even though that friend may not be particularly informed on the specific issue. During World War II Prime Minister Churchill leaned heavily on A. F. Lindemann (later Viscount Cherwell) for scientific advice though in retrospect, and even at the time, Lindemann's schemes often proved unworkable.[13] The decision maker can listen to the counsel of an expert who shares a similar ideological bent. During the height of the Cold War the Eisenhower Administration preferred to seek its advice on atomic energy from the hawkish Dr. Edward Teller, the "father of the H-bomb," than from the more dovish Robert Oppenheimer, the "father of the A-bomb." When Sternglass first raised his charges that radiation was causing death, the AEC assigned Tamplin and Gofman the job of refuting his research, not evaluating it. After their analysis convinced the two scientists of the basic dangers of nuclear power plants, the AEC refused to accept their conclusions. It sought evidence more compatible with its own bureaucratic ideology.[14]

Two alternatives remain for the nonexpert decision maker. He can acquire the expertise or he can abdicate responsibility. If the decision maker is the President of the United States, educating himself in the intricacies of nuclear physics is probably unrealistic. The superficial knowledge he might gain would be only the verisimilitude of what he really needed to know. If, however, the decision maker is a congressman on the Joint Committee on Atomic Energy or a nonexpert member of the Atomic Energy Commission, acquiring the expertise is logical. JCAE and AEC members serve for many years, have comparatively few other responsibilities, and are frequently called upon to utilize their expertise. After a few years' service a congressman or a commissioner can learn enough to understand much of the technical information he confronts. The opposite alternative of abdicating responsibility for expertise is logical for one charged with a duty he wishes to avoid. Congressmen interested primarily in their constituents or in other committee assignments find acquiring expertise an inefficient use of their scarce time. The abdication may be partial. They devote their JCAE effort to issues like land acquisition, commercial purchasing, or security clearances, which are not technical, while avoiding issues like radiation standards, research plans, or thermal pollution, which are. The problem with completely abdicating responsibility for making technical decisions is that it may not be legal. The Atomic Energy Act and other laws on the federal and state level often fix responsibility explicitly with the President or the AEC or the state governor. The best strategy for the decision maker seeking to duck responsibility is to assign the task to a special committee. The President has the AEC. The AEC in turn has its Advisory Committee on Reactor Safeguards and Atomic Safety and Licensing Boards. The Maryland governor, to cite an example from the state level, appointed a seventeen-member Task Force on Nuclear Power Plants in 1969, when ecologists became agitated about the Calvert Cliffs nuclear station. This solved the political problem, though not necessarily the technical one.

In addition to the legally allowed level of thermal and radiation pollution that the Calvert Cliffs plant daily spews into the Chesapeake Bay, the used atomic fuel must routinely be disposed of. Once a year this (or any other) reactor shuts down to remove and replace the depleted uranium. The used fuel rods are immensely more radioactive than when they were new a year before. Remotely controlled mechanisms handle the uranium behind thick shields. The "hot" rods are placed in water vats to cool for a year. The rods then go by truck in heavy lead caskets to a reprocessing plant, which extracts the uranium and plutonium for reuse. Yet not all can be recycled. Disposal of the radioactive wastes stymied the AEC. After some years the agency had 80 million gallons stored "temporarily" in metal tanks under ground. As a permanent solution the commission decided to bury the wastes a thousand feet under the surface in an abandoned salt mine. Once buried in a pit in the floor of the mine the heat from the radioactivity would melt the salt to form a permanent seal around the container. Unfortunately the Kansas salt mine the AEC picked for the Federal Waste Repository turned out to be one of the few wet salt mines in America. Rather than seal the tanks, the mine would have corroded them, allowing the radiation to escape. Robert J. Dole, senator from Kansas and chairman of the Republican National Committee, moved to block the AEC plan, explaining sardonically that: "We're eager for new industry in Kansas but we have grave doubts about whether or not this is the type of industry we want."[15]

Public concern with the environment has influenced President Nixon's choice of AEC chairmen. In 1971 he appointed James Schlesinger to head the agency. Schlesinger was an economist then serving as assistant director of the President's Office of Management and Budget. He came to the OMB to oversee the Pentagon budget because of his previous research on nuclear proliferation. Once at the OMB he branched out to include the responsibility for environmental funds as well. This sprang from his lifelong hobby of bird watching. His expertise in budgets, atomic weapons, and the environment seemed to Nixon to be the perfect combination for the AEC. He stayed only a year and a half, however, for Nixon named him first director of the Central Intelligence Agency and then Secretary of Defense in rapid succession.

To succeed him the President picked a woman marine biologist, Dixy Lee Ray. Dr. Ray was already a member of the commission when elevated to the chairmanship. She came with no particular expertise in physics but a strong concern for ecology. Her nomination symbolized the administration's desire to satisfy demands both for a clean environment and for advancement for women. Some observers charged that the appointment was little more than symbolism, that Nixon, who has not been notably devoted to either protecting the environment or advancing women, saw an easy way to throw a sop to both groups in making this unconventional choice. Dr. Ray's life-style was as unconventional as her appointment. She first lived in a mobile home parked near the agency's headquarters in Germantown, Maryland, but moved after neighbors complained she was lowering property values. Her two dogs, a poodle and a Scottish deerhound, accompanied her to her office, which is decorated with artifacts of the Kuakiutl Indian tribe of which she is an honorary member.

In their concern with the environment the two Nixon appointees reflect the contemporary political milieu just as have their predecessors. Truman named David Lilienthal to be the first chairman of the commission in 1946 because of his New Deal ideology and his administrative skill. Lilienthal had served as TVA board member and chairman for 13 years, proving his ability to run a massive and innovative federal project. Some of Lilienthal's problems as AEC chairman stemmed from applying TVA methods. The Republican majority of the joint committee during the 80th Congress was anxious to discredit the New Deal. Attacking Lilienthal seemed to be a good way. The new chairman became particularly vulnerable when he tried to apply some of TVA's penchant for free and open discussion to nuclear issues. The joint committee attacked him for lax security. The second chairman, Gordon Dean, likewise was an administrator and a lawyer. Since the agency was more established and the Republicans no longer in control of Congress, his job was easier.

Eisenhower continued the tradition of appointing administrators. His first chairman was Lewis Strauss, a New York financier and old friend of Herbert Hoover, who went into atomic energy affairs via wartime service as an officer in the Naval

Reserve. Truman had appointed Strauss as a commissioner to serve under Lilienthal in 1946. The citizen-admiral's chief concern in his term as a regular commissioner was national security. He urged the United States to launch a crash program to develop an H-bomb, opposed exporting radioactive isotopes to Norway for research, and took a hard line on internal security clearances. As such he was a prime candidate for the new Republican administration. In the election campaign Eisenhower had pledged a firm stand on national security. The H-bomb fit in with Secretary of State John Foster Dulles' brinksmanship and Secretary of Defense Charles E. Wilson's "more bang for the buck." Strauss's tough stance on internal security pleased the party's right wing, which applauded Senator Joe McCarthy's anti-Communist crusade. The issue of the AEC's role in supplying power for civilian use came up during Strauss's tenure. The admiral had little interest in advancing the reactor program, preferring to concern himself with weaponry. President Eisenhower rewarded Strauss for his AEC service by appointing him Secretary of Commerce. But his curt manner and unwillingness to admit he had ever made a mistake alienated key senators, so he could never secure confirmation and had to give up that post. Eisenhower's second AEC chairman was a more diplomatic version of Strauss. John A. McCone was a Los Angeles businessman. He had no expertise in nuclear energy but was able to restore a smooth working relationship with the joint committee senators who had taken their revenge on the AEC by blocking Strauss's confirmation as Secretary of Commerce.

President Kennedy broke the tradition of choosing an administrator as AEC chairman by naming a scientist. Glenn Seaborg was a superstar. At the age of 28 he discovered plutonium, then went on to discover eight other transuranium elements. For this he won the Nobel Prize in 1959. When Kennedy persuaded him to be chairman of the AEC he was Chancellor of the University of California at Berkeley. When reporters asked him how a scientist would do heading a major federal agency he said that "it might be easier to let a capable scientist learn political reality than to teach a politician science." Seaborg typified the dominant position of science during the 1960's. Scientists were the men who could get things done, physicists more than others. They could build bombs to defend the country or launch rockets to orbit the earth. Biomedical researchers seemed nearly as potent. Given enough money they could cure disease and transplant hearts. Some even believed that social scientists could stop riots in the cities and bring world peace. The vision of the future was one of scientific omnipotence. Given enough resources massive federal agencies could mobilize technology to solve any problem. TVA revitalized the Tennessee Valley. The wartime Manhattan Project built an A-bomb. The AEC built an H-bomb and developed reactors to provide electricity. NASA landed men on the moon.

By the end of the 1960's, however, the federal government's faith in technology waned. When Seaborg ran for election as president of the American Association for the Advancement of Science in 1970 many members opposed him because of the AEC's callous disregard of the environment. They charged that the A.A.A.S.'s responsibility was to remain neutral and objective, not to blindly promote government projects. When Seaborg left the AEC the following year Nixon took stock of these criticisms and appointed the ecology-minded Schlesinger to succeed him. His successor in turn, Dixy Lee Ray, while a scientist, is a biologist rather than a physicist.

As Dr. Ray looks to the future she faces the tribulations of two new methods of producing nuclear power. Both present formidable problems. For the first, it is radiation pollution; for the second, it is practicality. Yet both present hope for virtually limitless fuel supplies.

The first of the two methods in terms of the readiness of its technology is the "fast breeder" reactor. "Fast" refers to the process that utilizes neutrons traveling at fast speeds in contrast to the conventional process that slows them down for better control. "Breeder" refers to the fact that as the reactor burns its uranium 238 (or thorium-232) fuel it produces ("breeds") fissionable plutonium-238 (or uranium-233) along with the energy used to generate electricity. This new fuel can then be burned in the same or other reactors to release more energy. The breeder reactors' implications for safety and the environment are mixed. They release less waste heat and radiation. But the fission products they produce are lethal, and the AEC has yet to come up with an adequate means of eventually disposing of them. Its ineptness to date in disposition of spent fuel offers little hope. The temporary measures and abortive plan for burial in a Kansas salt mine can be tolerated as long as the amount is small, but once breeder reactors come into use the quantity of deadly waste will grow exponentially.[16]

While breeder reactors will come into use about 1980, the second method is still far from practical. This is the fusion process, which will literally burn water. Deuterium, the heavy isotope of hydrogen, can be extracted easily and cheaply from water. The potential energy of the deuterium from a gallon of water equals the energy of 300 gallons of gasoline. This is the fuel of the sun and the hydrogen bomb. The scientists' problem is how to harness it in small quantities, since the hydrogen "fire" is so hot it would burn through any container. The answer seems to be to hold it with magnetic force rather than a physical vessel. The AEC now believes fusion to be practical within two to three decades. Once, and of course *if*, this happens man will have cheap and abundant energy. It appears as well that this form of energy avoids the risks of pollution that the breeder reactors present. Until the fusion millennium arrives, however, the AEC must confront the present realities of generating electricity with fission reactors.[17]

The fact that the nuclear reactor produces power in the form of electricity suggests that the two energy arenas share many physical and political characteristics. They do, of course, but not as many as the commonality of their output might connote. Once the nuclear power plant generates the electricity it is regulated much as the electricity generated by fossil fuel plants. The Atomic Energy Act of 1954 does, however, direct specifically that all nuclear produced electricity come under the jurisdiction of the Federal Power Commission. Fossil fuel output would escape FPC regulation if it did not enter interstate commerce. Yet prior to generating the electricity the two types of production are treated much differently.

Nuclear power has shared fully in the contention between the advocates of public power and the advocates of private power. The battles of the 1930's over the New York State Power Authority, the Tennessee Valley Authority, the Rural Electrification Administration, and the rest re-echoed in the 1950's. Public power zealots argued that nuclear power should be public power because it began that way. The confiscation of the property of existing private utilities and the competition with them that had raised the ire of Wendell Willkie of the Commonwealth and Southern Company were not an issue. The federal government had a monopoly on nuclear power; let it remain that way. While the public versus private battle recurred, the outcome merely perpetuated the status quo. As noted earlier, the Atomic Energy Act extended the same division of the spoils for nuclear power as existed for nonnuclear power. The basic system would be private utilities subject to FPC regulation and including the preferences for public, municipal, or cooperative distributors that the New Deal wrote into law during the 1930's. The public power advocates' concept of a yardstick by which to measure the efficiency of private power fell by the wayside, largely because the pricing for nuclear plants never became realistic. The AEC began subsidizing civilian reactors in an attempt to gain experience through the actual operation of demonstration plants. A chief lesson learned from these was that nuclear plants were not competitive, so the AEC continued to subsidize the plants because it by then had the mission of promoting nuclear power whether or not it was efficient. Although the commission is no longer authorized by Congress to subsidize the private utilities directly, it effectively does so by supplying them with uranium and plutonium at an artificially low price, by recycling used fuel, by disposing of radioactive wastes, and by funding research.

The problems of finding suitable sites for generating stations are similar whether the fuel is fossil or atomic. While the electricity produced is clean, the power plant is dirty. One type pollutes its environment with smoke and dust, the other with hot water and radiation. States such as Maryland and Minnesota that have established procedures for official site selection include both types of plants in the same legislation. This is not so at the federal level. Nuclear plants must undergo an extensive AEC evaluation procedure. No comparable appraisal exists for fossil fuel plants. As a consequence a utility may choose to build the latter type because the licensing procedure is simpler; the plans must undergo only state scrutiny, not the elaborate federal examination. For plant construction to fall behind schedule can impose ruinous costs on a utility. And virtually all nuclear plants built in the United States have fallen behind schedule. Public objections can block the builder's timetable. Delays at the final stage are the most costly. If the AEC will not issue an operating license once the plant is finished (the last hurdle of the evaluation process), the postponement will cost the company thousands of dollars a day. In some cases intervenors at hearings for the operating license have argued, with some success in postponing plant openings, that the facility should never have been started. Even if true the proper place for such an argument would be at an early hearing before the construction begins. The intervenors counter, however, that the utility companies are so secretive about their plans that they do not learn of the generating station until the AEC issues the construction license. Utilities caught at the last minute have proved vulnerable to intervenor demands for modifications to assure less pollution or more safeguards. The wise intervenor seeks such changes rather than ultimately wasting his efforts by completely opposing the nearly finished facility. While environmentalist opposition increasingly is heard, the chief reason the nuclear reactors are behind schedule is delay in delivering equipment. Only a few companies manufacture the equipment and many cannot meet their delivery dates. The single company that supplies all the boilers for the reactors is one to two years behind schedule. Delays, whether from opposition to granting a license or nonavailability of equipment, raise the cost of the nuclear alternative. Utility companies, therefore, tend to opt for fossil fuel plants.

The nuclear arena is unmatched in the extent to which its politics derives from the physical properties of the fuel. Indeed, the physicist has often dominated the politician in deciding policy issues.

The fuel's unique property of exploding with cataclysmic might when it reaches the critical mass long dictated that its military role predominate. Only some years after the AEC was an established agency did it turn its attention to producing controlled energy for civilian use. Even this project had military origins, for the first successful reactor was developed for a Navy submarine. Concern that atomic fuel and technology from civilian reactors might be perverted to build bombs explains many policies. The chief argument for a complete government monopoly prior to 1951 was to prevent nuclear proliferation. Even after the AEC began to allow private industry participation, it maintained strict supervision. Power companies had to obey detailed regulations in their operations. The AEC retained legal title to the uranium fuel. Eisenhower set up the international Atoms for Peace program as a means to maintain American control of technology and material that could be used for weapons. The purpose was not to aid foreign nations but to keep them in line. In the face of growing world knowledge of nuclear physics the United States could no longer depend on ignorance to keep nuclear facilities out of the hands of heretofore nonnuclear nations. Hence it offered a bargain: the United States would share the technology and fuel if the other countries would abide by American safeguards against misuse.

At home as well as abroad esoteric knowledge of the physical properties of radioactive elements conferred political power. Since the AEC had a near monopoly of knowledge of nuclear energy, the agency could make decisions without outside participation. In its earliest stage even the commissioners and the members of the joint committee were so awed by the expertise of the scientists that they deferred to the General Advisory Committee led by Professor Robert Oppenheimer. As they later gained expertise of their own and as the GAC scientists proved to be fallible, the commissioners and the JCAE members asserted themselves. Even today much of the influence of the AEC and the JCAE derives from expertise as well as from the unique role given in the 1946 and 1954 legislation.

The physical properties of the fuel are particularly important in the face of the recent concern with environmental protection. Nuclear power is two-faced. It is clean insofar as it does not spew sulfur and ash into the air or spill crude oil into the water. Hence some see it as the environmental fuel of choice. But its pollution is all the more insidious. It is insidious because radioactivity is long-lived and its full consequences are still unknown. Radioactive wastes persist for many lifetimes, perhaps accumulating faster than they can be accommodated. And it is insidious because the pollution is lethal. The tiniest amounts can poison entire cities or disfigure generations. It is insidious because it is unpredictable. A nuclear power station is good for the environment until its boiler explodes, spreading fallout across a continent; or until its coolant fails and it melts down, burning a fiery pit into the ground. While all energy sources present risks, atomic fuel is more difficult to deal with because the probabilities of accidents are still unknown and the potential dangers are catastrophic.

In comparison to the properties of the fuel other variables pale in their power to explain the politics of the arena. Since uranium and other radioactive ores are widely distributed, geography plays but a small role. America's original dependence on ore from the Belgian Congo caused military strategists to develop domestic mines. The AEC paid artificially high prices to Colorado producers in order to develop the industry and thus stigmatized the miners, their children, and their mountains. Though less widespread, uranium spoil banks disfigure the Rockies much as coal spoil banks disfigure the Appalachians. In spite of this, uranium mining has never been a big enough industry to dominate the politics of a state. Only in Colorado has it been an issue at all.

Market forces were long ignored in the nuclear arena. Contrary to the rampant official optimism of the AEC and the joint committee, the atom did not become an economically viable fuel until the late 1960's. Even now it is competitive only because the AEC contributed over a quarter-century of research and development. Prior to the construction of Jersey Central Power and Light Company's Oyster Creek plant, all reactors had had some amount of federal subsidy. The rationale was that the facility was experimental or a demonstration, but the reality was that it was not competitive. This balance, however, is shifting rapidly in favor of nuclear power as rising prices for oil and natural gas change the cost equation.

Because of its recent invention, nuclear energy has experienced less change in its general political environment than have the other four forms of energy. The dominant issue shaping its development was national security, which has influenced it in a number of ways. The first was to retard its early emergence. The AEC's initial orientation was to support the military. Thus it concentrated on building bombs rather than generating electricity. Even when the AEC turned to research on reactors it was in order to develop a power plant for missile carrying submarines. The civilian applications were by-products of the military. National security dictated that the AEC maintain as strong a monopoly as possible. It was only with the greatest reluctance that the commission shared its expertise and fuel with private industries and with foreign governments. Throughout the 1950's the AEC used anti-Communism to justify policies ranging from Atoms for Peace to revoking Professor Oppenheimer's security clearance.

Although civilian nuclear power did not emerge until the 1950's it was still heir to the New Deal legacy. Since nuclear energy is transformed into electricity in order to give it a useful form, the industry fell partially into the pattern of the electrical industry. Many legal and institutional provisions were borrowed directly. Among these was the ritual polarization between public and private ownership. While the emergence of the atom heralded a new battle, the outcome echoed the old division of the spoils.

The transcending issue of protecting the environment has also penetrated the arena. While nuclear energy promised many advantages over conventional fuels, its opponents tended to be more strident and better armed. In recent years groups intervening to block construction have mounted formidable arrays of scientists to testify to the dangers of radioactivity and have taken advantage of new laws such as the National Environmental Policy Act of 1969.

By the mid-1970's the "energy crisis" itself had become an issue influencing the nuclear arena. While the basic problem was shortage of oil, the atomic arena felt the impact in several ways (besides the obvious one of changing market forces). Environmentalists lost public support and came to be viewed as obstructionists rather than protectors. The AEC gained in esteem, for if it could unlock the secret of fusion, could it not also unlock the secrets of solar, geothermal, wind and a host of other energies? If AEC technology could build bombs and reactors, could it not solve other technical problems? Hence the commission became the logical locus of energy research.

The outcome of the interaction of these various forces has been a highly regulated arena. The complex technology limits participation to a small elite composed of scientists and a few laymen who have mastered the requisite knowledge. Those few participants lacking expertise generally respond on the basis of ideological or emotional commitments to private (or public) ownership, environmentalism, anti-Communism, or faith in technology.

Notes

1. National Petroleum Council, *U.S. Energy Outlook* (Washington, D.C., 1972), p. 20; *Newsweek*, December 10, 1973, p. 137.

2. Harold P. Green and Alan Rosenthal, *Government of the Atom* (New York: Atherton, 1963), *passim*; Morgan Thomas, *Atomic Energy and Congress* (Ann Arbor: University of Michigan, 1956), *passim*.

3. Peter Metzger, *The Atomic Establishment* (New York: Simon and Schuster, 1972), *passim*.

4. Green and Rosenthal, *op. cit.*, p. 125.

5. Congressional Quarterly, *Congress and the Nation* (Washington, D.C., 1969), pp. 935—36.

6. *Ibid.*; Green and Rosenthal, *op. cit.*, p. 125; Philip Mullenbach, *Civilian Nuclear Power* (New York: Twentieth Century Fund, 1963), pp. 147—86.

7. Mullenbach, *op. cit.*, p. 285.

8. Metzger, *op. cit.*, pp. 115—44.

9. Sheldon Novik, *The Careless Atom* (Ann Arbor: University of Michigan, 1969), pp. 5—10.

10. *Ibid.*

11. *Ibid.*, p. 156.

12. Timothy Ingram, "Nuclear Hijacking: Now Within the Grasp of Any Lunatic," *Washington Monthly*, January 1973.

13. C.P. Snow, *Science and Government* (Cambridge, Mass.: Harvard, 1961), *passim*.

14. Ralph Lapp, "Four Fears," *The New York Times Magazine*, February 7, 1971.

15. *Ibid.*

16. Glenn T. Seaborg and William Corliss, *Man and the Atom* (New York: Dutton, 1971), p. 34; Federal Power Commission, *The 1970 National Power Survey*, Vol. IV, Ch. 1, pp. 65—69.

17. Seaborg and Corliss, *op. cit.*, p. 48.

7

Conclusion

Putting energy politics in perspective calls for more than an analysis of the five arenas based on the three-part model introduced in Chapter One. It calls for an evaluation of the model itself. Have the three sets of independent variables explained the dependent variables of policy outcome? Do different physical properties, market forces, and political environments elucidate the different politics in each area? Do similarities in inputs lead to similarities in policies? Which independent variables yield the most understanding and which yield the least? Is the model adequate to explain the complex politics of each form of energy, or is it too simplistic?

Evaluating the model's strengths and weaknesses requires reviewing a few key features of energy politics, classified this time not by industry, but according to the three major sets of independent variables. The following presentation will accent the conceptual framework, making the analytical categories stand out from the chronology. Otherwise the idiosyncratic history of each arena's politics may obscure the underlying themes common to all.

Physical characteristics of the fuel clearly do much to aid the analysis. That coal was easily mined by small enterprises using a simple technology led to its early exploitation. Easy entry into the industry meant that competition would be intense. The coal mine operator who paid his miners better wages would be driven out of business by his rival. The operator who restored his surface mine could not compete with the one who creamed the contours. Furthermore, coal mining is labor intensive—it requires a large number of workers in relation to its capital investment. In none of the other industries are the workers so important a component. Thus the physical properties of the fuel decreed that many should labor in the mines for low wages. This formula for oppression led toward the conflict and violence so typical of the coal arena.

Oil's underground pools and liquid state required a more advanced technology and greater capital investment for its production and transportation than did coal. In addition it had to be refined before it could be used. This meant a later development and larger corporations. Since entry was more difficult, the industry was less competitive. Less competition, combined with less need for labor, meant fewer and better-paid workers. Standard Oil, because its production was less labor intensive, could afford the Rockefeller Plan as the price of industrial peace.

The physical properties of the fuel are particularly useful in understanding the development of natural gas. First, because it is generally found with oil, its production shares many of the features of the oil industry such as the 22 percent depletion allowance and common ownership of the wells. Second, because until recently it could be transported economically only by pipe, its widespread use did not occur until the 1930's; and because it is a natural monopoly, it was a likely candidate for government regulation. Third, because it is burnable as it flows out of the ground it requires virtually no labor, hence no labor unions. Like oil and coal, natural gas deposits lie hidden underground. This makes assessing the value of these reserves a matter of speculation. Natural gas producers have used the unknowability of the reserves to frustrate the government's attempts to set prices.

The electric industry, in contrast, cannot hide behind the indeterminable value of its inputs to frustrate government regulation. Since it is easy to calculate an electric company's costs, regulatory commissions have less difficulty in setting rates to give "a fair return on capital." Because, like the natural gas industry, the electric industry must make a large capital investment in transmission and distribution, it too is a natural monopoly and in need of regulation. Since the industry is capital intensive rather than labor intensive and since the complex technology makes entry of competitors difficult, the industry employed few workers who would support the trade union movement.

Physicists did not unlock the secrets of the atom until the 1940's. Because the controlled nuclear power of the reactor was so closely related to the uncontrolled power of the bomb, civilian applications fell under many of the same processes as the military. Security dictated a tight government monopoly at first. When this was no longer viable, it was replaced by detailed AEC control. The esoteric knowledge required, combined with this AEC emphasis on security, confined participants in the arena to a small elite. Another physical property of the nuclear fuel is that it cannot be used directly but must be converted into electricity. This means that nuclear power shares many of the features of the electricity arena.

The physical variable of geography is less complex than that of the fuel's properties. The location of the fuel explains much of its politics. Coal fields underlie the Appalachian mountains so extensively that mining of that fuel dominates the politics of Pennsylvania, West Virginia, and Kentucky. While the nearness of these deposits to the major cities of the East and Midwest long made Appalachian coal cheaper, Montana and New Mexico are now subject to the scourge of mining. In a similar fashion geography decrees that Texas, Oklahoma, and Louisiana be oil states. Alaska and Florida are just now joining that elite group. The geographical pattern for natural gas roughly follows that of oil, but since gas is not as big an industry as its petroleum twin its location has less impact.

More important than the domestic location of petroleum is its international location. Worldwide, petroleum is scattered about unevenly. The largest and most cheaply exploitable sources lie about the Persian Gulf. The Arabs' political exploitation of this concentration in their boycott begun in October 1973 confounded the industrialized nations, which depended on oil imports. Europe and Japan were at the Arabs' mercy. The United States, which as Israel's protector was the prime target, fared better because its domestic sources were adequate for 80 percent of its needs. Yet the importance of the international dimension was inescapable.

Geography is less useful in understanding the politics of electricity. The key factor in siting a power plant is the location of the consumer rather than that of the primary fuel, unless that fuel is falling water. Hydroelectric generation is subject to the physical constraints of geography. In the past these constraints have led to development in the Pacific Northwest and in the Tennesee Valley. Today most of the suitable sites close to cities are in use, and future development will have to be in remote areas. Alaska, for instance, may become an ideal location for the manufacture of aluminum, since the process uses vast amounts of electricity.

Likewise nuclear power is little influenced by geography. Because the radioactive fuel is so concentrated, transportation is not a factor. Uranium mining is on the decline in Colorado because stockpiles are high and reactors are switching to plutonium.

Market forces, like physical characteristics, determine the politics of an energy arena. This has been the case for coal. From a high point in 1919, demand for coal began a long-term decline. World War II and the 1973-74 crisis brought only brief respites from this pattern. As a "sick industry" coal often displayed a corresponding political pathology. The decline in demand caused John L. Lewis to seek the intervention of the federal government.

Oil followed a different pattern. The boom and bust cycles up to about 1930 meant frequent alternation of sickness and health. The appeals for government intervention came during the busts when a field ran dry or when the opening of a rival field brought a decline in demand for the old field's crude. Producers at the booming, newly discovered source did not want regulation, of course, but the end result was the prorationing schemes of Texas, Oklahoma, and Louisiana backed up nationally by the Interstate Compact and the Hot Oil Act.

Market forces played less of a role in natural gas. Demand was high as cities like Detroit sought the natural fuel to replace their synthetic coal gas. But the monopolistic holding companies prevented a free market from ever emerging. The enactment of the 1935 and 1938 laws assigning regulation to the FPC and the SEC precluded market forces from operating from that time on. In spite of the FPC's everlasting economic analysis, the official prices have not reflected the true cost of production. The consequence has been a fuel priced unrealistically low. While this has been a boon to the consumer, it has fostered wastage and shortage. While electrical rates are also regulated there has been less distortion of the market.

Yet in both the gas and the electric industries the market has been the result of policy rather than the cause of it.

Because nuclear power is a source of electricity its market forces derive from the electrical arena. Although the electrical market is itself the product of government intervention, the federal government long chose to subsidize nuclear plants for symbolic or ideological reasons. Congressional Democrats urged federal support for atomic energy for reasons paralleling the Democratic support for hydroelectric power two decades earlier. Nuclear energy thus fell heir to the same polarization between public and private ownership.

While physical characteristics and market forces do much to shape the politics within an arena, transcending issues of the total political environment penetrate to influence policy as well. The political milieu at the time the fuel first comes into widespread use is of particular importance.

The legacy of the laissez faire era falls most strongly on the industries that emerged earliest. Coal and oil are privately owned at all levels from production through distribution. Since natural gas flows from the same wells as crude oil, production is private even though the fuel did not come into widespread use until the political environment had changed. The private sector of the electrical industry traces back to the laissez faire era as well.

The reform movement of the early twentieth century had its impact on energy politics. In the coal industry it brought the beginning of federal intervention on behalf of the workingman. In oil it took the form of trust-busting, the most notable example of which was the dissolution of the old Standard Oil Company, a court decision so far-reaching that in 1971, when the Jersey Standard successor of the old "S.O." sought a new brand name, it was still forbidden to use "Esso" nationwide and had to settle for "Exxon." In the electricity industry the reform era left a legacy of state and local regulatory commissions and, in some cases, municipal ownership.

Mobilization for World War I had its greatest impact on oil, for it reversed the federal policy of promoting competition. The U.S. Fuel Administration's coordination of the industry laid the groundwork for cozy cooperation between the producers and the government. War mobilization had less of an impact on coal since the industry was already well developed and there had been no prior policy of trust-busting. Federal intervention reinforced the ongoing policies. Though unrecognized at the time, President Wilson's decision to build a dam at Muscle Shoals to generate electricity to manufacture nitrates for explosives was to have far-reaching influence.

Of all the political environments whose influence penetrated the various energy arenas none was so pervasive as the New Deal. For those well-established fuels whose political arrangements were already set, the 1930's were a period of consolidating existing patterns and beginning some new ones. For those fuels just emerging it was a more critical period of structuring the arena's politics *de novo*. Even for nuclear power, an arena not yet in existence, the New Deal was to shape the mold in which it would be cast.

The Roosevelt Administration was a high point for the United Mine Workers. Labor found a friend in the White House, an ally in the Labor Department, and a home in the Democratic party. Congress sought to stabilize the market in passing the National Industrial Recovery Act and later the Guffy Coal Act. For the oil industry as well this was a period of consolidating past gains and stablizing the market through government intervention. But since oil had followed a different course, the beneficiaries were the owners rather than the workers.

The New Deal's impact was greater on natural gas and electricity. The politics of coal and oil were already seasoned and hence less mutable. But natural gas was completely new and electricity partially new, and hence both were vulnerable to change. The political history of gas is short and simple. It emerged in the 1930's, ran head-on into the New Deal, and has been subject to detailed federal control ever since. Electricity's story is more complex. Steam-generated electricity has a history dating back into the nineteeth century and is thus more like coal and oil. Water-generated electricity resembles natural gas. It emerged in the 1930's as a New Deal answer to economic depression and has fallen under the federal government's aegis ever since. Rural electrification followed a corresponding course. One remarkable feature of the political environment of electricity has been its symbolic role. Franklin Roosevelt identified himself closely with public electrical power as a panacea. In 1940 Wendell Willkie used his opposition to public electricity to win the Republican nomination to run against Roosevelt. After Roosevelt's death, Democrats continued to rally around public electrical power. It was in this way that the political environment of the New Deal structured the politics of nuclear energy.

Compared to the First, the Second World War had relatively little impact on energy politics. The postwar concern with national security had a far greater effect. Texas oil men justified the oil import quota system on these grounds. The Senate refused Leland Olds a third term on the FPC in the name of anti-Communism. Republicans opposed TVA as "creeping socialism." Because it emerged at this time and because of its relation to weaponry, nuclear power felt the strongest impact from the national security issue. The AEC deferred research on civilian applications while it moved forward on military applications. The commission restricted access to nuclear fuels and technology to preserve American control.

By the late 1960's national security no longer so dominated the political environment. The new issue was protecting the natural environment. For coal this meant that strip mining and sulfur emissions came under attack. For oil it was spills and nitrogen oxide. Siting a steam or nuclear electric plant became a major confrontation between the power company and the environmentalists. As the only nonpolluting fuel, natural gas enjoyed a surge of popularity. But FPC regulations meant that the price system was incapable of properly allocating that scarce resource.

Environmental protection was scarcely installed as the dominant issue in national politics when it gave way to the "energy crisis." A country long accustomed to profligate use of power suddenly came to the stark realization that plentiful supplies of power at low cost were at an end. Electrical blackouts and natural gas shortages heralded the crisis, but the central problem was oil. While sharply increasing its demands for gasoline, jet fuel, heating oil, and fuel for electrical generating plants, the United States confronted rising prices for imported crude and a shortage of refining capacity.

Then in October 1973 the Arab boycott began. All forms of energy felt the political effects. In their scramble for fuel Americans seemed willing to abandon such policies as environmental protection, low prices for consumers, and support for friends abroad. Congress hastily approved the Alaska pipeline. The Interior Department allowed drilling to resume in the Santa Barbara Channel and leased new fields off the Florida coast. It prepared to open public lands in the West to strip mining and the outer continental shelf to drilling. The FPC hastened to deregulate the well-head price of natural gas. The U.S. Environmental Protection Agency suspended clean air standards. President Nixon proposed a plan for converting electrical power plants to coal. The crisis even weakened America's longstanding commitment to Israel, the foreign policy change that was the specific aim of the Arab boycott.

The foremost methodological conclusion to emerge from this restructuring according to the three sets of independent variables is that the original model presented in Chapter 1, while basically accurate and useful, was too simplistic. It did not deal adequately with the complexities of politics within each arena. Simplicity in itself is not a liability; indeed it should be considered an asset. Analysis may be viewed as the process of simplifying the complex to a point at which it becomes intellectually manageable. Yet the process may go too far. An analytical model should not be simplified to the extent that it loses the capability for explanation. Since the original model is too simple, it needs to be elaborated upon in order better to explain the political outcome.

The model needs elaboration first to take into account the extent to which the fuel's physical characteristics influence both the market forces and the general political environment to which the industry will be subject. Of these two, the way in which the fuel's physical characteristics determine the political environment is clearest because the time the fuel first emerges is critical. Fuels that required the simplest technology for their exploitation emerged earliest. Hence coal, oil, and steam-generated electricity trace many of their political features to the laissez faire policies of the nineteenth century. In contrast natural gas and hydroelectric power are subject to FPC jurisdiction because their physical properties required a technology not available on a large scale until the 1930's, at which time the political environment was much different. The physical properties of the uranium nucleus confounded scientists with problems insoluble until the 1940's and 1950's, thus giving birth to a new industry in a political environment dominated by the Cold War (and with a lingering spirit of the New Deal).

The indirect influence of fuel's physical properties on its politics via transcending issues from the overall political environment has its counterpart in the indirect influences via market forces. The market represents the equilibrium between supply and demand, and the physical characteristics of the fuel do much to determine the supply (but not the demand, which is determined by consumer preference). Production, transportation, refining (if necessary), and distribution all depend on the fuel's properties and location. Appalachian coal's proximity to eastern cities long gave it a competitive advantage. But its high sulfur content today makes it less valuable since it cannot meet new antipollution standards. Natural gas's low energy value for its volume made it unavailable to northern cities until pipeline transmission became practical. Physical properties structure the market in ways other than supply. Economies of scale determine the size of firms and hence the degree of competition. At all levels of the coal industry small operators can enter the market and compete successfully. Thus there is no need to regulate on behalf of the consumer but a great need to regulate the external costs. Because the market is so competitive, firms have a strong incentive to let others bear the burden of the scarred landscape, sick miners, and polluted air. Oil demands larger operations, hence it is less competitive but also less likely to impose external costs. Natural gas and electricity require large-scale operations in order to bring down costs. The large amounts of capital needed especially for transmission and distribution make entry of a new firm nearly impossible. Since these natural monopolies are noncompetitive, government needs to regulate them to protect the consumer. It finds less need to guard against externalities. Since water and nuclear-generated electricity require the greatest capital investment, government ownership is most appropriate.

Even after this tracing of the indirect influence of the physical variables via market forces or the political environment, the model remains too simplistic. This is because the politics of an arena often structures the market. Natural gas furnishes the most vivid example. Since 1938 FPC regulation under the provisions of the Natural Gas Act has determined price. The consequence has been a greatly distorted market. The price was about half what it would have been on a free market. While this gave cheap fuel to a few consumers, it caused wastage and shortage. It also gave natural gas companies an incentive to thwart the FPC through endless litigation, false reporting of reserves, and lobbying in Congress. Although electricity is subject to similar regulation by the FPC and state commissions, the more easily calculated inputs have kept electricity rates closer to an optimal distribution, which in turn lessens the utilities' incentive to sabotage the process. Nuclear energy, as a source of electricity, takes its structure from the electricity market as determined by the FPC.

The role of politics in determining oil market forces is the most byzantine of all. Governmental policies distort the free market by (1) regulation and (2) toleration of externalities. Government regulation is a well-known phenomenon. State, federal, and foreign governments all intervene to distort the market forces. From 1959 to 1973 the import quota system split the market into two tiers, with domestic crude costing about $3.00 per barrel and imported crude costing about $1.50 per barrel for those possessing a quota licensing them to buy it. The import fee, which replaced the quota, aimed to phase out gradually the two tiers and bring about a unified market. But events were to be otherwise. The Arab boycott, "leakage" from abroad, and the Federal Energy Office's allocations fragmented the market. The intervention of many governments further destabilized the market. This economic chaos in turn made itself felt in the policy process as panic and haste led to political confusion.

Toleration of externalities is a less widely recognized means of government's distorting the market. Until recently there has been little doubt that the right to pollute outweighed the right to a clean environment and that the right to profit outweighed the right to health. Electric power plants could spew forth ash and sulfur. Strip mine operators could leave the spoil to deface the landscape, and uranium companies had no responsibility for radon-induced cancer. This violates the conditions of a pure market system, for in such a system each firm must bear its full costs in order for prices correctly to reflect the true costs. If the government allows a firm to externalize its costs, its product will be artificially cheap, and resources will not be optimally allocated.

While the political process often influences the market, as illustrated by the foregoing examples, only rarely does the political style of a single arena feed back to influence the overall political environment. The chief instance of this phenomenon was the impact of electrical policy. Roosevelt's advocacy of public power did much to shape the New Deal. It brought about federal participation in areas of the economy theretofore considered the province of private business. Reaction against it brought the Grand Old Party under the sway of eastern liberals from 1940 to 1960. During the 1950's it gave Democrats a shibboleth, and structured the nuclear arena.

A second instance of the political process of an arena influencing the overall political environment is less direct. There was feedback from the politics of coal insofar as John L. Lewis and the United Mine Workers furnished leadership to the labor movement. The coal miners' role in founding the C.I.O. and in leading the massive shift of workingmen into the Democratic party had an impact extending well beyond the coal industry.

Although the interrelations among the major sets of variables could be elaborated upon endlessly, the foregoing discussion serves to suggest the chief revisions needed in order to make the original model more useful (see Figure 2). The changes involve the indirect influence of the fuel's physical characteristics and the feedback of the arena's politics. Physical characteristics on one hand determine supply and economies of scale, thus influencing the market, and on the other hand determine the time at which a fuel will emerge and thus the general political environment to which it will be subject. In some arenas the political process in-

Figure 2
Revised Conceptual Scheme

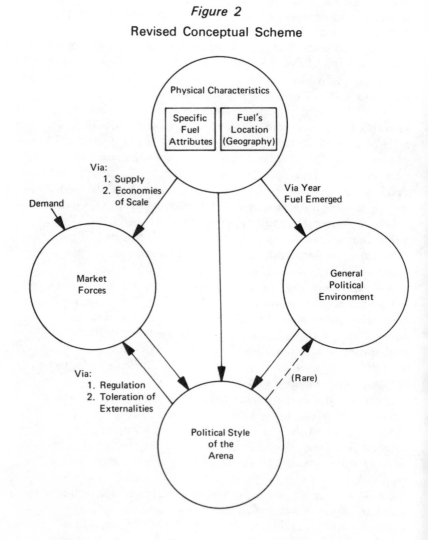

volves extensive government regulation and toleration of externalities which distort the operation of market forces. More rarely
there is feedback from the arena's own political process that influences the general political environment.

Revising the original analytical model suggests that it deserves
further testing. A fuel antedating even coal was wood. Do the particular physical properties, market forces, and political environment affecting firewood give it a distinctive political style? While in
the United States this is a challenging but passé exercise, it does
have relevance elsewhere. In South Korea, for example, firewood is
a political issue. Due to the Japanese occupation and the 1950–53
war the country is barren of forests at the same time that demand is
high for firewood. The consequence is that the government
carefully regulates tree-cutting.

Closer to home, natural resources other than fuels offer appropriate cases with which to test the analytical model. Metals
often have distinctive political arenas. Looming shortages of
copper foretell its possible politization. Silver and gold have been
political issues for so long that they are scarcely viewed as metals
any more. In 1896 William Jennings Bryan won the Democratic
presidential nomination because of his policy on one of these
metals, and throughout the 1960's General Charles de Gaulle
shook the international system because of his policy on the other.
The politics of timber, water, and land itself may prove amenable
to analysis starting with this model. Beyond the realm of natural
resources it may prove less satisfactory.

Some recent developments suggest that the division of energy
politics into separate arenas may be ending; the five arenas show
signs of converging. One indication is that the recent crisis is
viewed as an *energy* crisis, not an oil crisis or an electrical crisis.
Observers on all levels stress the interrelationships among the
various fuels. President Nixon sent Congress a series of *energy*
messages. The National Petroleum Council published a report on
the *U.S. Energy Outlook*. The same tendency to examine the subject as a single arena appears as well in newspapers, journals, and
books.

Convergence of the arenas also has appeared in the attempted
reorganization of political institutions. The Johnson Administra-

tion suggested that a Department of National Resources be established. The Nixon Administration attempted in 1971 to merge Interior with Agriculture and assorted other agencies. The farm lobby blocked that when the legislation went to Congress. Farmers did not want their captive department diluted with conservationists from Interior. In January 1973 Nixon tried to accomplish by executive order what he could not accomplish by legislation. He named the Secretary of Agriculture to serve as a presidential "counselor" to oversee natural resources affairs. Widespread opposition from environmentalists, combined with the President's general vulnerability from the disclosures of the Watergate investigations, aborted that scheme within six months.

The Nixon Administration's most comprehensive reorganization plan came in June 1973. The President proposed to create a Department of Energy and Natural Resources, an Energy Research and Development Administration, and a Nuclear Energy Commission. The core of the proposed department was to be the old Interior Department. The natural resources additions would include the U.S. Forest Service from Agriculture and the National Oceanographic and Atmospheric Administration (NOAA) from Commerce. To supplement Interior's traditional energy-related divisions, the new department would include the civilian functions of the Corps of Engineers and the Atomic Energy Commission (minus its licensing and regulatory functions). The new Nuclear Energy Commission would have these last responsibilites, thus meeting the criticism of the present AEC that the agency can not be trusted to license and regulate reactors because it is also charged to develop and promote the use of nuclear power. The Energy Research and Development Administration would aim at a wide range of new technological advances. It would inherit R&D divisions of the old Interior Department (such as the Office of Coal Research) and of the AEC, and would seek more exotic energy such as that from wind, tidal, geothermal, and solar sources. In the past such merger proposals have seldom succeeded. The Agriculture Department has held on to the Forest Service despite earlier attempts to transfer it. The Corps of Engineers' close ties with Congress precluded any shift not wanted by that highly autonomous agency. The AEC was not eager to be split three ways.

Similarly, Interior resisted giving up any divisions. NOAA, as a new and frequently reorganized agency, was the most vulnerable.

Bureaucratic, congressional, and interest group inertia frustrated the administration's reorganization scheme. To circumvent the immutable status quo President Nixon created a temporary Federal Energy Office by executive order in December 1973. Once Congress acted this was to become a permanent Federal Energy Administration and become a constituent division of the future Department of Energy and Natural Resources.

To head the new FEO Nixon appointed William Simon, the Deputy Secretary of the Treasury. Simon became the nation's fifth "energy czar" of the year. Until the previous January, General George A. Lincoln, director of the White House Office of Emergency Planning had had the responsibility. As early as the spring of 1972 General Lincoln had warned of an imminent shortage of oil but had found few receptive to his bad news, for the re-election effort made campaign strategy and fund raising primary. It was no time for doomsaying or threatening to upset the intimate relationship with the oil industry. In January, General Lincoln retired, and the OEP was abolished. Having tried an Army general, the President next appointed a diplomat as his special advisor. James E. Atkins was a State Department specialist on the Middle East. Atkins argued that the United States should take the Arabs' threats seriously and institute drastic measures to conserve fuel and build up inventories. His reward was reassignment to the State Department. The year's third energy advisor was Charles J. DiBona, a systems analyst who gave hope of bringing the magic of the computer to bear on the problem. DiBona's numbers, however, showed a looming shortage of oil. Obviously the President needed a man capable of transcending statistics with an understanding of the political questions involved. Thus in midsummer Nixon appointed Governor John Love of Colorado to become DiBona's boss. Governor Love would be a true "czar," able to apply both his political expertise and his political prestige to solving the problems that had confounded those less experienced in the real world of practical politics. But the governor fared little better than the general, the diplomat, and the systems analyst who had preceded him. His warnings, based on projections of a diminishing supply and a growing demand, found no more welcome than had those of his predecessors. Love complained that while he had the sobriquet of "energy czar," he in fact lacked both the staff and authority to cope with his assigned responsibility. Nixon showed no interest in supporting the governor or even listening to his advice. Worse than lack of manpower and access to the President, in the fall of 1973 Love faced a rival center of power in the Treasury. Under-Secretary Simon headed an interdepartmental committee on oil policy. With less responsibility and more manpower, the Treasury staff grew in influence as the energy crisis worsened. Simon's proposals meshed with Nixon's, whereas Love's did not. Love had issued gloomy predictions of a serious, long-term shortage at a time when the President was belittling it as temporary. The governor proposed gasoline rationing, which went counter to Nixon's longstanding aversion dating back to his wartime service rationing tires. Simon, who himself viewed the shortage as serious and long-term, managed to muffle his alarmism and opposed rationing. Love's White House-based group quarreled with Simon's Treasury-based group, leading to a breakdown in cooperation. Meanwhile the Interior Department launched its own fuel allocation program under the directorship of a crusty Navy veteran, Vice Admiral Eli T. Reich, who brought 15 admirals, generals, captains, and colonels from the Pentagon to bring some military efficiency to Interior's new Office of Petroleum Allocation.

To end the chaos President Nixon in December named Simon to head the temporary Federal Energy Office. Governor Love, seeing little reason to pretend he had any remaining influence, resigned and flew back to Denver. The salty Admiral Reich was not so willing to quit. When the reorganization transferred his allocation office to the FEO, Reich resisted losing the power he enjoyed while nominally under the Interior Department umbrella. After checking that a face-saving job was available for him back in the Department of Defense, Simon fired the contentious admiral.

Simon's reward for bringing at least some order to the chaotic situation was appointment as Secretary of the Treasury in April 1974. His successor at FEO was John C. Sawhill, a 37-year-old economist with a background in finance and management who had been Simon's deputy. When the temporary FEO became the permanent FEA in July 1974, Sawhill became its first official Administrator.

The executive branch's unification of energy responsibility into a single agency had its counterpart in the legislative branch. The Nixon Administration's creation of a temporary Federal Energy Office in December 1973 was matched by Congress' debates on a series of laws designed to treat energy as a unified arena. Throughout the winter of 1973-74, the 93rd Congress debated emergency energy legislation and conducted hearings probing more deeply into the causes and cures of the crisis. Senator Henry Jackson seized leadership of the congressional advocates of a strong, united energy policy with a fervor seen as the beginning of a race for the 1976 Democratic nomination for President. Yet Jackson's central role in energy policy came from an established familiarity with the problem. As chairman of the Senate Interior Committee and an Atomic Energy subcommittee he had long sounded the alarm, urging the government to develop a unified policy on energy. Under Senator Jackson's leadership Congress passed and sent to the President the controversial Emergency Energy Act. The act contained broad authority for the President to ration gasoline, conserve oil, and reduce environmental safeguards. Its most disputed provision required a rollback of domestic crude oil prices to $5.25 per barrel. Chiefly because of that provision President Nixon vetoed the bill.

Though the wide-ranging Emergency Energy Act was dead, Congress continued to treat all aspects of energy in a unified fashion. In May 1974 it passed the Federal Energy Administration Act, which typified a number of piecemeal successors to the vetoed Jackson measure. Even though more limited in scope, these legislative proposals pointed toward convergence of all fuels into a single energy policy arena.

An additional force pointing toward convergence is the concentration of ownership among the energy-producing companies. The typical pattern is for an oil company to purchase a share of a coal company. The oil men see coal as the fuel with the greatest future. Oil reserves may soon give out, whereas coal will last hundreds of years. The oil companies gain a tax advantage since they can charge up to 50 percent of their oil depletion allowance against their coal production. A House subcommittee reported in 1971 that major oil companies controlled 30 percent of the coal reserves, 50 percent of the uranium reserves, and 72 percent of the natural gas reserves.[1] The economic implication of the trend toward consolidation is that competition among fuels will lessen. The political implications are that the various separate arenas will merge and that the oil companies' techniques of seeking and obtaining special benefits will spread to coal.

Yet while popular analysis, new institutions, emerging legislation, and business consolidation point toward the separated fuel arenas converging into a single energy arena, the trend is far from unobstructed. Indeed close analysis of recent events indicates that the five arenas are politically still highly independent of one another and that the "crisis" of the mid-1970's can be best understood in this context.

In political terms the situation is not so much an energy crisis as an oil crisis. The extent to which it is a coal, or natural gas, or electrical, or nuclear crisis is secondary to the central role of oil. While the oil crisis does have impact on the other fuels, it is chiefly via market forces. Shortage of oil means more demand for substitute fuels and to some extent this modifies their political milieu. But the key to the situation is oil.

The political centrality of oil shows in many ways. A stark example came just before Christmas 1973. On December 19, as Congress rushed to complete its first session, President Nixon publicly announced he would ask for legislation to deprive the oil companies of "windfall profits." Because the oil companies needed an incentive to produce more, the President's Cost of Living Council would allow the producers to raise the price of their crude even though it would be counter to the administration's anti-inflation program. But in the name of fairness the government would recover undeserved profits with what the President called an "Emergency Windfall Profits Tax." At first glance it seemed that President Nixon had rebuffed the oil industry's $5 million of campaign donations. Yet closer examination revealed that the proposal was really not a tax on windfall profits but a tax on crude oil prices. Furthermore the tax would not go fully into effect until 1977, whereas the producers would begin to enjoy their windfall profits at once.

Even this presidential sleight of hand was too much of a threat for the oil-state senators, as they showed when Congress debated the provision on December 22. They objected to any sort of windfall tax and also to provisions of the bill that would reveal statistics about the petroleum companies' reserves and refinery production to the Federal Trade Commission and the General Accounting Office. Senators beholden to the oil industry for campaign contributions began a filibuster that threatened to last until Christmas. Foreseeing defeat and anxious to adjourn for the holidays, the rest of the Senate yielded to the oil-state senators' demands. The House of Representatives, less beholden to oil contributors and more consumer oriented, thereupon defeated the emasculated Senate bill.

This legislative climax, however, was far from the end of the matter, for when Congress reconvened for the second session the problems were worse then ever. Diesel-short truck drivers blocked highways and demanded aid from the federal government. After snipers killed several truckers who were ignoring the strike, the governors of a dozen states mobilized their National Guard troops to restore order, thus recalling coal and oil field wars of the earlier days of the century. Meanwhile ordinary motorists waited two or three hours to buy a few gallons of gasoline. As an added insult the annual reports of the oil companies showed profits up as much as 60 percent. Exxon, for example, made profits of $2.5 billion, an increase of 59 percent over the previous year. With the federal government hesitant to act, the states took the initiative. To reduce panic Oregon instituted a system of selling gasoline to those with even-numbered license plates on even-numbered days of the month and to those with odd-numbered tags on odd days. While this was not a real rationing scheme because it did nothing to increase or allocate the supply, it did reduce public anxiety. The Oregon plan rapidly spread to other states that saw an advantage in having only one half of the citizens in a state of panic on a given day. Meanwhile in Washington the administration and the Congress grappled with various solutions and traded accusations as to who was to blame.

Thus in the mid-1970's the oil arena finds itself in an unsettled state characterized by much the same instability it displayed in the period prior to the New Deal. Many of the longstanding relationships dating back to that period and before are on the verge of change. So too are the more recent elaborations of the basic relationships such as the restrictions on imports. Oil politics stands on the threshold of basic reorderings comparable to those of natural gas and electricity in the 1930's and nuclear energy in the 1950's. On one hand public opinion endangers oil's privileged status. On the other the crisis offers the oil companies an opportunity to gain even more privileges such as access to public lands and off-shore sites, relief from environmental standards and antitrust laws, and subsidies in the form of government research and tax write-offs. That oil is already a well-established political arena suggests that the changes will not be as great as they might be for a newly emerging fuel. Yet the magnitude of the problem portends significant changes in oil politics.

The effect on the other arenas will be more modest. Since the so-called energy crisis is essentially an oil crisis, the other fuels will feel the impact primarily through market forces. Coal will become relatively cheaper even with "stack scrubbers" required to reduce air pollution. Increased demand for natural gas will reinforce the movement toward deregulation. Nuclear power plants will gain a competitive advantage. Inevitably, some of the new privileges and/or penalties destined for oil will spread more or less directly to the other arenas. Oil's twinship with natural gas suggests, for example, that if Congress requires producers to disclose publicly the level of their reserves of oil, it will also require them to disclose their reserves of gas. If Congress relaxes environmental safeguards for surface mining of shale to be crushed for its oil content, it will have to extend similar freedom to coal strip mining.

Another trend affecting energy politics in the future will be increased conflict between the need for energy and the need to protect the environment. The two goals are fundamentally incompatible. The advantages of coal aggravate the problem, since extracting and burning the fuel is more damaging to the environment than extracting and using oil, natural gas, or uranium. Yet high prices and diminishing supplies of these latter three fuels make coal the inevitable alternative for the future. The drift toward coal brings cries of alarm from the environmentalists. They warn of strip-mined land and polluted air. There are solutions, of course, but they are expensive. The coal can be deep mined at a cost 25 percent higher. Low sulfur coal can be mined instead of the high sulfur type. The degree to which the environmentalists will be able to impose these costs on the energy consumers, the industry, and the public depends on their political strength in passing laws. The coal consumer will not pay the higher price without coercion.

The other fuel of the future is nuclear. In spite of the radiation and thermal pollution it is a comparatively "clean" source of power. But the recent alarmism which argues that no nuclear plants should be built because they are all dangerous may force the utilities back upon the "dirty" and increasingly expensive conventional plants. Faced with the choice between "dirty" coal and relatively "clean" nuclear facilities, the environmentalists will have to accept the fact that they must compromise their pollution control and safety standards.

The choice, of course, is not entirely either/or. One environmentalist solution is to slow or stop the growth in energy consumption. Demand for electricity does not have to double every decade. The consumer does not need an 8,000-B.T.U. air conditioner and a 300-horsepower automobile. The "zeroists" propose that energy production level off at the present point. Further increases are superfluous. Indeed they may be dangerous, for mankind may be producing more waste heat than the earth's atmosphere can radiate, in which case the planet eventually will begin to warm up uncontrollably.

Those concerned with the earth's fate point out that man's quest for energy is not the only threat to the environment. The looming shortages of oil and gas are matched by the looming shortages of key metals. Known reserves of iron will last 72 years. Copper will last 38 years; zinc, 28 years; lead, 27 years; and bauxite, a mere 2 years.[2] These at least can be recycled. Coal and oil cannot. Yet even if new technology and recycling ameliorate the problem, the present rates of consumption cannot continue indefinitely. Extractive industry is by nature suicidal. The fate of scores of Appalachian ghost towns built in the coal boom gives warning of what can happen on a national scale, given enough time.

Science brought salvation many times in the past. Can it do so for the energy crisis? Insofar as new technology develops new means of production and increases the efficiency of old ones, the answer in the long run is "yes." The greatest hope at present lies with atomic energy. Breeder reactors now being developed will produce more plutonium fuel than they burn. If fusion power can be controlled it promises tremendous increases in the power available.

Yet consider two factors. First the energy situation for the immediate future is already apparent. Fusion energy is still several decades from practical application. Breeder reactors will not change the situation greatly. They are costly and slow to build and the lethalness of their radioactive wastes adds to the expense of pollution control, security, and ultimate disposition. While internally they are a step forward, externally they are not much different from existing reactors. They will cost somewhat less but pollute somewhat more. Solar and geothermal energy offer hope for the future. Energy farms in Arizona and satellites in space could convert the sun's rays into electricity. Tapping the hot core of the earth, as power engineers are doing currently in northern California, could provide steam to turn generators and heat cities. But these revolutionary technologies are far in the future. The United States will continue for many years in its already existing energy consumption pattern. The demand for oil and gas will not disappear even though the supply might.

Second, the politics of energy will not necessarily change the same way the technology does. The key political questions are ones not of science but of control. Revolutionary as the technology is, fusion power will have prosaic politics as long as it remains under AEC jurisdiction. Understanding the politics of fission energy gives understanding of fusion, for they are both in the nuclear arena. Thus an analyst may predict that energy politics of the year 2000 will be characterized by private utilities operating under close federal governmental supervision; that is the present pattern in the nuclear arena and this nuclear arena will presumably expand to furnish a greater share of the nation's total energy production. Once converted into electricity, that energy will be regulated much as it is today by the FPC. It is likely that the public versus private dichotomy will still be around. Oil, on the other hand, will supply a smaller amount of the nation's power. If the cost of gasoline doubles because of diminishing supplies and more competition from foreign users, the public will place demands on city governments to build mass transit facilities. As the oil companies fall on hard times they will demand more privileges from the government much as the United Mine Workers turned to the government for help when mining declined. Thus, while science is not a panacea for the energy situation in the immediate years to come, understanding its direction indicates the political styles of the future.

If science cannot solve the problems of energy, can economics? Would not a return to full reliance on the price system as a means of coordination solve the distribution problems? In strictly economic terms the answer is probably "yes"; it would distribute the resources most efficiently. The further question is whether it is possible to return to a pure market system. The history of all five arenas shows some degree of flight from the market. Oil is the worst offender. To allow the price system to operate freely would require repealing the tax advantages of the 22 percent depletion allowance and the drilling write offs. It would mean ending the import fees. It would mean ending prorationing under the oil compact. For their part, the oil men would stop contributing lavish sums to presidential candidates and the Senate campaign committees. This deprivation might be more than the Republicans and the Democrats could take. For natural gas, the producers would lose their tax advantages too, but in return they would gain freedom from FPC regulation. This would put them back to the pre-1935 situation. Since gas is a natural monopoly the free market offers no solution to determining the correct prices. Liquified natural gas, not available in 1935, is still not really competitive. The difficulties of determining prices for electricity are the same; the market system is not workable. It is workable for oil, uranium, and coal—providing that the producers bear the burden of the external costs. Strip miners would have to buy the land outright, not just the mineral rights, and would have to restore it fully afterwards. Coal and uranium producers would have to ventilate their deep mines and bear the costs of industrial disease and accidents. The economic prescription for assigning true costs is the beginning. Consumers would have to accept high prices for gasoline, natural gas, and electricity without complaint. Demands for keeping prices low have yielded shortages. Natural gas is cheap in Chicago, but new customers cannot get any. The Cost of Living Council's regulation of gasoline kept prices down but service stations ran out of their day's supply by 11:00 A.M. and exhausted their monthly quota within two weeks.

It has been one of America's political ironies that the administration of Richard Nixon strayed so far from the traditional Republican ideology of private enterprise. Republicans who attacked the New Deal as a mortal sin against capitalism in the 1930's and labeled TVA as creeping socialism in the 1950's found in the 1970's that it was their own party that was bent on controlling prices and production. A grievous example of federal government interference in the free market earned the code name Project Independence. In response to President Nixon's pronouncement that the United States should become independent of imported fuel by 1980 the Federal Energy Office outlined a plan to increase coal mining by nearly one half, oil by one third, and natural gas by one fifth. Nuclear power would increase tenfold. This ambitious goal would include such breaks with Republican tradition as strong central planning at the federal level, suspension of state rights to control land use, and federal direction of what private corporations may produce.[3] Even the most ardent New Dealer would have hesitated to propose such federal interference in the economy.

The basic weaknesses of Project Independence lie in its assumptions. Chief among them is that energy autarky is an overriding goal. The United States does not need self-sufficiency in fuel any more or any less than it needs self-sufficiency in other major sectors of its economy. Rather than autarky, the goal should be dependability. The problem was not that the United States imported oil but that the imports stopped abruptly and unexpectedly. And the reason oil imports stopped was political rather than economic. The Arabs cut off supplies because the United States supported Israel in the Yom Kippur War. Other OPEC members joined the boycott because of deeply felt resentment against years of American exploitation of their natural resources. Project Independence would solve the American foreign policy problem but at an exorbitant price. The import quota system in effect from 1959 to 1973 gives some hint of the cost of energy autarky. In exchange for a slightly higher level of domestic production at the time of the 1973 boycott the American taxpayer paid an extra several billion dollars a year. The cost of autarky was overrich southwestern oilmen and presidents and senators beholden to them.

This does not argue that the United States should abandon legitimate foreign policy goals, only that it should secure them at the least cost. To the extent the matter is purely economic, imports should be judged by price. If the cheapest way to get oil is to sell ownership in "downstream" facilities to foreign producers, that is good economics. A Venezuelan owning one's local service station may be preferred to a Texas "fat cat" owning one's senator. To the extent the matter affects vital aspects of foreign policy, control of importation should follow a political strategy. If the United States intends to continue strong support for Israel it should avoid Arab production in favor of Venezuelan. If the United States foresees continued rivalry with the Communist bloc it should eschew importing large quantities of oil or natural gas from Russia in favor of Canadian sources. To the extent to which the United States foresees major boycotts it should stockpile inventories large enough to last six months or a year. Autarky has its place insofar as it serves a foreign policy purpose, but as outlined in Project Independence the purpose appears to be tinged with zenophobia.

Short of the unlikely return to a completely free market system to allocate scarce energy resources, economic analysis suggests some future trends bearing on politics. Even if the market system remains distorted, increased prices will draw new fuel into exchange and simultaneously prompt consumers to conserve energy.

Production currently too expensive will become profitable. Many more nuclear plants will become economical as the price of electricity rises. Refining oil from Colorado shale is now too expensive. When this is no longer the case oil companies will begin mining and crushing the rock with a consequent impact on the state's environment and politics. Higher crude oil prices will cause drilling derricks to sprout along the East Coast as they already have along the Gulf and California coasts. Breaking the FPC congestion on natural gas prices will cause the drillers to tap the reserves they have heretofore refrained from "proving."

While higher prices will draw more supplies onto the market they will also cut demand. Consumers will seek to conserve energy. Smaller automobiles are one way. The trend is already apparent. After the oil boycott began some panicky Cadillac owners rushed to trade in their behemoths for Volkswagens. Although this trend has no direct political consequence the demand to relax curbs on pollution does. Auto manufacturers managed to get the U.S. Environmental Protection Agency to postpone the deadline it originally set for pollution control devices. Detroit finds the energy crisis a handy excuse for further delay. Environmentalists find some consolation in the fact that less gasoline consumed means less air pollution. Switching auto production to smaller cars takes about three years. Switching housing construction takes much longer. Better insulation would save fuel, but it must be installed when the home is built. Electrical heating is wasteful because it requires two conversions, one at the generating plant and a second in the home. Direct burning is much more efficient but again the choice is usually made when the house is built, and conversion is expensive. Governments could require heat conservation. The Federal Home Loan Bank Board could make it a prerequisite for mortgages. City building codes could require good insulation and forbid electrical heat. TVA could raise the low rates that make electrical heating economically competitive. Factories, offices, and schools have already turned their thermostats down to 65 degrees in the winter and up to 78 degrees in the summer.

An economic shift already underway promises to reduce the rate of increase in the demand for energy. The United States shows a tendency to be shifting away from energy intensive consumption. Manufactured goods tend to be energy intensive. A 3,000 pound steel and aluminum automobile has already used a lot of energy before it begins gulping gasoline at the rate of a gallon every eight miles. Spacious suburban houses crammed with electrical appliances are energy intensive. So are jet planes. In contrast many new goods and services are not. Computers take little electricity to run. Long distance telephone calls cost a great deal for the number of kilowatts used. Many items gaining popularity are labor intensive. Television repairmen, beauticians, and teachers consume money but not fuel. Medical care, the country's fastest growing industry, does the same. Leisure saves energy. Increasingly Americans prefer shorter hours and longer vacations. Since the leisure will give more time to enjoy nature, study ecology, and become politically active on behalf of the environmental and consumer movements it should reinforce the ranks of those opposed to big corporations. The tendency has exceptions. Jet travel and aluminum pop-top cans are highly energy intensive. But in general the future seems to offer some relief.

In facing the energy crisis of the 1970's, American society finds itself in a familiar, self-imposed paradox. It has faith in science to solve the problem, but that faith is not justified since the problem is not really scientific. In the long run science may expand the resources available, but in the short run the country must make do with what it has. On the other hand society lacks faith in an economic solution, although this is exactly what it needs since economic decision-making is designed to allocate scarce resources in the short run. The result is to shift the problem into the political system—a common phenomenon known as the primacy of politics. The incentive to shift the decision-making process from economics to politics comes from participants who believe that they have more to gain in the latter than in the former. Thus John L. Lewis sought government assistance when U.M.W. membership fell to 84,000. Domestic oil producers first asked for an import quota after the United States became a net importer in 1949. The city of Detroit led the fight to break up the holding companies after the holding companies refused to sell it southwestern gas.

Upon becoming a political matter an issue is resolved according to the political resources the parties can bring to bear. The history of energy politics shows these often to be lobbyists, campaign donations, demogoguery, and violence. Too frequently these are the bases on which political institutions make policy. Policy is the net effect of the equilibrium of the forces acting in an arena at any one time. This temporary equilibrium may lack any rational basis. In recent years Congress has shown signs of breaking out of this form of decision-making by being more self-consciously analytical. It has deliberately tried to evaluate environmental costs against energy benefits. Was the aid to national security provided by a protected domestic oil industry worth the $500 million tax loss from a 27½ percent depletion allowance and the several billion dollar burden to the consumer from the import quota system? Congress and the President decided no, not quite. Is the Alaskan oil worth the damage to the arctic tundra? Congress decided yes. While neither of these decisions is completely rational in cost-benefit terms, they do represent consideration of the trade-offs.

Striking a rational balance among the various costs and benefits is a more self-conscious process in the executive branch. There the analysts will go so far as to assign "shadow prices" to replicate the economic features abandoned when the issue moved from an economic to a political mode of decision-making. Since a tendency toward central political planning has been going on since the New Deal, there is a certain irony in an attempt to make the process more rational by reinstating the economic characteristics the shift was intended to remove.

The trend toward rationality, weak as it may sometimes appear, promises the emergence of a new type of politician. The old style politico was skilled in balancing political forces. A senator deciding how to vote on a tax bill had to balance his desire for a campaign contribution against the ire of his constituents if they realized how much his vote cost them as taxpayers. Or a governor had to balance the needs of the coal operators against the needs of the miners. The new style politico faces much more complex problems. He may be not an elected official at all but an AEC administrator. He must balance the costs of safety devices on a nuclear reactor against the number of babies who would die from any radiation that might escape and at the same time consider balancing the political forces as well. He must know both the technical and the political sides, in contrast to the old style politician who needed to know only the latter. The politician of the future will need to understand all aspects of the policy arena.

Notes

1. "Common Ownership," *CQ Weekly Report*, May 6, 1972.
2. "Resources: Using Them Up," *Newsweek*, May 21, 1973, p. 78.
3. Federal Energy Office, Office of Policy Analysis and Evaluation, "Project Independence," February 11, 1974 (draft report). See also Ford Foundation Energy Policy Project, *Exploring Energy Choices*, March 31, 1974; and "Energy Self-Sufficiency," *CQ Weekly Report*, June 8, 1974.

Index

About the Author

David Howard Davis teaches political science at Rutgers University. He received his A.B. from Cornell University and his Ph.D. from the Johns Hopkins University, where he held a Woodrow Wilson Foundation Dissertation Fellowship. As an army artillery officer he served as a forward observer in Vietnam and later as commander of a 175 mm. gun battery. Professor Davis was on leave from Rutgers in 1973—74 as a NASPAA Public Administration Fellow assigned to the U.S. Environmental Protection Agency headquarters in Washington, D.C., where he worked in the Office of Planning and Evaluation and the Office of Legislation. He has previously written *How the Bureaucracy Makes Foreign Policy.*